Sharing Recovery Through Gamblers Anonymous

Published by
Gamblers Anonymous
P.O. Box 17173
Los Angeles, California 90017
(213) 386-8789

First Edition

Third Printing 1997

Printed in the United States of America

———————————

Library of Congress Catalog Card Number
84-080686

———————————

ISBN 0-917839-00-5

DEDICATION

This book is dedicated to Jim W. our founder
1912 -1983

May we also dedicate this Book to those members
who came before us and those who will come after.

ACKNOWLEDGMENT

The Fellowship of Gamblers Anonymous wishes to thank the Committee who contributed their time, effort and guidance in making this book a reality.

TABLE OF CONTENTS

FOREWORD

Pathological (compulsive) gambling is a destructive, dangerous and potentially deadly disorder. Yet, this devastating problem is treatable and Gamblers Anonymous (GA) has been and is the single most effective treatment modality for the pathological gambler. This book presents the principles and guidelines of GA which have been used by thousands of people who are being successfully treated.

Lack of in-depth knowledge of GA is the primary reason for any misunderstanding about its purposes, methods and activities. Simply, it is a voluntary fellowship of compulsive gamblers gathered for the sole purpose of helping themselves and each other to stop gambling. It is a program of 12 steps that provide a framework of hope, structure and friendship for those who have lived the program and successfully adapted to life. This book describes the routes on the road to this successful adaptation to a life without gambling. This road can be smooth or rocky, but in any case, it is never a painless journey while recovering.

GA is effective because it (a) undercuts denial, projection and rationalization, (b) identifies the serious implications of gambling, (c) demands honesty and responsibility, (d) identifies and corrects character problems (e) gives affection, personal concern and support, (f) develops substitutes for the void left by the cessation of gambling, and (g) is nonjudgmental.

The more a person understands Gamblers Anonymous, the more one respects and admires it for its principles, accomplishments and effectiveness — and the lives it has saved.

Robert L. Custer, M.D.
May 1983

INTRODUCTION

The editors believe that through the dramatic devices of fiction you will gain an enhanced awareness of the emotional and physical pain endured by compulsive gamblers and greater appreciation for the support and encouragement — required for their recovery — which the members of Gamblers Anonymous share with each other. This can be observed in Chapter II.

You will also see that Chapter VIII, the largest chapter in the book, consists of many pages of personal remembrances voluntarily contributed by members of the Fellowship and that Appendix "1" consists of a sizeable extract from the biography of Jim W., the founder of Gamblers Anonymous.

Thus, it is apparent that a considerable portion of this book is devoted to personal reminiscences and biographical sketches of compulsive gamblers telling how they started on the path of recovery through the Fellowship.

Our emphasis upon personal stories of recovery is necessary in order to correctly present the view of our members who, as pragmatic behaviorists, are more concerned with the process of recovery from compulsive gambling than they are with reasons why they became compulsive gamblers.

Consequently, this book is not a text book on psychology, theories of compulsion or systems of treatment, nor is it a polemic against recreational gambling. It has been organized in a particular order for the benefit of those who wish to read it from the beginning. But each chapter has its own internal cogency and you may choose to read chapters or sections of the book at random.

If you are a family member or close friend of a compulsive gambler you may choose first to read Chapter VI. If you wish to know more about treatment facilities turn to Chapter VII; those concerned with the therapeutic system used by Gamblers Anonymous turn first to Chapter III. As to the personal stories, they are the shared emotional experiences which bind together the members of the Fellowship and provide the inspiration for this book. No understanding of the suffering and hopeless degradation experienced by compulsive gamblers, nor their remarkable recovery through the encouragement and direction of Gamblers Anonymous, can be truly comprehended without reading Chapter VIII.

The process of recovery for members of Gamblers Anonymous is more than a personal mastery over the compulsive desire to gamble. The continuing recovery for each member of the Fellowship is characterized by the desire to help other compulsive gamblers. This is why the Fellowship places a high value on what is called "Twelfth Step Work," which is explained in Chapter V, but to which many references are made at other places in the text.

Chapter I

COMPULSION AND COMPULSIVE GAMBLING

The most successful treatment for the psychological disorder of compulsive gambling is provided by the Fellowship of Gamblers Anonymous. The subject of this book is how Gamblers Anonymous succeeds where other forms of treatment have been less successful. But in order to understand the philosophy and therapy of Gamblers Anonymous it is necessary to know more about compulsive behavior and compulsive gambling in particular.

Gambling, for the compulsive gambler, is defined by the Fellowship of Gamblers Anonymous as *any betting or wagering, for self or others, whether for money or not, no matter how slight or insignificant, where the outcome is uncertain or depends upon chance or "skill" constitutes gambling.* Compulsive gambling, very simply, is gambling which is beyond the emotional control of the gambler.

There is probably no individual who has not gambled. Most people are able to monitor the frequency of their gambling according to their income, the enjoyment they receive and the appropriateness of the social situation in which gambling may take place. This is not so for the compulsive or pathological gambler. Unlike the social or professional gambler, the pathological gambler cannot stop—interest is focused solely on the next bet.

Gambling Is An Emotional Illness

For these afflicted people, gambling is an emotional illness, because the need to gamble is uncontrollable. The compulsive gambler gambles even

1

when it is not the appropriate response to a social or personal situation, and will bet just as readily to celebrate the birth of a child as to forget the death of a loved one. The need to gamble dominates the thinking and energy of the compulsive gambler. So much energy is spent by the compulsive personality in planning how, when and where to gamble that eventually the enjoyment fades and is replaced by anxiety over the ability to get money for the next gambling venture, and to pay debts.

Assuming that the propensity to gamble compulsively has been there to begin with, it may take only one incident to push an individual over the edge into compulsive gambling. This incident might be the death of a close relative or friend, a marriage or change of jobs. Once the gambler has yielded to the urge to wager, the compulsion to continue becomes stronger than any desire to stop. Life for the compulsive gambler becomes unmanageable. The pathological gambler loses self-control and eventually may be convinced that it is impossible to refrain from gambling, which in turn becomes another excuse to continue gambling.

Those who gamble compulsively usually feel that they have no choice in carrying out their actions. Compulsive gamblers feel compelled to gamble, and even though they know gambling is harmful, they are powerless to stop.

Such powerlessness, however, should not be considered "moral weakness." Until the "Age of Psychology" (the beginnings of which conform roughly to the generation of experimental psychologists who preceded Freud), those who gambled or drank to excess were considered to be "weak"; their habits were called vices and as habitues they were thought to lack "sufficient strength of character to resist temptation."

While not all human behavior is random or habitual, neither are all human actions premeditated nor consciously deliberate. Each of us seems to be a unique mixture of biological and psychological potentials realized through our own personal and social biographies. This realization makes it impossible to write about any aspect of human motivation and need in terms which are sufficiently general to apply to all. Such attempts almost invariably lead to superficial and even fatuous statements easily proved to be scientifically invalid.

Therefore, this book will try to avoid using random generalizations concerning human behavior, and where such generalities are unavoidable, it will be important for the reader to maintain a sense of proportion between the generalities of the statements and the "uniqueness" of each individual.

This is particularly true in a discussion about the causes of compulsive gambling as opposed to the behavior modification or treatment of this pathology. As we shall explore later in this book, Gamblers Anonymous has discovered an animalistic irony — that behavior modification or therapy may be generalized or standardized even for a behavioral disorder which originates from very complex situations that are unique to each individual. This standardization of treatment is possible in part because compulsive gamblers share sufficient psychological characteristics for the development of a composite personality profile, distinguishing them from the non gambling and social gambling public. The social gambler has no difficulty in recognizing choices — to bet or not to bet — and the result of this recognition is seldom painful. However, the pathological gambler has no such objectivity. Even the realization of the harm the pathological person does to him or herself or to others is secondary to the overriding compulsion to gamble.

The compulsive gambler lives in a perpetual state of tension, unable to relax for any length of time because of the obsessive need to make bets and to raise money to gamble or pay gambling debts. While gambling may be stressful, being away from it can be even worse. Furthermore, the compulsive gambler cannot cope with the stress and pressures of everyday living; the circumstances of life seem to be fraught with tension. This cycle of behavior becomes more and more destructive. Even though there are alternatives, the compulsive gambler does not have the perspective to see them or the control to choose a healthier behavioral pattern.

Another element of the compulsive gambling personality is the inability to handle responsibility; any of the responsibilities and obligations of adulthood such as those that come with a job, marriage or children can trigger a compulsive gambling response in these individuals. The compulsive personality does not know how to cope adequately with responsibility, looks away from it, preferring instead to retreat into the unreal world of pathological gambling.

Theories of Compulsive Behavior

Compulsive behavior is described as a strong irrational impulse to carry out some particular act. Although this behavior can be a one-time action, it is usually repetitive. This behavior can take a variety of forms: gambling, drinking, excessive cleanliness, church-going, working and others. Most analysts, although they may not agree on what causes compulsive behavior, agree that almost every individual is compulsive to some degree. But we must be careful to remember that every "habit" is not necessarily compulsive, in part because every habit is not necessarily irrational.

There are many theories of personality and approaches to what is generally called "behavior," and more specifically, to the compulsion complex. Entire schools of therapy have been created around the theories of the great philosopher-psychologists Sigmund Freud, Alfred Adler, Carl Jung and others. Many of these schools or systems of therapy have influenced the treatment of compulsive gamblers and we should know something about the concepts of personality they represent in order to better understand the problem of compulsive gambling and the therapy developed by Gamblers Anonymous.

Sigmund Freud believed that compulsivity is at least partially rooted in the pleasure principle, which he differentiated from the reality principle. The pleasure principle, according to Freud, governs immature behavior. For example, a child requires the pleasure of instant gratification, which it demands from a selfish point of view. The maturing child, however, becomes aware of the reality of the outside world and learns to adapt the desire for self-gratification to the demands of the society. The mature individual, according to Freud, is one who has integrated the pleasure principle with the reality principle. Conversely, the inability to integrate these two principles results in immature behavior and the continuing need to carry out acts of self-gratification. Freud noted that compulsive acts often stem from this desire to satisfy the individual's childish pleasure-seeking.

Franz Alexander linked obsession with compulsion and formed a new theory of obsessive-compulsive neurosis. An obsession is a persistent feeling, idea or influence that dominates a person's thinking or action —and from which the person cannot escape. Obsessions often tend to be antisocial in nature, such as the desire to kill, have incestuous intercourse or to harm oneself. Alexander postulated that because these actions are not acceptable to society, the obsessive individual represses them into his subconscious.

Although these desires are buried, they still manage to motivate the individual's conscious behavior. The result is that such obsessions are acted out in compulsive conduct, often in exaggerated acts of socially acceptable behavior. But since compulsion is a subterfuge, according to Alexander, it can appear in the behavior of the obsessive individual in any number of ways — from uncontrolled anti-social acts to rigid conformism.

Another theory of compulsion neurosis was developed by Alfred Adler, who believed that *all* neurosis is based on the attempt to free oneself from inferiority feelings by replacing them with superiority feelings. According to Adler, the compulsive person is motivated by the "compulsion idea," a belief which is the activator or motivation for carrying out the compulsion, and is never absent from the individual's actions.

The compulsive person achieves superiority feelings by replacing the will of others with his own. This type of person is motivated to obey only the compulsion, which becomes sacred and irresistible, and leads to feelings of being all-powerful and in control.

Adler also noted that even though compulsion can appear in any kind of behavior, all compulsions produce worry and torment. Moreover, any attempt to suppress the compulsion produces severe anxiety. Eventually, he said, all compulsions degenerate into alcoholism or drug addiction, or become connected with them.

4

Adler identified several traits common to the personalities of compulsive individuals, such as: an attitude of being unapproachable, based on feelings of little love for humanity; few friends; a sense of being weighted down by family influence; a pessimistic outlook built on feelings of inferiority; and lastly, hostility towards the demands of society. In fact, Adler pointed out, compulsions exist in large part to exempt the individual from carrying out the normal duties imposed by society.

While the individual is sometimes aware of his compulsivity, this is rarely the case, according to Adler's observations. And even when such an awareness does exist, Adler found that far from having a curative effect, the individual's recognition of his own compulsivity tends to give the affliction an even freer reign. For the gambler, this might well amount to the aforementioned rationale of helplessness, where the afflicted individual acknowledges that he is sick while at the same time deciding that nothing can be done about it.

Adler also noted that a second born son, an only girl in a family of boys, and an only boy in a family of girls were more likely to become compulsive personalities than others. Whatever the individual's position in the family structure, he concluded, the compulsive person wastes a great deal of time that would more normally be spent carrying out necessary tasks.

Carl Jung, a contemporary of Freud, Alexander and Adler, also contributed to the theory of compulsion neurosis. Jung believed that one cause of compulsion is the inability of the individual to place moral restraint upon himself: compulsive symptoms, i.e., the need to commit irrational acts, are a cry for help.

More recently, another theory of compulsion neurosis has come from Frederick S. Perls, a leading proponent of the Gestalt school of analysis. Perls believes that compulsivity stems from retroflexed behavior, when the individual does to himself what he originally tried to do to others or to objects. At the root of this behavior is the person's recognition that he cannot change society or make it conform to his demands. Instead of accepting this state of affairs or trying to work constructively towards positive change, the compulsive individual substitutes himself in place of the outside world, as the target of his "reform."

According to Perls, this substitution of self for society precludes any satisfaction with the desire for change. Because no meaningful resolution can be achieved, compulsive behavior is repetitive. Sadly, each misdirected effort begets only another more futile attempt.

Perls believes that all of us are compulsive in some way. He calls compulsivity the outstanding "neurotic" symptom of our era. Not surprisingly, he observes that compulsive personalities accomplish very little, spending most of their time in preparing, deciding and making sure, but making very little headway in executing what is planned. Unfortunately, compulsive persons are trapped in their behavior patterns because they don't have the opportunity to grow by the successful completion and assimilation of their tasks. Their approach to problem-solving is rendered ineffective by fixed and archaic attitudes.

It should be noted that the American Psychiatric Association most recently eliminated the term "neurosis" from the revision of its official diagnostic manual. Nowhere in the manual do the words "neurotic" or "neurosis" now appear.

According to Dr. Robert L. Spitzer, who was chairman of the task force to revise the Association's diagnostic manual, the term "neurosis" originally referred to a neurological disorder. Later, it took on other meanings and the term finally came to be defined "more by what it is not than by what it is." It was because of this lack of clear definition that the term was dropped.

Many psychiatrists believe that the elimination of the concept of "neurosis" has been the most important decision of the psychiatric profession since the end of WWII.

Behaviorism: A Pragmatic Theory of Therapy

Behaviorism is the name of the most recent psychological theory to have achieved sufficient professional endorsement to be considered a major "school" of thought. Behaviorists are not primarily concerned with what motivates a person to act in a particular way. Behaviorists concentrate more on objective, observable behavior. Their aim is to modify the way a person acts so that regardless of the cause of psychological maladjustment, the person learns how to operate successfully around it. In the most general terms, the Behaviorist method is to positively reinforce, or reward, productive behavior and negatively reinforce, or punish, destructive behavior.

The goal of changing behavior rather than of dealing with or changing theories of psychological structure is the basis for Alcoholics Anonymous, the first major support therapy established to deal with a compulsive behavior. The founders of Alcoholics Anonymous were instinctive behaviorists. Indeed, Gamblers Anonymous and other "Anonymous" fellowships, such as Overeaters Anonymous, are patterned directly after Alcoholics Anonymous. These support groups have been consistently more successful with their therapies than have been most of the other theoretical approaches to changing the behavior of individuals afflicted with problems of compulsive personality behavior.

In summary, we can see that while there are many theories of compulsion, it is not an easy matter to establish just what causes compulsive behavior. It is equally difficult to determine why one individual becomes a compulsive gambler and not an alcoholic, why another becomes an over-eater or drug addict, etc. or why some are afflicted with multiple compulsions.

Further, it cannot be flatly stated that any individual who has an antisocial or antipersonal compulsive habit is necessarily doing so

6

because of anxiety, jealousy, anger, guilt, shame, frustration or any other such emotion. While each of the psychologist-teachers we have cited has developed his own set of assumptions, all that we can conclude — particularly before we understand the individual, and the individual understands himself — is that compulsive behavior is almost always harmful to the best interests and happiness of the person.

Of course, the focus of our interest here is on compulsive gamblers in particular, their traits and the therapies used to restore them to healthier ways of life. In order to more fully understand the behavior and needs of those who gamble compulsively, it is helpful to know more about their characteristics as a sociological group.

The Sociology of Compulsive Gambling

A nationwide study conducted by the Survey Research Center of the University of Michigan in 1975 estimated that there were between 1.1 and 3.3 million compulsive gamblers in the United States. The United States Department of Public Health places the figure even higher, estimating that approximately nine million Americans are compulsive gamblers. This discrepancy can be explained by conflicting definitions as to just what constitutes compulsive gambling behavior and also by different survey statistical techniques. Nonetheless, both sources agree that the number of compulsive gamblers is growing, with the Department of Public Health projecting the growth rate to be about ten percent annually.

Typically, compulsive gamblers have tended to be men, but more and more women are turning up in research findings. Dr. Robert L. Custer, M.D., director of the U.S. Veterans Administration program on addictive behavior and the leading researcher in the study of pathological gambling estimates that females currently comprise about 20% of compulsive gamblers in the U.S. Dr. Custer believes that the proportion of female compulsive gamblers will continue to increase because the ability of women to earn and borrow money is also on the rise. According to Custer, money is the "drug" of the pathological gambler. As women's access to money and credit grows, so does the likelihood of their becoming addicted.

Other reasons cited for the rise in compulsive gambling by females are the greater levels of freedom and equality that American women recently have achieved. Women are now freely admitted to gambling facilities and accepted not just as men's companions, but as independent participants in their own right. Women have developed greater interest in competitive and professional sports, almost all of which have had some kind of association with gambling. Spurred, in part by Title IX of the Civil Rights Act, which mandated high schools and colleges to provide equal funding for women's sports, female interest in both spectator and participant sports has reached unprecedented levels and is still growing rapidly.

It should be noted that women always have been as susceptible as men to compulsive behavior. Formerly restricted by societal norms to such compulsions as excessive eating, cleanliness and drinking, women are now free to indulge their pathological urge to gamble.

Since the founding of the nation, Americans have been subject to social, political and economic pressures to gamble. As Dr. Custer notes, the United States has always been a gambling society. The thirteen original American colonies were largely financed by lotteries, as were Harvard, Yale, Princeton, Brown, Dartmouth and Columbia universities. Both George Washington and Thomas Jefferson strongly advocated the use of lotteries to raise public funds. This historical inclination to support state and federal operations by gambling was in part inherited from Great Britain, a nation which has long encouraged its citizens to bet on everything from political elections to sporting events.

Gambling is promoted in almost every one of the United States: some states have casino gambling, many run lotteries and almost all have had horse and/or dog racing for many years. In addition, many communities allow religious groups to hold Bingo games and "Las Vegas Nights" both to raise money and to provide a source of entertainment for their members. Fewer than ten states do not have any form of legalized gambling. Gambling is also an integral part of the travel and entertainment business in America. Airlines, buslines and hotels regularly advertise offers, such as a week in Las Vegas, a weekend in Atlantic City or a day at the track. Most luxury cruise lines also offer the attraction of gambling on board. And indeed, a number of Caribbean and Latin American countries and territories, such as Puerto Rico, Aruba and the Bahamas, promote attractive gambling packages of their own, competing heavily for the American gambling/travel dollar.

While the allures to gamble are varied and legion, horse racing deserves a special note. Horse racing, the sport most intimately connected with gambling, enjoys the greatest attendance of any spectator sport in the United States, drawing over fifty million spectators each year. Yet, according to a Louis Harris poll conducted for the Perrier corporation, the race tracks tend to draw the same fans again and again. Only about 4 percent of the adult population attend horse racing in a given year. This compares, for example, to baseball, which though smaller in overall attendance, attracts 16 percent of the total adult population over the course of a year.

Aside from the obvious advertising and promotional appeals, the urge to gamble is reinforced in much subtler ways. The daily newspaper, for example, lists stock market quotations, lottery numbers, as well as betting lines for baseball, football and other sporting events. Odds and inside tips on horse and dog racing are also regularly included. Books on how to win at blackjack, pick the horses, beat the odds, etc., reach a wide readership. In addition, there is widespread access to private gambling get-togethers, such as the weekly poker or mah jong games. Such rein-forcement need be no more blatant, or less persuasive, than a friendly invitation.

In addition to legal gambling, illegal gambling is common throughout the United States. Most forms of legalized gambling are also conducted illegally, such as illegal raffles, numbers games, bookmaking and even illegal casinos. While it is impossible to determine exactly the number of participants in these activities, it is clear that illegal gambling thrives due to the patronage of an extensive gambling subculture.

The image of the gambler, as promoted both in classical literature and in popular media, is strongly attractive to many people. Much of the imagery conveyed is strongly masculine, with the gambler depicted as glamorous and wealthy — commanding the respect of men and the desire of women. Even the losing gambler is portrayed frequently as someone in pursuit of a bitter sweet romantic ideal, as a man who takes risks, tempts fate, regardless of the consequences.

There are almost as many settings in which gambling is romanticized as there are personal tastes. The Mississippi riverboat, the elegant casino, the western saloon, the championship race; these and other exotic settings provide fantasy playgrounds for the compulsive gambler's mind. His daydreams are never affected by the horrible realities to which pathological gambling invariably leads.

Pressures to Gamble

Clearly, in the United States, the social pressures to gamble are intense and are increasing with each passing year. Whether or not these pressures are represented as specific offers, subtle suggestions or the invitation to day-dream, they can have a devastating effect on those individuals who are pathological gamblers. As Dr. Custer defines it, compulsive gambling is a disorder in which there is "a progressive increase in the preoccupation with and urge to gamble." This results in such excessive gambling that serious damage is inflicted on the gambler's personal, family and professional life. According to Dr. Custer, the compulsive gambler is characterized by an emotional dependence on gambling, by a loss of self-control and impaired normal functioning.

The need to escape into gambling inevitably leads to the creation of a fantasy world, usually including an elaborate system of rationalizations that support the need to bet. Such excuses can be manufactured as the need arises, shifting the blame to another person or agency, postponing remedial action for a more propitious time, etc. Rationalizations may also fit into larger schemes and fantasies carefully designed to sustain the impression of well-being. The operative assumption for most of these fantasy structures is that gambling will ultimately pay off, improving the quality of life for the gambler and his loved ónes. In his imagination the compulsive gambler sees this triumph as the vindication for past failures.

9

Much of the pathological gambler's time is spent fantasizing about the great things that will be achieved when the "big win" comes through — trips, glamour, sexual companionship, and/or respect. But the "big win" rarely comes, and if it does, the money is used for more gambling, with hope of an even greater triumph. Eventually, the winnings are lost. As the debts mount, so does the desperation with which the individual gambles to make the fantasies come true. Dr. Custer notes that as the desperation and frustration mount, ironically, the individual's proficiency at gambling usually decreases. Although even deeper disappointments are inevitable, the dreams go on, because without them the compulsive gambler's life would be intolerable.

The compulsive gambler is an immature person who wants to have all the good things in life without making any concerted effort to obtain them. The compulsive gambler feels a strong need to be taken care of, never having fully accepted the fact that there is a point past which one can no longer rely on others, such as parents, for support. Finding oneself out of the nest and in the adult world may provoke pathological urges as the result of resentment toward this harsh reality.

Seeking a refuge from the responsibilities of adulthood, the individual turns to gambling as a means of escape. Although at first perhaps no more than an idle pastime, the urge to bet and wager soon becomes overwhelming. Will power alone is no match for it. Often the compulsive gambler expresses the sincere desire to quit, and may in fact do so for a period of time. Inevitably, however, periods of abstinence are followed by spectacular gambling binges. With a sense of making up for lost time the cycle becomes more intense and frequent.

Compulsive Gambling is a Progressive Disorder

As the compulsion accelerates, the gambler is often forced into a pattern of lying, cheating and stealing to stay "in action." Wagering takes money, and eventually, the gambler's funds disappear. Obtaining money becomes of paramount importance, often necessitating such devious actions as writing bad checks, stealing money from a child's savings account, cheating on an expense account, or embezzling. Often such actions are rationalized by a sincere vow to rectify the immoral or illegal act. Frequently, however, compulsive gamblers are caught in their crimes, and spend time in prison.

Ultimately, to be rehabilitated, the compulsive gambler has to choose to break out of this destructive pattern. Realizing that such a choice exists is but the first step, however, and true recovery takes much more time and effort.

The question arises of where to go for help — to a clergyman, doctor, therapist or friend. While the choice of any one of these counselors represents an affirmative step, it is unfortunate that the chances of rehabilitation through any of them are slim. One-on-one analysis, by itself, has a very poor record of helping compulsive gamblers.

What does work well is support therapy, and that is what the Fellowship of Gamblers Anonymous provides. This group accepts as a member any person who expresses a desire to stop gambling. Many thousands of compulsive gamblers have been rehabilitated through Gamblers Anonymous, and it is the most successful and effective means toward recovery that exists.

Chapter II

"ABNER AND HOWIE" AN ORIGINAL STORY

Part One

For someone afraid of the ocean he was lying too close to the incoming tide —it had almost reached his feet. But for someone who had acquired faith in himself he wasn't at all concerned when the water would touch him and he refused to open his eyes — even though he didn't know how to swim.

This was the first time that Abner had deliberately come so close to the edge of the ocean without being overwhelmed by the urge to drown himself. So it was no small accomplishment for him to enjoy the experience of waiting for the water to cover part of his body. It was the ultimate test of a startling discovery he only recently had come to, he liked himself.

He heard his wife call out to him, warning him of the tide and reminding him not to fall asleep — how far away her voice sounded — but he smiled inwardly at her concern. Of course he did not want to fall asleep, so satisfying was the heat of the sun melting the cold out of his body, so pleasant the tingling sensation of the salt spray on his skin, so soothing the noise of the breakers sounding to him like the laughter of children —rising and falling in breathless sighs and giggles as the water skipped along the beach.

It was both rewarding and sufficient to know he could experience pleasure again and appreciate it. For years he had been oblivious to his body's requirements: he had gone without sleep when his body ar.d mind had needed it — had sometimes slept in a chair or even in his car, though his muscles ached for the comfort of a bed — and had made a habit of skipping too many meals and of avoiding exercise and all other interests while living each day under the tension of random luck.

But the worst punishment he had inflicted on himself was his failure to have learned how to restore his spirit through the rejuvenation of his body. He had taken all the discomfort and pain with the same desensitized view of himself: his body had been unskilled labor employed to satisfy the incessant demands of his childish will.

When, eventually, his body had rebelled and demanded rest he had either ignored the need or had gone into tantrums of self-inflicted punishment, insisting that his muscles and nerves work on unreimbursed overtime.

This was the seventh day of his first vacation in nineteen years and he felt a little proud — privately proud — of finally having done what millions of people did every year without so much as a second thought: he had paid the travel agent in advance for the air fare and hotel accommodations for this vacation with his wife and children.

Abner had insisted they take the children out of school, though he knew it would put them behind in their work. He had made a point of making them promise to study on weekends when they returned. But his wife had not objected. She understood the significance of this vacation, so much so that she had cried when they boarded the plane, for it was the first gift he had promised his children which he had not had to lie about, ignore or take back.

After they had checked into the hotel the children had changed clothes and gone horseback riding and Phyllis had called down for room service. She knew he wasn't hungry but had ordered lunch in order to give him something to do. He had spent that first afternoon sitting in their suite, afraid of going out. It had occurred to him with frightening irony that he didn't know how to enjoy himself — he did not know how to play tennis or golf or even swim — and he had become apprehensive of what he might do if he became restless or bored, or too aware of all the 'distractions,' as he had explained euphemistically to his wife.

So Abner had read for a while and then fallen asleep. When Phyllis awakened him in the late afternoon he had kissed her apologetically. He had to be crazy, he insisted, to pay all that money to fly down here just to sleep.

But Phyllis had understood his anxiety and was content to keep him company in their room until dinner.

Now he heard his wife call to him again, warning him not to fall asleep — but he had no intention of sleeping, the experience was too stimulating for him to become drowsy. Then something soft bumped his head. He opened his eyes and saw a beach ball resting near his shoulder. It was covered with damp sand through which he could see swirling bands of pale blue, white and brown. It looked familiar to him — like those

14

pictures he had seen of the earth from the moon (but smelling of sand, plastic and cotton candy) and he contented himself with squinting at the beach ball through his eyelashes and imagining what it must be like to stand on the moon and see the world so complete and far away.

"Hey mister! Grab that ball!" It was a boy's voice calling to him.

Reaching his arm in back of his head, he cradled the ball in the crook of his elbow and shut his eyes until he heard voices quite close.

He looked up at four brown knees supporting khaki shorts and higher up, as he squinted against the light which slipped through the fingers he had raised to shield his eyes from the sun, he saw two boys laughing and pointing at him.

"You wear beach ball shorts!" said the taller one and pointed to his swimming trunks — light blue with swirling diagonals of brown and white.

"We lost three volley balls this week. If we lose this beach ball we got to pay for it from our allowance."

"Where do you play?" He sat up on one elbow to see where they pointed. "Why don't you move farther back up the beach?" he asked, sounding like his wife.

"Isn't any fun," the smaller boy explained.

"If you can't lose, it's no game," the other one said with sophisticated logic.

"Makes it dangerous, eh?" Abner knew the need.

He watched them confer and then the bigger boy pointed to his swimming trunks. "If we lose our beach ball can we use your trunks?" The four knees unhinged to convulsed laughter.

"Not with me in them!" He tossed the ball to the smaller boy and lay back on the sand, listening to the sound of their laughter dissolve in the gurgle of water and the cries of sea birds.

Like a man who cannot yet tell that he has had a little too much to drink, Abner was unaware of the intoxicating effects of the warm sun and cool spray, so that without even being surprised he fell into the half world between dreams, memories and a sensuous awareness of his body in which the last thing he remembered was the sound of children laughing and the water tickling his feet like the tongues of puppies.

It was his brother's responsibility to keep track of the time. When you're eleven years old and seven years younger than your brother you can enjoy the water and let him worry about getting you home in time for dinner.

Their father had died when Abner was in the sixth grade and Danny was a freshman in college. It was the first non-fictional death he had experienced and the shock to his boyish assumptions about the unlimited adventures of life, which up to then had filled every day with excitement, was kept from morosely affecting his personality only by his brother's willingness to become their father's surrogate.

15

Needing the security and approval of a father, Abner had drawn even closer to his brother and despite the difference in age Danny had encouraged him.

His brother's friends had called him 'The Shadow,' but because of their affection for Danny had allowed him to accompany them. While he had been pleased just to be accepted by older boys so much stronger, more experienced and independent, the responsibilities of acting more sophisticated than he was, of pretending to be older, of imitating the behavior of his brother's peers, and of trying to think and understand the world from the limited perspective of the school books he read had been a strain on his powers of insight, wisdom and experience.

Likewise his attempts to power his skinny, pubescent muscles to hit a baseball as far as Danny (to slide into third base with as much skill), or shoot a basketball with as much grace, to swim or run with the stamina of his brother's friends was more than his body could endure. He never quit, but paid the penalty of physical exhaustion until he grew bigger and stronger.

The only games in which he could compete on equal terms with his brother's friends were games of skill. So he practiced with a secret intensity and determination that surprised everyone, including Danny. In rapid succession he became proficient at billiards, pool, card games, hand magic, balancing acts and juggling.

Money had never been a problem when he was a boy. He didn't need much and by the time he was thirteen he began to win at cards and pool with increasing frequency. He played cards with his friends for quarters and bet them hamburgers and milkshakes against his skills at juggling and balancing.

With those who were unaware of his talents he'd bet as much as they wanted — even five or ten dollars. Once he bet he could juggle four cans of tomatoes and had lost twenty-five dollars, but Danny had paid the bet without criticizing him or telling their mother.

All during these adolescent years Danny was his idol, his source of advice, guidance and protection. No boy could be closer to his father than Abner was to his brother. So he was unprepared for the second shock of his life when he discovered that Danny had been drafted.

He had learned in pain that he could not volunteer to follow Danny into the Army, that Danny would not be coming home on weekends. No, they would not be moving to stay near Danny's camp. That was adult business and he was still a boy unable to comprehend the loneliness he was to feel during the next three and a half years.

He envied his brother and all of his brother's friends, listening with aching wonder to their stories when they did come home on leave, wanting to be accepted by them, but having nothing to offer in exchange while they had stories of travel — as far away as California, and overseas. Several had come back with wounds and decorations and beer talk of battles, women and careers — all mysteries to him.

Then, suddenly, with the shock of genuine disappointment to him the war was over before it was his turn and again he felt cheated for he longed to go into the service just to be able to share with his brother and other teenage males that common initiation rite of manhood.

His brother came home an officer, his uniform decorated with symbols of his service, and Abner had assumed that life would continue where it had left off before the war. But his brother returned to college, took a night job at a medical laboratory and announced that he would become a dentist. That had seemed inconceivable to Abner: dentists were old men who filled cavities, put braces on children's teeth and lectured to them about dental hygiene. It was the only time Abner had thought Danny disloyal.

Suddenly the world had become older, cranky and selfish. It wasn't any fun any more and there was no one with whom he could confide. His brother's friends were either working, or going to college and working part time, or worse yet, were involved with girls who stole every hour of their leisure time so that few of his brother's old friends came over to the house to play cards or to take him cruising in their cars, or just to sit on the porch and drink beer and tell stories of the war.

The world had grown up, become serious and was no longer an audience for Abner's games and skills, even though he had learned to juggle six Spaulding softballs, which, by his admission, had been easier to do than to understand Danny's world of work, responsibility and obligation.

Then with innocent surprise he learned it was his turn to be drafted and he knew it would be a good thing, an escape from the experiences of adolescence and growing up that were beginning to strangle him.

His mother had not wanted him to go, correctly judging him to be so much less mature than Danny at the same age.

He remembered listening to Danny's voice in the kitchen arguing that it was a perfect time for him to be drafted: the war was over and he couldn't get hurt. It would help him to grow up, see a little of the world and find out what he wanted to do with his life. He had never loved Danny so much.

But he was not drafted. Or, more precisely, after he was drafted he did not serve. Heart murmur, a selective service doctor had told him. Unfit for military service. He had felt ashamed of his impaired body which made him unable to serve his country. This was the third disillusion for which he had tried to compensate.

While his brother had studied and worked at night and supported the family, Abner had worked at, quit or been fired from a hundred jobs. And all because of inattention and daydreaming — of wanting to please his brother and his mother, of trying in months to equal the accomplishments for which his brother had taken years.

It wasn't a bad thing to want to do, only it was frustrating to be so concerned with the goal of success, as to be unable to perform satisfactorily the elementary work necessary to achieve it. And it was self-perpetuating in a most debilitating way — the more he thought about the future the less he concentrated on his job, which made his work less efficient and therefore less satisfactory to his employers; while his poor job performance led him to spend more emotional effort in planning and in vicariously living through gambling the success he sought — and needed.

Not so with his brother: Danny had graduated with honors, had gone on to dental school and eventually specialized in oral surgery. To help him achieve the highest level of his skill as a surgeon he had designed numerous improvements in dental tools and when they could not be improved he had invented new instruments and new surgical techniques to complement each other. He had authored books on anesthesia, jaw surgery and a study comparing canine and human tooth decay and then, at the age of thirty-six, he had become the youngest professor of dental surgery at the state university.

His sleeping self felt a gentle pressure on his arm and that mysterious part of his brain which possessed self-awareness even while the rest of him slept, reluctantly insisted that he pull himself back from his dreams and open his eyes.

His wife was standing beside him in her beach robe, surrounded by the mauve-red haze of the late afternoon sun. It was time to dress for dinner, she reminded him and held out a beach towel while he stood up shivering.

Now it was different water running down Abner's back — cold needle-points from the shower head (unlike the sleep-inducing sensuousness of the ocean spray), hurrying him on in anticipation of a happy evening with his family.

He turned off the faucet and stepped from the stall feeling content and certainly healthier than ever in the past twenty years. As he dried his legs he noticed the contrast between the sun tanned back of his hands and the patches of pinker skin between his fingers. He hadn't seen his hands look like this since he was a kid spending his summer days on the playgrounds and at the beach.

They gathered in the hall and marched to the elevator — handsome wife and children, then walked to their table in the restaurant, conscious of the way the guests looked at them. His were the only teenagers in the dining room and it made him feel all the more pleased that he had insisted on sharing his experience with his children.

Could not everyone tell they were a close and happy family? How right they would be to envy him, but how surprised to know the struggle it had taken each of them to come to this closeness, this open affection for each other.

After dinner they strolled through the lobby, planning to window shop

18

until it was time to go to the movies. But when they came to a display of sporting goods his wife reminded him that if the children were to take tennis lessons they needed new shoes. Abner walked them to the doorway, whispered hurriedly that he would meet them at this store or at the newsstand on the far side of the lobby, if they finished shopping before he did.

Recalling that they had passed the store where he had left several rolls of film to be developed and printed, he hurried back, hoping the shop had not closed for the evening. He wanted to surprise his family by enlarging and framing the most attractive picture.

Though empty of shoppers the store was not closed and he was waited on immediately. Abner paid for the package of prints and before the clerk had returned with his change he had opened the envelope and began looking at the pictures. To his surprise and satisfaction all but two had been reproduced in sharp, color-balanced prints. There were so many excellent, even flattering pictures Abner decided to let the family select the one they thought best. He put the envelope in his pocket, thanked the clerk and left the store anxious to show the photographs to his wife and children.

Outside the store, in the lobby, the sounds of hundreds of visitors talking at the same time lay over the carpeting like ground haze through which he had to push his way. Above the drone of these voices — higher still than the dissonant chords of laughter, calls on the public address system for the assistant manager and the distant ring of a telephone — he heard — or thought he heard — someone call out a familiar name. It wasn't really his name or a diminutive of it, but a special name by which someone he had known years ago had called him. Nevertheless, Abner did not bother to stop walking or look around.

He was certain no one knew him here and, besides, the friend who called him by that name had been dead for many years.

But again he heard it, suddenly closer this time, just behind the hand he felt on his arm. When he turned he flinched inwardly at the sight of the man who touched him so familiarly: he looked like someone he knew — or used to know — but the remembrance of that person confused him, for this was an older man with gray hair and several days of beard stubble which made the skin of his cheeks look dirty, his bloodshot eyes darker, bloodier. Since it was disturbing to stare at the man's face Abner concentrated on the rest of his appearance: his shirt was stained with perspiration, the faded knot of a food-spotted green tie was pulled askew under his frazzled collar and his jacket was as rumpled as his uncombed hair. Even his shoes were curled and gray — the way leather dries after it has been immersed in water.

"Neddie?" The man stood with legs apart, holding the nub of a cigar in one hand and a checkered cap in the other. He giggled until bubbles of saliva jumped across his lips. "Don't know who I am! Can't guess? Fooled

19

you!" He grunted and wiped his lips. "Bad eyes. Always said you had bad eyes. But I knew you. Knew it was you across the lobby."

A name formed in his head and took shape in his throat, though he said nothing, his sense of recognition inhibited by fear that the reality of this man depended upon whether or not he said the right name.

"Really got you fooled, heh?" The lips pulled back revealing horse-like yellow incisors and Abner realized there was only one person he knew — had known — who looked like a horse when he smiled and who called him 'Neddie.'

It was Howie Packer, but Abner tried not to have to admit it, nor his curiosity to know how it was that Howie was alive when everyone had told him about his death. But he did not ask: he did not want to become part of Howie's world — again.

"Still got you guessing? Haven't changed that much." He turned his head to show his profile. "It's me — Howie!" Then he leaned forward to put his face closer and grinned.

Abner nodded slowly as though in a state of shock. He hoped his feigned surprise would justify why he did not reach out enthusiastically to embrace his old friend. His feelings toward Howie were ambivalent. They had known each other for more than twenty years and there were experiences they had shared together which even now warmed Abner's memory. Yet he had no desire to resume their old friendship: too much had happened to him since they had last seen or talked to each other.

Having come through more than five years of the most rigorous self examination, personal criticism and confession (as a result of which he was certain all of his pretenses had been burnt away) Abner felt a certain purity — not unlike the arrogance of celibacy worn like a papal seal by some priests — and he could not easily relinquish the secret superiority with which he looked at his old friend.

To Abner there was no greater contrast between what he had been and what he had become than the sight of Howie Packer: he was the symbol of everything from which Abner had escaped and to which he swore he would never return, and now — as if to protect himself from contamination — he stepped back and sealed himself off by folding his arms across his chest.

"I really surprised you, didn't I?"

Abner nodded slowly.

"How's Davie?"

He smiled briefly, at least he thought he had smiled, still uncertain as to how he should respond to the uninvited and unexpected intrusion of this old friend into his vacation — into his new life.

"You still married, Neddie?"

He turned his head and lifted his eyebrows in a gesture of disdain, as though a reply would be more rhetorical than the question. But, in truth, his wife had left him twice since the last time he had seen Howie and had

20

threatened, promised and prayed for divorce every day until his "SAGA" (as he called it) had begun.

"And Danny?"

"Huh?" he parried, pretending not to have heard the question.

"Your brother."

This was a question for which there was an answer, but Abner chose not to speak it. If he could avoid having to tell Howie that his brother was dead he could circumvent having to listen again to the same painfully useless questions and the necessity of his repeating the same frustrating explanations.

The fact was that his brother had been buried before Abner had learned about his death, and what specific information he possessed about the causes of it he had learned in a haze of guilt and self-recrimination. Furthermore, it had been too painful and too embarrassing for him to ask questions, the answers to which he should have known and would have known if his life had been less dominated by a private and selfish passion.

Abner had not known that his brother had high blood pressure, or heart disease and diabetes; Danny had never spoken about his health and even if he had done so, Abner knew he probably couldn't have heard his complaints or understood them.

So telling Howie what little he knew about Danny's death would result only in questions Abner could not answer and he refused to trivialize his brother's death for the sake of mere gossip.

There was also the matter of Howie's special friendship with Danny. From that day when, by a circumstance he could not avoid, Abner had reluctantly introduced them to each other (convinced that the self-esteeming prejudices of their disparate lives would keep them from comprehending what he knew was exemplary about each of them), he had been amazed by the genuine affection and high regard they had formed for each other.

His brother had correctly judged that, despite his appearance, Howie was possessed of innate dignity and courage, for he was totally without self-pity, guile or selfishness. And Howie had rightly recognized that Danny's accomplishments had required courage, unselfishness and the same guileless faith in the pursuit of truth. And so, incongruously recognizing in each other those attributes of personality, they were not consciously aware of possessing in themselves, but hoped to find in every man, Danny and Howie had become instant friends.

Abner, however, could not afford to reminisce about that past; he was afraid that giving Howie the chance to talk about Danny might evoke in himself such feelings of nostalgia he would be unable to maintain an impersonal relationship with Howie.

Without moving his head and with his arms still folded across his chest, he could see the face of his wristwatch and noticed the time. "I have an appointment," he said flatly.

"Got a woman?"

"Wha?"

"You tied up with some 'T and A'?"

"I'm meeting my wife."

Howie snickered. "Phyllis? You'd never bring her down here."

"Not only her but the kids, too."

"Com'mon, Neddie. Have a care! I think you're trying to put a feather in my ear. I know you love your kids but what could you do for action with them down here?"

"Rest."

Howie's mouth fell open. "Like the rooster rests when the chickens are running free!"

"I made plans to come down here six months ago."

"Now I know you're trying to diddle me. Nobody makes plans that far ahead. What's your game?"

"Tennis."

"Heh, heh — you don't play tennis, Neddie!"

"I've taken a lesson twice a day since we got here. Tomorrow the hotel pro's going to start me on golf."

"Golf? You?" Howie snickered and wiped his lips on the sleeve of his jacket. "Golf's for people with nothing to do in the afternoon. You must be hittin' the casino at night."

It had been Phyllis' idea to come back here for their vacation, Abner explained. This was the hotel at which they had honeymooned. "You know how some people are about things like that."

Howie neighed and stomped his foot. "You telling me you made reservations for *this* place knowing you weren't going to gamble in the casino? Heh-heh. That's hard cheese to swallow, Neddie."

Why did he feel compelled to extricate himself from Howie's honest, if painful insight? He knew he had no obligation to justify his behavior — let alone to apologize for it — to Howie, and yet he heard himself explain that he had been unaware that there was a casino in the hotel. They didn't have one when he was here before, he complained.

It was Molly who had noticed it first as they were waiting in line at the reception desk, startling them with her gasp of dismay. Intimidated by the presence of the casino, Abner had tried to find accommodations at other hotels, but at this time of year nothing was available.

He had suggested that they go home and he had meant it. But even to Howie he could not pretend that he had wanted to go home — after all of the planning, expense, anticipated pleasure and the significance of this vacation to his family. But he had been prepared to go home, even if he had been frustrated once again by the influence of gambling over his happiness and that of his family.

"I even called the airline office, but it was impossible to exchange our reservations for any other flight.

"So we've had no choice but to stay and to ignore that place." Abner concluded rather apologetically. He pointed toward the casino with his elbow without looking at it, hoping to convey the sincerity of his answer by the intensity with which he stared at Howie: "Phyllis and I—"

"— I know Phyllis!" Howie interrupted. "She hates gambling — she wouldn't come down here."

"Look at these," Abner interrupted in exasperation and took out the envelope of photographs. "We took these the second day we were here. That's Phyllis!" He was almost shouting now. "Recognize her? And that's the front of the hotel. And the boy and girl — that's David and Molly."

"Auh, com'mon, Neddie. Don't do that to me. I know what your kids look like. I used to take them to the movies. They're little — "

"That was almost six years ago," he interrupted. "They've grown up."

"No kidding? Makes me feel kind of strange. I want to see them, but I'm sort of— " he touched the lapel of his jacket and tried to straighten his tie. "Maybe tomorrow I'll come by. I've missed them. Uh — can we talk some place now, Neddie? I mean in private." He waved his cap at the lobby.

Abner wanted Howie to stop calling him 'Neddie'; it reminded him of the past and weakened his resolve to keep himself separate from that past. He could not remember when Howie had begun to call him by that name — it was so long ago — nor had he ever been able to understand the reason why Howie did it. 'Ned' was one of the diminutives of 'Edward,' but neither 'Ned' or 'Neddie' had any relationship to his name. Furthermore, to his remembrance he was the only person Howie had ever addressed by any nickname.

Since no one else called him 'Neddie,' Abner heard the sound of that name always exactly — and only — as Howie pronounced it: he might not even have recognized the name if he'd heard someone else say it. Perhaps this was why the sound of it now evoked such feelings of nostalgia.

Suddenly he felt compelled to say something, anything, which acknowledged that past which they had shared and he repeated the story he had heard of Howie's death. "They said the Colombians — or was it in Mexico or Caracas? — had shipped your body to Eleanor in Buffalo." His own voice sounded strange to him.

"God forbid Miss Eleanor should get me!" Howie shuddered. "She'd put a penny candle in my ear and lay me out in the city dump.

"It was frustrating, Neddie. They couldn't understand English and I couldn't speak Spanish. I was in the hospital eight weeks. Bus accident. Then I got blood poisoning. In their hospital! Lost my passport and all my clothes. Didn't know until they let me out that they thought I was somebody else. I couldn't leave the country until the embassy could prove I was me!"

"I'm glad to know you recovered," Abner said coldly even as he observed that Howie did not look well.

"Neddie, you act like you're — egh — afraid of me. I know I need to

23

clean up — haven't had any sleep in three days — but I don't have a disease."

Abner nodded gravely, his arms still folded across his chest. It wasn't a comfortable position to maintain for long without moving and his hands needed to be put down. But he tightened his grip on his arms, glanced again at his watch and reminded Howie that he had to leave.

"Let's go to the bar where we can talk. It's my lucky day, Neddie!"

Abner did not want to go to the bar. It would take too long. Besides, after watching the quiver at the corner of Howie's cheek when he said it was his lucky day, Abner was certain he knew what Howie wanted and he was determined not to lend him any money.

He did not think there was anything inherently wrong in borrowing or lending money. Neither was he afraid to spend or lend his own money. He was in no way parsimonious. To the contrary, his true nature was outgoing, prodigal, generous — even extravagant. He had always enjoyed treating money as a consumable commodity of pleasure.

But Abner wanted to avoid repeating his old habits, particularly that of becoming involved again with Howie. He was afraid even of indirectly contributing to Howie's gambling, for he was certain any money he would give him would be used either to pay off an old gambling debt or to make a new one.

"For old times," Howie prompted and waved his cap in the direction of the bar.

"I suppose you'll think I'm lying when I tell you I don't drink much any more. I taught myself not to want to drink unless Phyllis is with me. She's never finished a cocktail, so it's been a good way for me to cut back on my drinking, especially compared to the way I used to do it."

Howie made a noise like a horse, snapping his teeth and winked at him. "You mean she won't let you drink by yourself? I'd rather talk to you alone, Neddie, but you can invite her if you want to. I always liked Phyllis."

"She wouldn't drink now — we just finished dinner. Besides, she's shopping."

It wasn't the drinking that was important, Howie explained. He only wanted to talk where it was private. Besides, it would be better if Phyllis didn't see him today. He knew he looked scruffy. He'd had a hard week, particularly the last three days.

So here comes the 'pitch,' thought Abner, and he wondered what he would say when Howie told him he hadn't eaten for several days, or paid his rent. Or would he admit he wanted the money to pay a gambling debt?

"Howie," Abner said, speaking his name for the first time so that the sound of it was strange to him, "let me tell you now so you can save yourself a lot of effort. I'm not giving you anything. No cash. No checks. No barter. No money orders." He was talking as fast as he could in order to keep Howie from interrupting him. "If you're looking to put the arm on me — forget it." Unconsciously he put his hands in his pockets and twisted his torso so that he presented a narrower silhouette of himself to Howie.

"No loans." Abner promised himself aloud looking at Howie obliquely, across his shoulder, and jamming his fists deeper into his pockets. "No third party checks, no IOU's. And no credit cards — I don't use them anyway. I'm not supporting your dreams, Howie, they always turn into nightmares."

Howie's expression changed to bewilderment and Abner felt a kind of redemptive smugness knowing he had guessed correctly about what he wanted.

"You got it all wrong, Neddie."

"No, *you* got it wrong. You're still living the kind of life I gave up and don't want any part of, so don't press me." He felt secure about himself for this was, to his memory, the first time he had refused to lend Howie money — or to borrow from him, or to bet with him, or for him or against him.

"Heh?"

"I'm afraid of you, Howie, and that's the truth. You remind me of myself." It was not easy for Abner to admit his fear of succumbing to the temptations of the past, nor of trying to describe the struggle for self-control which had confused him for so many years — the daily tests of will between his frustrated aspirations for immediate success, wealth and recognition and the acceptance of himself as a person with limited intellectual, creative and financial potential. But he was too proud and insecure to explain to Howie his relapses and the suffocating pain of having failed his wife and disappointed his children. That was too private, too personal.

"I mean it, Howie, I'm not giving you even a dollar."

Howie closed his eyes and giggled. "I don't need your money." He salivated and smacked his lips.

"But you'd like my company's credit cards, eh? Or for me to co-sign a loan? Or is it something you want to sell me?"

"I don't want anything except to sleep. If it wasn't for seeing you I'd have gone home and flopped for the next ten hours. Haven't had any Z's since Sunday. I've been playing cards for three days and ni — "

"Lost again, eh? Don't expect anything from me!" Abner interrupted, not wanting to listen to Howie exaggerate his success, boast about how much he'd won, or whine about his losses — the jackpots he'd almost taken in — and his present need for 'just a little help.' It was an old story with which Abner was all too familiar and in his fear of becoming involved with Howie's faith in numbers, he called him a romantically retarded adolescent without a sense of responsibility even to himself. "You'd bet your house — if you had one. Or your wife — if you had one."

"What's come over you, Neddie? I never heard you ever talk like that!" Howie pulled at his tie and patted his hair. "Besides, it's my lucky day. And yours too."

"Then why are you asking me for money?"

"Neddie, you don't listen."

"I won't finance your gambling."

"It's just like I said — you don't listen! I just come down from a parlor game where I hit the cage. I racked it up!"

"Playing cards?" Abner looked at Howie incredulously, disbelieving what he'd heard. "You?"

He watched Howie fish amongst his pockets and take out first one, then a second, and third and now — incredibly — a fourth and finally a fifth packet of one hundred and five hundred dollar bills, crisp, and unwrinkled, bound together with paper wrappers and rubber bands.

"See this?" Howie stacked the packets on top of one another and held them out toward him. "This here is more than eighty-six thousand dollars! Eighty-six thousand five hundred and twenty strong green men and they're all mine! I don't need to borrow from you, Neddie. That's what I've been trying to tell you. It's my lucky day!"

His first thought was that Howie was holding flash rolls. Although he would not touch the money, Abner leaned forward and stared intensely as Howie slowly fanned the packets. It was all there — or at least it seemed to be there — eighty-six and a half thousand dollars!

"*You* won this playing cards?"

Howie looked up at him and showed his equine teeth. "I did it, Neddie! I beat the house! I won more than a hundred fifty jackpots in three days and nights. I knew I was going to do it. That's why I wouldn't leave the table to get some sleep. I felt it in my fingers, even when I was so tired I couldn't think. Some of the time I played dumb poker and I still won. You never saw such timing, nothing could stop me.

"They even set down a professor and a mechanic and I steam-rolled them both. Neddie, it was like going to church. I drew so many pat hands I had to start losing a few to keep the table going. They thought I was cheating, but I wasn't scared. I knew as long as I sat there I was gonna win." Howie turned the stack of bills upright so that his strong green men stood at attention, ready for parade, silently repudiating the self-assurance with which Abner had assumed Howie needed to borrow from him and the arrogance with which he had lectured to him about responsibility.

"We know each other more than twenty years, Neddie, and you never saw me play cards like that. For the first two days and nights I felt like I was somebody else — John Scarney, or Amarillo Slim and Texas Dolly Brunson! My fingers moved sometimes without my telling them what to do! By this morning I was so sleepy I could barely read the boards. The sweat burned my eyes so that sometimes I couldn't even see across the table. But it didn't make any difference. No matter what kind of game we played, no matter who was dealing, I kept winning. And I wouldn't leave

26

unless the house called a rest. I was afraid I'd break the spell. Nobody's had those kinda cards since they opened the place.

"You should'a seen the way they were lookin' at me, Neddie. Could you believe it — I iceboxed the game. Me! I was *the* king of the boards for the biggest pots you ever saw — zip code numbers!" He shook the packs of bills with both hands, raising them over his head. "Told me to come back as their guest! You hear? Their guest! They're gonna pay my table antes for a month. What d'ya think of that?"

"It won't take them that long to get their money back."

"Auh, Neddie, you sound like a bad sport. I'm invited to play in their tournament. I'm not gonna let you spoil it for me."

"If you can't stop waving that money in this lobby somebody will spoil it for you."

"By this afternoon they were standing around the table four deep." Howie stuffed the packets of bills into the pockets of his jacket. "All the Palookas and Lucky Boys had dropped out and I was playing against the house. You would'a been proud of me. I knew I couldn't keep going more than another couple hours. So I remembered my manners and told them I was quitting at five p.m. no matter what. If I'd won the last two hands I'd have more than a-a-a hundred thousand. But eighty-six Big Ones ain't bad, eh? Heh? Besides, if I'd kept playing I might not have seen you! And now it's all ours, Neddie."

"What do you mean, 'ours'?"

"I mean I don't need all this cash. I want you to have some of it."

It wasn't enough for Abner to be embarrassed because of his lecture to Howie: now he felt foolish, even ridiculous. Howie was offering *him* money!

"It's our lucky day, buddy. Even if I'd have lost I'd have come over to see you and Davie — I can hardly wait to see him tomorrow. Besides, I want you to have some of these Philadelphia Printers, or would you rather take McKinleys?" Howie took out the packet of bills and offered them to Abner. "Remember, Neddie, I owe you."

"Nonsense," Abner protested weakly and afraid of being trapped, of not being able to move, he took his hands out of his pockets. His palms felt hot and damp and he rubbed them together briskly, then folded his arms across his chest again. "Put that cash back in your jacket. Anybody walking by here can see it. You wanna get rolled?" He was becoming angry with Howie for the absurdity with which he displayed the money he had won and for his unreasonable and good natured generosity.

"You got to believe in fate, Neddie, when it's a fact. Can't you see it's no coincidence? The very first time I see you in more than five or six years is the day I leave a card game with eighty-six thousand five hundred and twenty strong green men! It's a double lucky day for me! How much you want?" He whinneyed like a little horse which had found its way to the barn. "Remember, Neddie, I owe you."

"Will you put that money away!" Abner protested, trying to remain detached from the experience even as he recalled days when the two of them would have celebrated if either had won a thousand dollars. "You don't owe me anything," he argued, trying to dissuade Howie from being more loyal to their friendship than it was his own intention of reciprocating.

"Neddie, we've known each other a long time and we always shared when either of us won. Besides, like I said, I owe you."

"Nonsense. If you did I'd remember."

"But you don't understand!" Howie did a little dance of frustration. "It's been in my head a long time to repay you. Now that I've got a bundle you got to let me do it! You got to take it."

He was overcome by Howie's stubborn insistence on sharing his winnings and knew he might give in if he did not find a way to defeat his persistence. Desperate to think of a satisfactory argument he suddenly challenged Howie to tell him how it had happened that he owed him any money.

"Go ahead," he prompted almost accusatively. "I want to hear you explain why you owe me any money. Can you tell me what it's for?"

Now it was Howie who seemed surprised and embarrassed. Abner watched him cram the packets of bills back into his pockets again, light a small peeling cigar with a kitchen match he struck against his shoe, and then put the burned out match in his breast pocket. It was exactly as Abner remembered him lighting a thousand other cigars. It even was the same type of cigar — short, dry and always peeling — so that when Howie lit it, the wrapper began to burn separately with little flares of fire. He even held the cigar in his mouth the same way — between his front teeth the way some people hold a toothpick.

Abner could not help but watch with fascination as Howie repeated the same mannerisms and facial grimaces he had seen him make so often, so many years ago. It was like watching a scene from a familiar old movie in which he could remember — and anticipate — the gestures of a favorite actor. Howie would take — he took — a quick puff of his cigar; then he would squint — he squinted — and then he would wave — he waved —his cap at the smoke. Then his nose — he would scratch his nose and put the cap under his arm: it was exactly as Abner remembered, except that Howie stopped to pat his hair.

It had been bothering him for a long time, Howie began, and asked if he remembered how they would bet for each other whenever either of them could not get a bookie. Howie stopped speaking and Abner realized that he had no intention of continuing until his question was answered, so he responded by acknowleding he had not forgotten the years they had spent gambling, nor all the suffering they had shared. But he hesitated to admit he remembered any particular episode for fear it might serve Howie with some credible example for whatever he was trying to prove.

"Remember the summer you bought that red convertible and parked it in my cousin's garage to keep it clean?"

"What's that car got to do with your money?" He was defensive about that car since it had been paid for by his brother. It was another loan he'd never repaid which his brother had never mentioned.

"It was just before the Fourth of July. That fall I went to Caracas. You gave me four thousand to lay down for you in my name with Charlie Eyes."

Abner pursed his lips. How could he recall all the bets he's placed with bookies, or those he'd given to Howie to place for him?

"When I got to the bookmaker I took a look at your sheet — you picked four morning glories! I knew you couldn't win — those four were gonna finish so far out of the money they'd have to pay parking tickets to get past the club house. You never were good at picking horses, Neddie." Howie's voice dropped to a whisper, "So-I-didn't bet your picks. You never found out because those four gave up before the half mile post."

Abner shrugged. "So how much did you win with my money and your picks?"

"Nothing. It's the only time in my life I can remember having a hundred dollars more than my rent and not laying down a bet."

"You didn't bet? What did you do with my money?"

"I-I'm ashamed to tell you. I paid a finance company and gave the rest to Miss Eleanor's lawyer. He was gonna get a court order to put me in the work house for non-support. How could I support her?" He whined and clicked his incisors. "That's why I took off for Caracas."

Abner expected to feel anger at Howie's confession, or at least resentment, but his true feelings were of astonishment and guilt, for he remembered that when the desperation to win had suborned the integrity of their friendship *he* had cheated Howie, though he could not recollect exactly the circumstance of when or how he had done it.

He could not pretend to express anger when it was so far from the truth of his feelings and he heard himself say that he could not remember when Howie had ever owed him more than he paid back. "Besides, that was a long time ago," he chided evasively. "Maybe there were days when both of us were chasing our losses and we held back on each other. Maybe — " It was hard for him to breathe.

"Not you, Neddie. You'd never do that to me. I've always respected you for being straight up with me and everybody. And I tried to be that way. Maybe that's why I've never been able to forget about what I owed you."

Abner could not ignore Howie's adulation: it was irritating to him because it was so far from the truth he knew about himself, and yet — in an embarrassing way — it was satisfying to his private sense of accomplishment.

He realized that everyone who knew about his past life was aware of the pain he had inflicted upon his family and friends (until he didn't have any friends); the lies he had told his employers and the merchandise and time he had stolen from them; and the lies he had told his family and the money he had embezzled from them. Even his children knew his past — his failure to have accepted responsibility, the years he had ignored them because of his selfish preoccupation with gambling. And he understood that no one who knew about his past could ever completely ignore it. He couldn't. Perhaps that was why he never gave himself enough credit for having been able to stop gambling. Perhaps that was why he put so much emphasis on remembering those years before the Fellowship. Was he purposely being unfair to himself in order to insure that he would never succumb again to the life he had led? Perhaps flagellating himself with his memories was the reason he needed the succor of Howie's flattering and romantic view of himself.

Abner knew it was child-like of him to put such value on Howie's judgment. Howie was the least successful, the least accomplished and the most naive of all his friends, or former friends. Why did it mean so much to him to maintain an image of integrity with Howie?

To his family and to his intimate friends at the Fellowship he was another member struggling for redemption — trying to create a new person from an old failure — and there would always be doubts. It was the natural scar tissue of every recovering gambler. But to Howie he had always been the very model of a dependable, honest, successful friend; a loving, responsive father who only played at gambling for the fun of it.

So Abner was embarrassed both by Howie's idealistic faith in his character and his own attraction to that myth and he tried to show indifference by shrugging off Howie's praise, but he could barely move his shoulders. His stomach was churning and he heard a ringing in his ears as loud as a siren. The secret pain of his conscience kept reminding him that he had not always been honest with Howie, but it was an experience so buried in his memory he easily could have convinced himself that it was only an empathetic fantasy to Howie's confession. But then how was he to account for feeling — for believing — that he was guilty? How could he explain this private shame?

Howie was still talking about repaying him for using the four thousand dollars, confessing that he had been afraid to tell him what he had done for fear of losing his friendship.

"That was the only time in my life I was ever scared to tell you the truth, Neddie. Besides, I keep thinkin' what I would have told you if one of your Clydesdales had won."

"If-if-if," he gasped out the words defensively. "That's all hypothetical — and a long time ago. Why don't we just forget it?"

"Now you see what you're doing? You see! You hear what you said? You're trying to keep me from paying you back! That's just like you, Neddie. You didn't even get mad when I told you I'd crimped your four Grovers."

"Why don't you visit Eleanor? Maybe she needs money."

"Heh! I don't owe Miss Eleanor a thing. She cleaned me out before she left. When I got back from Caracas she was gone and so was the house, the furniture, the car and all my clothes. Sold it all. She even took the lint on my socks and my old toothbrush. Didn't leave me a nickel. I know my obligations and she's not included on my list. But what I owe you is different. You and me've been buddies and you got to take some of my bundle. It'll make me feel better."

Howie took out the packets of bills again and offered them to Abner. "I've got ninety-one McKinleys and four hundred and ten Philadelphia Printers. They were gonna give me a dozen Grovers but I wouldn't take them. Heh-heh! Remember the time we won ten grand rolling craps in Vegas and took our winnings in Grovers? Drove to San Diego to see my uncle and nobody'd cash one of them bills! Thought we'd robbed a bank or printed them ourselves!" He began to laugh and dribble saliva from the corner of his lips.

"There's no monkey money in here, Neddie. No wallpaper or 'gimmy's.' It's all genuine Federal paper. Eighty-six thousand five hundred and twenty strong green men. Why don't you count them? Then you could believe me and you wouldn't feel so bad about letting me pay you back."

Abner shook his head and backed away, placing himself behind the corner of the sofa. He wanted to stand behind it, but he didn't want to exaggerate his fear — he only wanted to maintain an independent distance between himself and Howie's money.

Never, in all the years he'd played cards, had he won eighty-six thousand dollars on one bet or in one game. He'd never won more than maybe ten or twelve thousand dollars at one time — and seldom that much before losing it all, or most of it, in some other action. And Howie had never won more than eight or nine thousand — at least as Abner could remember — without giving most of it back.

So the stack of bills which Howie was holding out toward him — all those strong green men — caused Abner to wonder if time and experience had enabled Howie to become a more skillful poker player than he had been in the old days, and if he too would have become even a better player if he had not stopped gamb — ; Abner suddenly and abruptly interrupted this speculation. To make such a conjecture, even a rhetorical one, even if not made in absolute seriousness, was calamitous proof to him of the existence in his unconscious of some lingering fascination with gambling and it frightened him.

Howie moved closer, pawed at the carpet and held up the package of bills. "It doesn't have to be four thousand. You can take more if you need it."

'Need it?' Abner repeated to himself. Of course he needed four thousand dollars! His children were getting ready for college — next year for Davie and a year and a half later for Molly. He "needed" the unexpected gift of four thousand dollars as much as any middle class, middle-aged parent —particularly one who had gambled away so much of his family's savings. Now all he had to do was to hold out his hands and Howie would count off the bills! It was so easy, so tempting.

But Abner knew that to touch that money was to be trapped by Howie's generosity as surely as if he had bet it all himself.

Thus he grasped at the first defense of which he could think and he began to ridicule Howie for being so selfish and greedy that he had thought nothing of the suffering he had inflicted on the gamblers from whom he had taken so much money.

"What are you talking about, Neddie? I won this free and clear. I won it without cheating, in an open game. It's got nothing to do with anyone else. Not even you. I've been playing cards here for a couple of years waiting for this chance."

"And now you're proud to walk around with the guts of all those dumb gamblers in your pockets! I suppose you've already forgotten what it was like when you *lost*? " he challenged. "Maybe you enjoy feeling like a vampire."

For the first time Howie was not smiling. He shoved the money into his pocket, put the cigar in an ashtray, wiped his lips on the sleeve of his jacket and shook his head as though to free himself from a toothache.

"I don't pretend I haven't been a hustler, but this is *my own money* coming back to me! I probably lost enough the last five years to buy my own horse farm. I ain't no vampire. What I won the past three days is *my* money! It's only fair!"

Howie was not asking him for advice and Abner knew he had no right to lecture him. Were it not for their old friendship he would have turned away, in fact, he looked across the lobby to where he had told his wife and children he would meet them. But there were so many people in the hotel it was impossible for him to see the newsstand.

"What do you expect me to do?" Howie continued. "Give it back? Heh! Heh! I ain't such a silly fool as to do such a silly thing."

"But you want to give me some of the blood you scraped off that table! Just to ease your conscience!"

"I can't understand why you're trying to make me feel bad for winning in a card game and at the same time you're telling me not to feel guilty for having used your money. You never acted this way when you were losing. All you ever talked about was getting back your money."

"Money doesn't mean the same thing to me any more. It isn't a challenge to my self-respect."

"But you never won a hundred and fifty jackpots and eighty-six thousand five hundred and twenty dollars in one game! Maybe that's what's bothering you? I've been playing cards here three and four times a week for more than two years and most of the time I've lost, so don't get mad at me for winning back some of my own money. Danny wouldn't've called me a-a-a vampire. And he'd've let me pay him back."

"How you won that money or what you claim you owe me has nothing to do with *my* brother," he corrected, emphasizing the personal pronoun by purposefully referring to Danny in terms of that familial relationship which excluded Howie. It was meant to be an unfair and hurtful answer which Abner hoped would demoralize Howie from speaking again about Danny.

"Listen to me, Howie," Abner ordered and began to back away, talking as he walked, trying to redirect his fear into anger. "I won't touch your money. Even if you owe it to me I won't let you pay me back with what you won playing cards. It's gambling money and I won't have anything to do with it." He continued to walk backwards.

"What's come over you, Neddie? I never heard you talk like this. Where you going?"

"To meet my family. We're going to the movies." He looked at Howie and saw the forlorn expression with which he was staring at him, but he had no intention of asking him to come along. In the old days they were always taking Howie with them, but not tonight. He was too afraid of Howie to invite him now, too afraid of what he might say to his children — or what he might do. Howie was always a gentleman in his own way, but he was a romantic fool and he might even give his children the four thousand dollars!

"Can I come by tomorrow, Neddie, after I clean up? I want to see Davie and Molly."

It was difficult for him to say no. He knew his children would be disappointed if they knew he had denied them the opportunity to see their former babysitter and companion. Howie was that rare adult with whom all children instinctively know they may share their most intimate secrets and David and Molly loved him as though he was their brother.

Having observed their tears when they had learned of Howie's death, Abner knew the joy with which they would now greet their old friend. And yet he was certain it would be better if they did not see Howie again.

Maybe tomorrow, he promised vaguely. The difficulty was that they had signed up tomorrow for lessons in the morning in tennis and for private lessons in the afternoon for golf. His ambivalent feelings about discouraging Howie were evident in the elliptical and awkward syntax with which he tried to explain their schedule.

"You wouldn't let me down, Neddie? I know I can count on you tomorrow."

Abner tried to walk sideways in order to move faster and still watch Howie.

"I don't think this is how old friends should act," Howie whined. "Why are you running away from me?" He was trotting along trying to keep close enough to talk to him and shove the packet of bills into the pockets of his jacket at the same time.

"It isn't important, Howie. I mean the money. That was a long time ago. I forgot about it. It isn't important any more."

"It is to me."

Now Abner was almost running sideways across the lobby in the direction of the newsstand and the security of his family. But still he kept watching Howie, afraid he would follow him even as he stumbled into a luggage cart, scraped his knee and mumbled an apology to a startled bellman.

He saw David first and then Phyllis and waved for rescue like a drowning swimmer to the captain of a ship, unable to hide the fear and anxiety which his meeting with Howie had provoked.

It was obvious that they had not recognized or probably even seen Howie, and yet why did his wife and daughter greet him with kisses and his son with such a reassuring squeeze of his arm?

He gave one last furtive glance back at the lobby, but Howie had disappeared.

Part Two

Abner sat up in bed trembling. His skin was cold and damp. His heart was beating as though he had been running. He looked at his watch: it was ten minutes after six.

In the pale light which filtered through the curtains and shimmered from a corner of the picture mirror he could read the familiar contours of his wife's figure in the adjoining bed. She was asleep. Then he looked for the dresser, the night stand, the chair across which he had thrown his slacks. All were in their accustomed places. What had awakened him? He inventoried his body: he didn't have a headache, his stomach wasn't upset, he wasn't thirsty. Furthermore, he had no recollection of dreaming. And yet this was the third time he had been awakened.

He lay back on the pillow and tried to recall the activities of the previous evening. They had gone to the movies — though he could barely recollect the picture, nor what they had talked about afterward. He remembered they had walked back to the hotel, stopping for ice cream and then at the newsstand in the hotel lobby for the morning newspa — ; suddenly he saw himself running across the red and gold carpeting in the hotel lobby and that incredible meeting with Howie began to retrace itself in his consciousness. There was Howie waving the packets of bills in the air — eighty-two, four, or was it eighty-six thousand dollars? — urging him to take four thousand dollars, or more, if he needed or even wanted it! What had he called them? His green men, his strong green men. And then he saw himself running across the lobby again toward the newsstand and the entire episode repeating itself in an endless loop of personal

34

examination and criticism: why had he run away? Why was he afraid he might not be able to resist Howie's offer?

If Howie's story was true then it was his own money which Howie was offering him and it was not easy to refuse the return of his own money. Then, too, there was his awareness of needing to put aside more money for his children's education. And finally, the money could be difficult to refuse because he knew Howie could easily afford to give it to him. And yet he had not forgotten that it was all tainted money: it was gambling money years ago when he had given it to Howie and it was gambling money yesterday when Howie wanted to give it back.

And so he had protected himself and his loyalty to his family and the Fellowship by running away. But he recognized the irony that in attempting to escape from repeating the selfishness of his gambling life he had acted just as selfishly. He had dishonored the memory of an old friendship, had acted like a coward and had denied Howie the opportunity to make restitution. He had been totally preoccupied with what was good and bad for himself without any thought about what was good or bad for Howie — or even for his children, who would be ecstatic, he knew, to see their old friend.

He threw off the blanket, jumped out of bed, dressed hurriedly — careful not to awaken his wife — left a note on the dresser and took the elevator to the main floor. It was seven-thirty, but some people were already gathered at the checkout desk and a few at the entrance to the casino. Nevertheless, the first sounds he heard were the hum of floor polishers and vacuum cleaners as the maintenance crews finished their work. The smell of tile wax, brass polish and carpet cleaner stimulated his appetite, but he knew that until he had apologized to Howie he would not stop for breakfast.

Abner remembered that Howie had complained that he had not slept for three days and nights during the marathon poker game. Surely he must be sleeping now, but where did he sleep? Where did he live? Most likely some of the local hustlers would know, he told himself, and walked toward the casino.

The entrance was a large doorless archway edged with a band of blood-red neon tubing. It gave the archway the appearance — at least to Abner — of a huge open mouth and he approached it cautiously, obliquely, from the side — as if he might be pulled in.

When he heard the card calls, the clink of chips and the clacking of the roulette wheels, his chest tightened, making it difficult for him to breathe: the sounds reminded him of a panther crunching on the bones of the gamblers and he shivered, gulped at the air and moved farther to the side, feeling the exhilarating fear he imagined he would experience in the immediate presence of that rapacious carnivore.

The light darkened when, from his perspective, someone crossed in front of the entrance and Abner flinched as though that giant mouth had snapped shut on another victim.

At this early hour there was no one in front of him waiting in line to enter the casino and he could have moved closer to the entrance. Nevertheless, he had determined that he was as close as he dared allow himself.

There was no legal or moral prohibition keeping him from entering the casino. But he knew there was the danger that if he did go inside he might succumb to the psychological stimuli and persuasive atmosphere of the casino and begin to gamble.

He knew that those who were unimpressed with the emotional obsessiveness of compulsive gambling might consider his fear of entering the casino proof that he was a fool. But as they got closer he noticed that they looked like hotel guests and were not likely to know Howie: they were over-dressed for all-night gambling, their business suits were creased from long hours of sitting, their vests were unbuttoned and they had loosened their collars and ties.

As they approached the exit they seemed to walk closer together, almost touching arms as if they needed mutual support and yet they did not speak to or even look at each other. They walked with a shuffling gait, too exhausted to lift their feet or their eyes from the carpeting.

Abner looked into their gray, expressionless faces and felt embarrassed as though he had invaded their privacy, for he knew and understood the pain they were trying to hide.

Four losers, he said to himself with sympathy, and looked away as they passed him.

Then two men wearing cowboy hats came out. By their raucous laughter it was obvious to Abner that they were winners. They stopped to listen to his question, but they were from El Paso and had never heard of Howie.

It became apparent to him that if anyone knew Howie it probably would be someone from the hotel staff and he waited until a cigarette girl and then two security guards walked by, but none knew Howie.

Finally, he stopped a waiter who came out holding a serving tray under his arm as if it were a battle shield. He was from room service, the waiter responded to Abner's questions, and although he had just carried a light breakfast for several of the all-night gamblers, he had no idea or recollection of how many guests were in the casino.

But perhaps he had served breakfast to the players in the marathon poker game which had ended upstairs yesterday afternoon? Howie prompted.

"Maybe you know my friend, Howie Packer? Little fella. Wears a checkered cap and smokes dry cigars?"

The waiter looked at him dourly and mumbled that his job was to pay attention to the food and the check.

"My friend was the big winner yesterday. I'm trying to find somebody who knows where he lives," he explained and repeated the description.

"If he was a winner yesterday he'll be back today. That's the way it is

36

with all of them dummies. They can't stay away until they're flat broke."

"I just served breakfast to a couple of 'high rollers' from New York, but I couldn't tell you what they looked like. All I know is if they would've had to pay cash for their food they'd have had to go hungry. But they just charged it to their room bill. They better have their return tickets or they might have to swim home. I've seen their kind before. What'd you say his name was?"

"Howie Packer. Sometimes he calls himself Howie Parker, or Harvey Pasteur when he wants to dress it up."

The waiter pointed to the reception desk. "Did you ask them?"

"Oh, he's not a hotel guest."

"Why don't you go in and see if you can find him? It's not a private club. Otherwise try the Melbourne Room around four this afternoon. That's when they start playing again." The waiter picked up his tray.

Although Abner had no intention of entering the casino he also was determined not to wait until the afternoon. That would be too late, he told himself, and he looked around, desperately seeking an answer.

Before he was aware of her she was standing in front of him, blocking his view into the casino, smiling provocatively, almost carelessly, her bosom full, temptingly exposed.

The shock of her smile pleased him. He had forgotten, but of course he recognized, that she was a hostess and smiled at every patron. Nevertheless, he heard himself ask apologetically if she knew a card player by the name of Howie Packer. "Sometimes he calls himself Howie Parker, or Pasteur. Little man with big teeth — almost like a-a-a horse. Wears checkered caps. Smokes little — "

"Why not come in and play a few games while you wait for your friend?" she interrupted. "There's a table over there that's ready for a winner."

"No, no. Thank you. I'm just looking for my friend — maybe he comes in here to play craps or blackjack?"

A roar of approval and applause from a table directly opposite to the entrance way attracted his attention and he watched a winner embrace and then shake hands with the patrons who surrounded him.

Abner remembered that feeling of victory, confidence and power. He saw himself in the person of that blackjack player, watched him pocket his winnings and realized it always had been the challenge of winning that consumed him, the challenge of putting his ingenuity, his tenacity and courage — his intelligence — against the odds and against the skill of others. That was always what had excited him. The money had always been second to the challenge.

Even though he was standing outside the casino Abner suddenly felt a rush of passion to gamble which was so physical it made him nauseous. It was, for an instant, as powerful as any sexual urge he had ever known. In that moment he recalled all the sensations of winning against the biggest odds and of being so high on the excitement of beating any challenge that he was gasping for breath.

He was startled at the momentary intensity of his desire to gamble, but not by the idea of gambling, for he had long ago accepted the fact that, like a man with a malfunctioning kidney who requires blood dialysis, he needed a kind of emotional dialysis in order to purge himself of what was a weak but still existent attraction to the competition of gambling.

This is crazy, he told himself and instinctively moved backward from the entrance a few steps. I am not going inside. I'm only looking for Howie. But even as he undertook to control himself he was aware of thinking about the satisfaction of pyramiding a small bet into a pile of chips — a bundle of cash as big as Howie's (he had always been a better gambler than Howie) and of staying awake for three or four days and nights just like Howie in order to play out the game until he showed them all how it was done.

The blackjack winner was leaving the table and Abner studied the width of his shoulders and wondered if he could juggle six cans of tomatoes or eight softballs or walk across a metal spiked fence in his sneakers without falling off.

Floating through his memories came the high pitched defiant cry of kids: "...I'll bet you can't hit it over the Great Bear Sign...What d'ya wanna bet?...I dare you to walk over that ledge...I'll bet you won't dive in there...Your buck against my five you can't make eight baskets in a row from here...I'll put up my two best baseball cards you can't juggle...."

Some people were lucky. They could accept any challenge and yet remain unaffected even if they lost: their self-esteem was never damaged by losing — and they did not become egotistical as a result of winning. Less fortunate were the poor losers, the complainers, the brooders and the apologists who rationalized excuses for losing. But by far the least fortunate were the few, like Abner, who were driven to succeed, to practice secretly — even at night, if necessary — until they could defeat any challenger in any game.

Yet theirs was as much the futility and frustration as the determination of champions, because they could not win all the time. No one could. However, they did not complain or whimper when they lost, but drove themselves more relentlessly to win.

Abner had been such a boy. He had never known, or at least acknowledged his limits, and had kept pushing himself to excel. And it had led to his taking chances, testing his self-confidence and determination, gambling not for money at first but on his ability to be the best until the success of gambling on anything and eventually to his discovery at the age of thirty-six that he was still a little boy.

But Abner would never know if he could beat that blackjack player at any game, for all of his questions were unspoken and all of his challenges were silent — muted by the recognition of something he had known, but until this moment had not had to admit: the exhilarating freedom and fun of childhood were gone forever. He had finally — and sadly — grown up.

He turned and walked from the casino entrance past the front desk, the cashier's office and a bulletin board which listed the activities and meetings for the day. Unable to decide what next to do he scanned the messages as fast as he could read them, skipping across the lines as though he truly expected to find Howie's address:

> Welcome... American Drug... Plenary Session...9:45 A.M.... 20th Ann...Reun-ion... Offi-Crew USS Daviso ... Flori... Suite... Robi-bi-tron-on-ics...Wilson Room ... Chrysanth...Tours...luncheon...district manag-... Telephone Compa- Telephone! Perhaps Howie had a phone!

He began to run toward the phone booths and the telephone directories. If Howie had a phone his address would be listed, though by which of his names he might be listed he had no idea.

He was halfway to the booths when he noticed two feet in yellow and orange striped socks, resting on a chair which stuck out from behind a hedge of artificial privet. The socks were so ugly he was certain they could belong to only one person and with mounting expectation he walked around the hedge. There was Howie. He was asleep on a couch, his legs and stockinged feet resting on an adjoining chair, his curled shoes and checkered cap placed neatly under the chair.

It was obvious that he had not gone home — he was wearing the same clothes, even the same green tie, only it was uglier and more spotted than it had looked yesterday.

"Howie?" Abner shook his arm and watched as he yawned, wiped his eyes and stared up at him as though still asleep. "What're you doing here? How come you didn't go home?"

"I meant to. But I got tired and took a nap. What time is it?"

"Eight-fifteen. I want to talk with you."

Howie swung his feet onto the carpeting and sat up. "What d'ya wanta talk about?" He pulled at the toes of his socks, but made no effort to put on his shoes.

"About yesterday." Abner was still uncertain what he was going to say other than to apologize, but he knew there was something else.

"I woke up this morning and realized that I didn't treat you right. There was no good reason why I should've run away from you. I suppose I was concerned with protecting myself."

Howie rubbed his eyes with his wrists and yawned again. "Na — na. That's alright, Neddie, you were surprised to see me."

Abner glanced around the lobby; he need not have feared being overheard, the lobby was almost empty, particularly when compared to the crowd with which it had been filled the previous night.

"But it was selfish of me — and I apologize."

"Forget it, Neddie, I understand." Howie smacked his lips and rubbed his stomach. "I think I'm hungry."

"You can have breakfast with us. I'm gonna meet Phyllis and the kids here in the lobby in a little while."

Howie jumped up and patted his hair. "But I ain't cleaned up, Neddie. I couldn't let them see me." He pulled the brim of his cap over his eyebrows, sat down and hunched over to make himself less noticeable.

He could wash in their suite, Abner suggested. "I'll take you up after Phyllis leaves. You can wear one of my shirts."

Howie shook his head and smacked his lips in anticipation. He stomped his feet with a kind of rhythmic glee, but his gratitude for what was a small generosity embarrassed Abner and he urged him to gather up his clothes.

While Howie struggled to put his feet into his warped shoes and tie the laces Abner went to the house phones and called his wife: she was already dressed and waiting for his call. Abner asked her to cancel their golf and tennis lessons and to take the children to the coffee shop for breakfast. "Start without me. I'll be a little late. I have a surprise for you," he added mysteriously, wanting to keep his wife from asking questions or waiting for him in their suite.

When he returned he found Howie pacing in front of the couch on which he had slept, already smoking one of his peeling cigars and absorbed in such concentration that he did not notice him.

"Are you ready?"

Howie flinched and then like a baseball pitcher going through his windup, proceeded with the motions of his cigar smoking ritual. He was ready, but first he wanted to ask a question and he closed his eyelids until they were almost touching, as if he believed he could magnify his sight by limiting his field of vision. Abner knew this grimace. It almost always anticipated a question to which Howie attributed an important answer.

"How much money have you made gambling since the last time we saw each other?"

It was such an unexpectedly naive question Abner refused to treat it seriously. "Let me think a moment," he paused, pretending to be calculating. "It was eleven and-a-half or maybe twelve million before I quit. I got tired of paying so much taxes on my winnings."

"Awh, com'mon, Neddie. It must be a pile if you won't say how much it is. You can tell me." He sucked in the saliva glistening at the corners of his lips.

In what manner could he, or anyone else, report the truth to Howie and assume he understood it? Howie's brain seemed to respond to different currents of stimuli, for he heard, saw and believed only in that which from his total experience agreed with his pre-conceived faith in the goodness of nature, the reasonableness of chance and the reliability of people. Abner wondered if any man could be more romantic and foolish.

The truth was that he had not won so much as a fat quarter in almost five years, he reported.

"Well then, how much have you lost? You must've hit the worst plague of bad luck ever! What's the most you've lost at one time?" His lips curled away from his teeth as though he had bitten into a sour plum, but he seemed equally excited by the mention of any large sum of money, regardless of whether it had been won or lost.

"Big money interest you, heh? Well I'd consider it big money if I bet five dollars and won and even bigger money if I bet five dollars and lost."

"That's hard cheese to swallow, Neddie. I remember you betting mo —"

"Told you I haven't gambled for years," he interrupted. "Not for money, buttons, match sticks or my school lunch. I have a good job. I work hard at it and my salary doesn't depend on figuring odds and covering long shots. I don't gamble any more, understand?" he challenged, then looked at his watch. It was time to go and he pointed to the elevators.

But Howie pulled back, complaining he did not want to use the front elevators for fear of meeting Abner's family.

"You don't look strong enough to walk up sixteen flights."

They could use the service elevators, Howie suggested, and led him around the clusters of people beginning to fill the lobby, through a gilded door to the pantry and along a corridor whose chipped and marred walls were partially hidden by stacks of folding chairs, lecterns, carts, flagpoles and table tops for banquets in the grand ballroom, stored on edge like lids for enormous cans.

As he followed Howie the level of noise began to rise in the passageway, becoming louder and more discordant until at a turn in the corridor they came upon the loading area for the freight elevators.

The entire hall was filled with room service waiters standing in line with red and white covered serving carts, watching for the lights which signaled the arrival of the elevators.

It was, to Abner, like visiting backstage during the performance of an opera — the waiters, dressed as resplendent members of the soldier-chorus in starched linen jackets with gold buttons and epaulets, adjusted their bow ties, smoothed their hair and fidgeted with their carts as they paraded from the kitchen to the loading area and then onto the brightly lit elevators.

Although there was no hotel policy of which Abner knew forbidding them from riding on the freight elevators with hotel employees, and even though he was a registered guest of the hotel, Abner felt uncomfortable — as if he and Howie might disarrange or soil the spotless carts or uniforms of the waiters merely by brushing against them.

"Found your friend?"

Abner turned toward the voice and recognized the waiter he had stopped in the lobby. Yes, he nodded and patted Howie's shoulder. "I

41

thought you worked in the casino?"

This was the worst time of the day for them, the waiter grumbled. Most of the hotel guests ate their lunch and dinner in restaurants. But it seemed to him as if they all wanted to have breakfast in their rooms.

The waiter stared at Howie and shook his head as if in disbelief. "You the one who knocked down the house yesterday?" He glanced at Howie's disheveled appearance. "Looks like you smacked it just in time." He nodded to Abner and pushed his cart onto the pantry hall at the next floor.

Bus boys, waiters and chamber maids squeezed on and off the elevator at various stops, carts were maneuvered artfully and trays held overhead until the elevator reached the sixteenth floor where Abner and Howie pressed their way to the front and got off.

Abner knocked at the door to their suite and when there was no answer he turned the key and motioned for Howie to enter.

"This is some room, Neddie! It's like a suite. You got a separate bedroom. Cost you a couple of horse shoes, heh?"

Howie sat down and suddenly began to breathe heavily through his mouth as though he were hyperventilating.

"Do you feel alright?" Abner asked and pointed to the complimentary carafe of orange juice provided by the hotel every morning. "Want some of this?"

Howie nodded, and held a glass in both hands while Abner poured, then gulped down the orange juice. Instantly — even while Abner turned to put the carafe back on the tray — Howie groaned, dropped the glass on the floor and clutched at his stomach.

"Cramps," he gasped, making whistling noises in his nose and holding his sides as though he were in labor.

Abner helped him into the bathroom and made him sip warm water until he had recovered. Then he turned on the faucets in the tub.

"Take a bath and shave. Use my razor and soap. It's all here. Meantime I'll get the valet to spot clean and press your suit."

"I'm sorry, Neddie. I forgot I didn't eat yesterday or the day before that. I was too excited with the game."

He closed the bathroom door, picked up the phone, requested the valet and then on impulse asked for room service: Howie needed nourishment. Then he walked to the bedroom, took out a clean shirt, shorts and a pair of socks from the dresser, picked a tie from the closet and carried the clothing into the living room and placed them on the table next to the couch.

"Empty your pockets in my bathrobe and give me your suit," he hollered through the door.

By the time Howie came out of the bathroom in Abner's robe, looking thinner, smaller, older and more fragile, the valet had taken away his rumpled suit and run down shoes and the room service waiter had knocked on the door.

Howie glanced at the serving cart appreciatively. "That's beautiful!" He sat down and lifted the food warmers. "Ham and eggs! Home-fries! Say, this is some breakfast, Neddie. How much did it cost you? I want to pay — "

"Eat. Don't worry about the cost. You're my guest."

Howie buttered a slice of toast and squashed it into the eggs and then put down his fork. "You said I could have breakfast with you and Phyllis and the kids. Why'd you say that if you didn't mean it?" He stared at the plate of food but kept his hands in his lap.

Nothing had changed, Abner explained. This breakfast was just something to fortify him until they went downstairs to see his family. "I ordered it because you said you hadn't eaten for a couple of days."

Howie picked up his fork, glanced at him for conformation that he had meant what he had said, and then began to eat, making little grunts of pleasure as he swallowed each bite of food.

"Many thanks, Neddie, many thanks. You're a true friend. A real pal. This is a repast fit for the King of Sardinia. But where's your plate?"

He did not want to eat now, he explained, holding out his cup while Howie poured from the coffee pot. There would be time enough later in the morning when he could have breakfast since he had cancelled the family's golf and tennis lessons for the day. "You can visit with the kids and then we'll all go on a picnic." Just like the old days, he almost added, but thought better of it.

Howie's teeth almost burst out of his mouth as he giggled. He did a little dance on the table with his fingers.

"Awh, Neddie, I knew you didn't mean it yesterday. And now you've cancelled your lessons. I always knew you were my friend. Won't it cost you a lot?"

"No, no," Abner interrupted, but trying to hide his impatience. It was all to be a surprise for Phyllis and the children — he hadn't told them about meeting him last night.

"What a real pal you are, Neddie. I owe — "

"No. I owe *you* an apology for yesterday, for running away. That's why I came looking for you this morning. I was afraid of all that money you won, and maybe I was a little envious of you. I admit I never won that much in any game. Then you embarrassed me by offering to give me four thousand dollars for a dumb thing I had done years ago and forgot about. But, of course, you never forgot."

"I just wanted to pay back what I owed you, Neddie."

"Don't you understand how I felt? I didn't think I deserved that money just because you claimed you owed it to me after five years. And I wasn't going to take that money simply because you could afford it. Besides, you had already told me you had won it gambling."

"What's happening to you, Neddie? You're talking to me like I was

43

your mama's preacher. Of course it's gambling money! Won and lost, won and lost. Over and over again."

"And that's why you won't have any of it left in a month."

"Howie did not answer immediately. He appeared to be contemplating something which made him feel uncomfortable and caused his lips to quiver. "What would you do with them, Neddie, if you were me?"

"With what?"

"My strong green men."

"I'd sign them to a long term contract before they could desert and take a job with somebody else. I'd bank the whole bundle."

"I can't do that."

Abner sighed. "How much do you owe?"

"I don't owe much to anybody except you and five-and-a-half weeks back rent to the YMCA. I got a pawn shop ticket for my watch and a couple suitcases of clothes."

"Pay the 'Y' and get your clothes out. Don't worry about what you owe me. You can pay me whatever amount you want — whatever satisfies you — whatever makes you feel good." Abner sipped at his coffee. "But I got a right to feel good too. So, whatever you give me I'm going to give to charity."

Howie slid out from the table, turned and supported himself by holding onto the arms of the chair in which he had been sitting. He twisted his head and looked at him sideways. "Would you feel just as good if I gave you only part of the money?"

"So long as that's what you want to do."

"It'd make me feel better to give it all to you, Neddie. But I haven't got it all."

Abner gave a nervous laugh. "I suppose you put it in the stock market?"

"Na — na — na. I mean I lost some of it last night."

"Your bundle? Your money? Abner dropped his cup onto the saucer splashing the coffee on his hand. "You got rolled? Mugged?"

"Awh, I'm too smart for that."

"Lost it? Flim-flammed? Dipped?" He rose from his chair. "I told you not to flash those bills!"

"Na — na — na. Don't worry. It isn't serious, Neddie. I went to the casino after you left me."

"Whatss" the pronoun left his mouth in a squishing sound like air escaping from a balloon. "You went — in there?" He sat down.

"I thought if I'd win some more green men you wouldn't feel so bad about letting me pay you back. Besides, I enjoy playing roulette. I like the sound of the wheel and the little ball."

Abner jumped up. "You couldn't wait until today?" Why didn't you call me? I'd have — "

"I was afraid Phyllis or the kids would answer and I didn't think you wanted me to talk to them."

"I know you a long time and you never needed an excuse to make a bet! You know you would have gone to the casino no matter what I said, or whether you had half a million or half a hundred!"

It was easy to rebuke Howie for losing money in the casino: Abner had admonished himself so often for chasing his gambling losses it was as though, while looking at Howie, he was actually talking to himself. Just as it had never been sufficient for him to know simply that he lost (he always had to know to the penny *how* much he lost and *why* he had lost) so it was that almost reflexively he asked Howie how much he had lost in the casino and if he knew why he had lost it.

"Maybe I lost more than I wanted to," Howie confided and gulped from his coffee cup.

"That's an answer? I'll bet you counted it five times. Put it on the table and count it again."

He didn't have any of the money with him; he'd put it in the hotel's safe before he took his nap.

"Howie, you never lied to me — except maybe just that once — but you're avoiding my question. How much did you lose?"

"I got seventy-five."

"You lost ten thousand dollars in the casino last night?" Abner asked quietly, trying to avoid the panic he was beginning to feel. "Yesterday I wouldn't have cared if you had lost it all. Now it hurts me almost as much as it does you."

"Awh, it's only money, Neddie. I can win it back."

"And you could lose another twenty thousand trying to get back the first ten.

Howie got up suddenly and went into the bathroom. Abner heard him turn on the water faucet in the wash basin and he waited until he came out wiping his face with a towel.

He looked ill, Abner judged, but he had less sympathy for Howie since hearing of his child-like unconcern for the money he had lost. Besides, in a convoluted way, he was angry with Howie for causing him to be angry with himself. Abner believed he was partially to blame for what had happened to Howie.

He knew he never should have left him alone with eighty-five thousand dollars in cash in his pockets — that was like leaving a child alone to play with matches!

But Abner also reminded himself that he had no responsibility for the way in which Howie had won his money and he could not accept responsibility for the manner in which he had lost any of it. His responsibility was to himself and the continuing struggle for his own recovery. If he had felt a need to keep away from the temptation of Howie's money, if he had felt some danger in succumbing to the nostalgia of his old gambling life — even though such dangers or temptations were only in his imagination — then he had done what was necessary for his self-protection, just as he had known to stay out of the casino.

Nevertheless, the conscience of the Fellowship was so persistent in reminding him of Howie's desperate inability to manage money that Abner finally volunteered to help him.

"I'll tell you what we'll do," he suggested. "When we go downstairs we'll take your cash out of the hotel safe and walk it around the block to a bank. That way we'll keep your green men from setting fire to your pockets every time you pass the casino."

Howie poured the last of the coffee into his cup and although it was less than half full he added several spoonfuls of sugar, stirred the spoon with a nervous twisting of his wrist and drank noisily.

"I got to tell you something, Neddie." He held the coffee cup in both hands close to his face — the way he often held his cigar — almost hiding his mouth. "You didn't understand what I said — before." He set down the cup and wiped his mouth with the sleeve of the bathrobe, but he did not speak. Instead, he picked up his fork and touched the crumbs of food on his empty breakfast dishes.

"Alright, tell me what I misunderstood," Abner urged, unable to continue watching Howie's irritating behavior.

"It's like I said, Neddie, you misunderstood me. I got seventy-five *hundred* left. Not — egh — not seventy-five thousand."

Even in the limited time Abner had had in which to become reacquainted with Howie he had been reminded that Howie's peculiar mannerisms almost always indicated his mood and what he was thinking. But nothing in Howie's behavior prepared Abner for the shock of what he heard him say and he tried to act as if he had not understood him, and that was a mistake because Howie repeated it.

Abner wanted to throw up. He felt such frustration and rage that he accidentally knocked an ashtray off the nightstand as he flailed his arms. His eyes filled with tears, he felt the perspiration run down his back sticking his shirt to his skin and to hide his hands which were shaking uncontrollably he crossed his arms over his chest and shoved his hands under his armpits.

Of course it was the money that mattered even though it wasn't his. But there was something else that angered him; which always angered him when he lost at cards or at the track or at trying to hit a ball over the Great Bear sign. He knew he could do it — he'd done it — and yet so many times when it counted, when he was competing against himself and the world — he had failed. It was failing that angered him, it was being defeated that frustrated him, even Howie's defeat — of losing and not knowing or understanding why. Of not being able to comprehend the logic of losing — only to know that all the planning, rehearsing, practice and control stood for nothing! It meant giving in, capitulating to a force stronger and more impersonal than he was — than Howie was — or than either of them could ever be, that made Abner angry.

46

He looked at Howie and saw that he was trying to appear nonchalant, although he was obviously surprised at the merciless speed with which he had lost so much — and like a boy whose kite suddenly snaps the string and sails off with the wind, Howie kept looking up at the ceiling as if he were searching there for an answer, while his fingers kept touching the tassels at the ends of the belt which was part of Abner's bathrobe.

"You dropped eighty thousand dollars like that?"

But Howie could only shrug his shoulders in a kind of hopeless dismay and mumble that everybody couldn't be lucky every day.

"I ask you how could you lose eighty thousand dollars in a few hours in the casino and you tell me, 'Everybody can't be lucky everyday?' Do you have any idea what eighty thousand dollars would buy? Do you know how hard most people work without ever saving eighty thousand dollars?" He was shivering.

"Why're you so upset, Neddie? It's my money — or at least it was. I'm not angry with anyone — not even with myself."

"I care because we've been friends for a long time. And maybe because I think I'm responsible for you. I care because it was obvious to me from your appearance that you didn't have any money before you won that marathon poker game. I care when you use me as an excuse for hurting yourself. Now I understand why you slept in the lobby!"

"I 'm sorry if I disappointed you, Neddie. I never wanted you to know. It came out unexpected. I'll give you thirty-five hundred now and send you five hundred next month. It that alright?"

"That's part of your trouble. You don't have a place to sleep, you lose eighty thousand dollars and you're planning to pay me back four thousand dollars!"

"It's only right. I owe you."

"Howie, you're two years older than I am and what've you got to show for all these years of gambling?

"No bank account.

"No business.

"No home.

"No job.

"Oh, but you're wrong there, Neddie. I got a job." He smiled proudly and pulled the bathrobe tight across his thin chest. "I'm the night manager of Pete's Pita-burgers."

"Wha?"

"I'm not a very good night manager. Pete says I give away too much food to the drifters who come into the place. He says I'm too poor to be so extravagant. But he trusts me with the cash register. I guess that's why he lets me stay. But I haven't been there for four nights so — maybe he fired me."

"Then it's like I said: no job.

"No car.

"No wife.

"No nothing.

"Where'd it all go, Howie?"

"I suppose it goes into The Game so that we can win it back again."

"You think you're gonna win eighty-five thousand again? Playing cards? How many times have you done that?"

"Only this once, Neddie. But I won some big pots in other games. And I'm a good horse player. If I don't think I can win, I don't bet."

I'm going to tell you something I might not have said to you yesterday: you're a compulsive gambler, Howie. You're like me. I'm a compulsive gambler. And you've got to do what I did. I can't say it was easy. Maybe that's what challenged me. It was the most difficult thing I ever did in my life — but you've got to quit gambling."

"Quit? What would I do? I don't know anything but hustling."

"And you don't know anything about winning. Can't you understand that for people like us winning is always a loan? It's temporary. Only losing is permanent."

"Gambling never scared you, Neddie."

"The hell it didn't!" Abner shouted. "I wasn't smarter than you, or even luckier. I just had one thing you don't have — a successful brother."

"But, Neddie, you always had good wheels and expensive clothes. You know how to live — like this hotel suite and this shirt and tie. I never had such a shirt like this. I've been proud you were my friend. And I always knew I could count on you. Just the way you came through for me today.

"I tell everybody about you and Phyllis and the kids and Danny. It makes me feel good, sort of like being part of a family. I wish I could be like you. Or make you proud of me, like I am of you. And Danny."

Abner could barely breathe. He walked to the air conditioning unit, turned up the thermostat and with his back to Howie closed his eyes and inhaled. He had said the same kind of words to his brother and he knew how self-destructive they had been.

"Don't say that to me, you hear? Or to anyone! You don't want to be like me or anybody else. I spent twenty years trying to please my brother, trying to catch up with him, trying to impress him and then — ('after he died,' he wanted to add, but managed not to say it), I learned it wasn't necessary. He loved me even when he found out I had lied to him, even when he knew I was immature and selfish."

"You, Neddie? What're you saying? You were never selfish. You were always honest with everybody and fair."

"If you talk about my past, you must be more accurate," Abner warned him. "I'm not trying to be pretty — just honest with myself.

"I was never more than a fool with too much money and I don't want credit for having been anything else."

"But you done nice things for lots of people, particularly for me. Just like this breakfast and this shirt and tie and the socks you're loaning me.

Say, this is just like the old days. You'd win at poker and I'd win at the track or at craps and then we'd — "

"Nonsense!" Abner interrupted irritably. "You think I was a good gambler, a winner? I *never* won more than enough to cover my losses. Toward the end, I was losing all the time.

"You know why? Because I don't know how to gamble. I never did. I couldn't make a few bucks and quit and I couldn't lose a few bucks and quit. I don't know how to quit. And you don't either. And when you don't know how to quit, you don't know how to win."

"I quit the poker game yesterday at 5 o'clock, just like I said I would."

"You didn't quit. You just interrupted your gambling for a few hours. And that's all I ever did, day by day, for more than thirty-one years."

Why was he talking like that? Howie asked him, squirming in his chair.

"Because it's time you see me for what I am — or was — and yourself too. I was no success," he admitted. "I want you all to know I was dishonest with money and unrealistic about my life. I spent a lot of time lying and cheating to make up for having lost so many jobs, so many friends, so much money while I — " Even before he finished speaking Abner recognized in the sounds and rhythm of his words a familiar syntax and he realized he had indeliberately repeated a sentence verbatim from the catechism of his therapy — just as he had spoken it at a thousand group meetings.

At those meetings he would wait his turn to recite with uncompromising and unequivocating accuracy the autobiography of his sickness and then listen to the all too familiar stories of others: these were not confessions, however, but the principal means by which the members of his Fellowship kept in touch with the reality of their past. Such revelations were not given as exercises in self-punishment but as exercises in self-awareness, not so much as expressions of their guilt for the past, but as the starkest reminder of their mutual and unending vulnerability.

Could his self-deprecating therapy shock Howie from his nostalgic romanticism with the past? It would depend upon his ability to disturb Howie by repeating the same squalid and degrading autobiography he gave in his therapy, revealing incidents in his life he had rationalized or hidden for so many years that even Howie was not aware of them.

Yet he also debated whether or not it was right for him to interfere with Howie's child-like faith in a just world or with his compulsive need to gamble. Howie hadn't asked for his help and seemed to be happy enough — or at least content with himself and the world he had constructed.

Abner knew that to try to change whatever gave meaning and continuity and satisfaction to Howie's life was a dangerous and selfish thing to do. If Howie were forced to abandon his faith in an understandable and just world (even tough he had naively self-constructed it from the exaggerated idealism of his own personality) he might become ill. If he destroyed that which Howie needed in order to hold together the fortunes and misfortunes of his life in reasonable equilibrium, Abner would have to offer him an adequate emotional substitute. But just as it was useless to offer honor to cynics, so Abner realized it was useless to present truth to the naive.

Nevertheless, Abner was uncertain whether he came to an unconscious decision to give his therapy to Howie and then began to recite it, or whether he first began to recite his therapy and then concluded it was the right thing to do. All he was able to recognize was that after the second sentence of his therapy ('My gambling problems began when I was eleven years old') he stopped and was unable to continue. He had not forgotten the events in his past nor the words required to describe them. But he kept reminding himself that if the principal purpose of telling the story of his gambling life was the benefit he was to derive from repeating it, then it was self-serving of him to repeat it to Howie. There had to be another way he could achieve the same result.

"So you think I was a success in gambling? It was my brother who made me look like a success. He bailed me out, paid my fines, my bills, my court costs. It was Danny who got me jobs and who set me up in business. He was the success, not me."

"You're making up these things."

"And you've been trying to make me into something I never was! You're hoping to make the future fit your dreams about the past. You can do whatever you want with *your* past, but I can't let you change mine. Even if I'm not proud of it. If I did, I'd be cheating myself — and my family and a lot of people who believe in me — in spite of everything I've done."

"Why're you playin' this game with me, Neddie? I know the good times we had, the money we won. You're the best gambler I've ever known. You understand sports and you're good at making odds, figuring points. You were always calm and slick and you never cheat. I was always proud of you for that. You know how to win like a gentleman."

"Do you remember me losing?"

Howie laughed triumphantly. "Not often, Neddie! You were too smart for — "

"As smart as when I gave you four thousand dollars to bet on those Clydesdales?"

"You never had a good eye for a horse, Neddie."

"Did you come with me many times when I took cash to pay bookies and street sharks?"

"Like you said — only now and then."

Howie's graciousness made Abner even more determined to destroy his idyllic picture of the past and he reminded Howie of the times his brother-in-law had come to visit and they had gone to the track every night for three weeks.

"Do you know how much I owed Sam for all of the side bets I made with him and the cash I borrowed?"

Howie acknowledged only the vaguest recollection.

"When he took my check to the bank what happened?"

"I think they said you couldn't cover it. But that happens to everybody, Neddie. It didn't mean you were going to stiff him."

"I might have, if he hadn't been your brother-in-law. Do you remember how I made it good?"

Howie rubbed his teeth with the side of his finger. "You left the cash with Danny. I picked it up at his office."

"That wasn't my money — it was his money, Danny's money! He loaned it — gave it to me. Do you know I borrowed from him until I was forty-three years old?"

"But he's your brother. You'd do the same for him! Why're you making up these stories?"

"You think I'm inventing my past! If there's nothing beautiful in what I'm telling you why would I invent it?"

"I don't know, Neddie. You got a good wife and kids and a kind brother. You always had clothes and plenty of money. Look at your suit! You ain't no 'loser.' I got thrown out of the YMCA last week for not paying my rent. But you got style, Neddie. That's what makes you a successful gambler."

He was not a successful gambler, Abner answered loudly and leaned forward across the table, wanting to cram the words into Howie's head. He had never been successful at gambling and he did not want to be successful at it now.

"I haven't touched a deck of cards or placed a bet in four years."

"You talk like somebody I don't know."

"That's what I've been trying to tell you!" Abner agreed. "I'm not the same person you knew. Could you believe I've passed this casino a half dozen times every day since I've been here and I never went inside? Even this morning when I was trying to find somebody who knew where you lived.

"I stood by the entrance waiting for somebody to come out so I could ask about you. I could hear all the action and even see some of it but I stayed outside in the lobby. Can you imagine me doing that in the old days?"

It wasn't so much boastful as it was satisfaction — proof — to Abner that he had been able to control himself in such a dangerous environment.

But Howie only snickered, curled his lips and remarked that it didn't take any effort to leave the casino without betting: he'd done it hundreds of times when he was broke.

He often went to the casino when he had no money, hoping to find someone from whom he could cadge a small loan. If he didn't see anyone he knew, he'd stroll around the tables and watch the action while looking for chips which had been dropped on the floor. He would bet whatever he could borrow or whatever was the value of the chips he found. "And I always felt better for having chanced it, even when I lost and was forced to walk out without a nickel in my pockets."

Abner had heard it all before: it was the credo of the quintessential romantic — someone who believed it was more honorable and courageous to gamble on the unknown, even if one chose incorrectly, than it was to find ways to solve even the smallest problem through an understanding of predictable events.

But before Abner could respond there was a knock on the door and he flinched, fearing it was his family. But the voice announced it was the valet service. Abner tipped the porter and hung Howie's suit over the closet door. It was still ugly but it was pressed and the lapels had been spot cleaned, even his shoes had been shined to a surprising brilliance.

Howie examined the suit and seemed pleased. He picked up the clothes which Abner was lending him and carried them to the bathroom, then came back for his suit and shoes.

They were late and at any minute Abner expected to hear his family at the door. He had failed to influence Howie and the time left for them to talk was rapidly vanishing.

Impulsively, from his own sense of failure and desperation, Abner told him to wait before he dressed and in a voice which surprised him by its sincerity he asked if he remembered how much they had won on their trip to Las Vegas with Howie's brother-in-law. Abner knew he could hold Howie's attention with any gambling story — true or imaginary — and, in fact, Howie stopped, suit and shoes in hand, and waited for him.

"We pooled our money and divided it before we left the motel for the casinos. You didn't forget that, did you?"

Howie nodded slowly, the full recollection of that adventure apparently only now beginning to enter his mind. "Oh I remember as if it was yesterday because if it hadn't been for what I won I wouldn't have been able to visit my uncle in San Diego."

"That's right. But how much did I win?"

"Nothing. You played blackjack, I think. But I know you tapped out. So did Sam. Why're you asking me about that—"

"Because I had to lie to Phyllis why I was taking a trip. I told her I was going to St. Louis for a job interview and she even borrowed the money for my plane ticket." That part was true. "So how could I forget winning more than fifteen thousand dollars?"

"Where? On that trip to Vegas? Naw," Howie giggled a little and then frowned. "You got it all mixed up. You lost, Neddie, just like Sam. I was the only winner."

"How do you know?"

"Because you had no cash left, no chips. I know because you told me so."

"Well, I didn't tell you the truth," Abner tried to confess, his voice sinking with his self-esteem. "I won fifteen thousand, but I needed every cent of it. I'd been lying about my job — how much money I was making — and I got trapped — everything came at me at once. I had to prove good faith. I had to come up with cash for Phyllis, the bank, two shylocks, and a marshall who had at least four judgments against me.

"That's why I went to Vegas with you. If I hadn't won I might not have gone home."

"But you're saying you lied to me, Neddie. You never did that to anybody." Howie shook his head in disbelief.

"That's how it is for people like me. At least that's how it was. When you owe enough you get desperate enough. You know that." Abner sat down and looked away from Howie's bewildered gaze.

"So the way I figure it, I owe you a third of fifteen thousand. If you keep the four grand you owe me then I'll owe you just a thousand. Seems practical to me."

Howie didn't answer, he stood transfixed in the hallway like a traveler who had just discovered he was on the wrong train, headed in the wrong direction, unable to salvage the time, or the price of the ticket, let alone the power to turn the train around.

For a moment consternation — even panic — seemed to overwhelm him. He leaned against the wall as though to steady himself. But then he suddenly squinted at Abner in his strange manner and waved his shoes at him as if he was patting him on the back and reprimanding him at the same time.

"I know what you're trying to do, Neddie. You're trying to keep me from paying you what I owe you. You're even trying to make it seem like you owe me money! That's what Danny would do." He walked to the bathroom, hung his suit on the door and came out still holding his shoes. "I ain't so dumb so as not to understand you're trying to get me to quit gambling like you done." He waved the shoes again. "And I'll tell you a secret I wouldn't admit even to Danny — it isn't much fun any more. But I can't quit, Neddie.

"I'm by myself. I haven't got a family, I mean a real family with kids, like you got. Going to the track or to the casino and playing cards is like being with my family. I need that even more than the money or the action."

He walked up to the bathroom but paused and looked back at Abner admonishingly. "Don't ask me to give it all up, Neddie. I can't."

The door closed and Abner was left to consider how ridiculous he had been to try and rescue Howie. Rescue him from what? From the little happiness he found in his miserable existence?

He thought back on his own life and the miserable existence from which he had been rescued by strangers who had introduced him to the Fellowship. They had owed him nothing and yet they had saved his life. He recalled the suffering of that year. Recovery was so painful when it was real — even for those who had helped him — that for several years it had been difficult for him to understand why they had not given up on him when he had admitted to gambling after he joined the Fellowship. But they had never threatened to let him sink — always someone had been there to help pull him out.

Didn't he owe it to Howie not to give up on him? But what did he have to offer Howie besides money?

Suddenly he thought he understood what it was all about and he ran to the closet, ripped off his clothes and put on his shorts, pullover, sweat socks and tennis shoes.

He was tying his shoe laces when Howie came out of the bathroom wearing his old shirt with the frayed collar and his ugly green tie. He carried Abner's clothes back to the table near the couch and put them down side by side as if they were medals of honor. The tie first, then the shirt, the underwear and lastly the socks.

"It's a nice shirt," Howie volunteered and gently brushed his fingers against the fabric. "But it wouldn't fit me," he said with forgiving grace.

Howie hadn't looked up at him until this moment but Abner could see that he was as surprised to notice his change of clothing as he had been to see what Howie was wearing.

Why had he changed his clothes? Howie asked. "Aren't we going downstairs to—"

"I'm going to play tennis," Abner lied and picked up his wife's racket. "There's no point to your seeing Phyllis and the kids. You told me you didn't have a family and said it was the casino that was important to you."

"But I didn't mean your family, Neddie. I want to see them. I've missed them."

"You? Missed my family? What do you need a family for? What's the purpose of a family anyway? You think you got all the answers."

"A family is people who care about you, who love you," Howie volunteered.

"You couldn't be a member of a family," Abner sneered.

"Yes I could!" Howie challenged.

"You're too selfish to be a part of a family. Even Eleanor left you because you only thought about yourself — what're you going to contribute to a family? What've you got to give? Poker chips? An old deck of cards? Parimutuel slips?"

"You don't have to be rich to have a family," Howie argued. "Even if I haven't got a lot of money I can give other things."

"Like what? Cheating? Lying? Spending every penny on yourself? Taking your family's money? Destroying their financial security and their faith and trust in you? Family? Hah! You don't know anything about being part of a family!"

"Yes I do know," Howie squealed. "I've watched you and Phyllis. I was your babysitter. I gave up gambling lots of times to stay with David and Molly."

"David and Molly! They thought you were dead. It's better for them if they don't know how far down you've gone.

"You actually compared my family to the swill you've been hanging around with — deadbeats, pimps, card sharks, dildocks and buncos! That's a family?"

"That's not fair, Neddie," Howie cringed.

"I don't think I should let you see my family. What do you want with them anyway — they don't have much money."

"Please — " Howie gasped.

"Are you going to try to bribe them with your seventy-five hundred bucks?

"No. I don't think you understand what a family is. You might try to ruin mine."

"Neddie, Neddie, what are you saying? I love them. I wouldn't do anything to hurt them. It isn't fair of you to talk like this. I'm going to call Danny and ask him."

Abner recoiled at the sound of his brother's name. It was the last name he would have thought to hear mentioned in this conversation. But, of course, Howie knew nothing of Danny's death. So maybe it was only logical that he would seek help from that same person upon whom Abner had depended for so many years.

"Danny? You want to call Danny?" Abner repeated the name and suddenly it sounded strange and remote — like a foreign name for which he could not determine the nationality or even the gender.

"And that's another thing. Stop talking about my brother. You can't call him, you poor fool."

"And why not? I don't have to charge it to your room. I got enough money of my own. I'm going downstairs and place a call by myself. Danny'll understand. He'll make you let me see David and Molly. He—"

"Danny's dead!" Abner sat down.

"Don't tell me another lie, Abner—" But something in Abner's expression or the tone of his voice or the way he had changed his posture caused Howie to wobble on his warped shoes and he sat down, facing Abner but not looking at him.

"You are making it up. It's a lie just to scare me."

It hurt Abner to see the change which was taking place in Howie's face and yet he felt vindicated by the change. Wasn't this what he had wanted?

"Danny couldn't be — he couldn't," Howie mumbled in disbelief. "He told me—" and he felt amongst his pockets and took out a faded personal card and smoothed it with his fingers. "That's his writing — his own writing. It's the only thing I owned I managed to save in Caracas."

Danny had told Howie to call him at any time if he were in trouble but Howie had resisted in spite of the times he had needed help. He had been content to keep that card in his pocket like a talisman, believing in its power if he should ever want it.

"This card's been my ace. I thought that as long as I had it I had something special I could always count on."

Howie held up the card and turned it over several times. "It was like having my own family, my own little family." He smoothed the card carefully and put it in his breast pocket. "What'm I gonna do now?"

Abner saw at last what pain, humiliation and love could do.

"So, Danny was more than just luck, or money to you?"

Howie nodded.

"He was someone we both could count on. And that's what a family's for."

"But he's gone. I haven't got a real family any more, Neddie."

"The hell you don't. You got two of them! Com'mon. Put on my shirt. We're going downstairs to see Phyllis and the kids. And then we're going on a picnic and I'll tell you about the other one."

Chapter III

INTRODUCTION TO GAMBLERS ANONYMOUS

Gamblers Anonymous is a fellowship of men and women who share their experience, strength and hope with each other that they may solve their common problem and help others to recover from a gambling problem. In the hundreds of local group meetings held each week in the United States and abroad, members of the Fellowship gather to reinforce their efforts, as well as those of other compulsive gamblers, to abstain from gambling and to grow personally and spiritually. Recovery does not entail gaining the ability to gamble normally, as a social gambler would. Gamblers Anonymous members realize that testing themselves in this way only leads back to the old patterns of destructive behavior. Rather, members seek to channel energies that would otherwise be expended in gambling into activities that foster productive character development. Such participation in the Fellowship's program is intended to be a lifetime endeavor, for although an individual may control the compulsive gambling disorder, one can never really eliminate the illness from one's psychological make-up. Adherence to the Gamblers Anonymous Program leads not only to a life free from gambling, but also to a higher level of moral and spiritual values and conduct for members as they succeed in the program.

As the name implies, Gamblers Anonymous is guided by the principle of anonymity, which takes two basic forms: public and individual. At the level of press, radio, film, and television, the anonymity of Gamblers Anonymous members is carefully preserved. Only first names are used, both to safeguard the identity of the members representing the Fellowship and to keep emphasis where it properly belongs — not on individual spokespersons but on the Gamblers Anonymous group as a whole.

Gamblers Anonymous works to attract, rather than recruit. The Fellowship does not seek to promote its own image, nor that of individual members. Gamblers Anonymous simply wishes to inform the public that help is available for someone with a gambling problem. Hence, the Fellowship uses the public media to advertise itself, and encourages members of its public relations committees to make its existence known to the general public. Some who respond to the Fellowship's message do so of their own accord, but a great many come through the efforts of someone else, such as a spouse, other family member or friend.

Once introduced to the program, the newcomer is actively encouraged to stay with it. Frequently, members of the Gamblers Anonymous chapter will telephone the newcomer to encourage attendance at meetings and to help with any problems he or she might have in adjusting to the program. Success in the Fellowship depends upon the efforts and determination of the new member. While the decision of whether or not to continue gambling is ultimately left to the individual, Gamblers Anonymous members energetically support a new member to stay with the program and refrain from gambling.

Regular attendance at meetings is strongly urged for all members. Experience has shown that recovering members attend at least one meeting per week. Prolonged or repeated absence results in trouble, where the old pattern of compulsive gambling and destructive behavior recurs.

The Fellowship believes that compulsive gambling can never be cured. Gamblers Anonymous knows, however, that compulsive gamblers can recover control over their lives by abstaining from gambling and by changing their destructive behavior. Such rehabilitation is accomplished through the Fellowship's Recovery Program, which is designed to arrest the disintegration of the compulsive gambler's life and to foster new, healthier behavior.

The GA Recovery Program

This program consists of the Twelve Steps of Recovery which are based on practical experience and insights developed over many years. Most importantly, the Twelve Steps of Recovery *work*, and they are therefore the cornerstone upon which the Fellowship is built. Although Gamblers Anonymous is not a religious organization, the Recovery Program is based on certain spiritual values and concepts. The Recovery Program is based on the faith that compulsive gamblers can be helped by yielding to a force greater than themselves, be it God, the Fellowship or both.

Gamblers Anonymous can be described as a spiritual fellowship because it asks its members to have faith and to develop the highest and finest qualities of human character. Such virtues as kindness, honesty, humility, empathy, generosity and integrity are advocated as the best principles for a new way of life. Through practicing these virtues members have learned to strive for spiritual progress as the means for personal recovery and for the perpetuation of the Fellowship.

Compulsive gamblers who have been rehabilitated through the Gamblers Anonymous program come to realize that they have been launched on a lifetime of self-examination and self-improvement. They learn that there is no short-cut for building a new future. Because rehabilitation takes time, and also because of the need to be ever vigilant against the impulse to gamble, members come to realize that participation in the Fellowship is an ongoing commitment — one to which they must strive. It is only from within the Fellowship that these rehabilitated gamblers have the power to overcome their compulsion and to effect the changes in their character they desire.

The Group Meeting: Core of the Fellowship's Existence

The Fellow's principles are put into action by means of the group meeting. Although Gamblers Anonymous maintains local and national service offices to keep the Fellowship functioning, it is through local group meetings that compulsive gamblers are actually rehabilitated.

The structure of the group meeting is basically similar all over the world, although the individual groups are free to run their meetings according to the wishes of members, provided that meetings conform to the general philosophy of the Fellowship. Meetings are held on a weekly basis. They can be held anywhere, but usually nonprofit organizations such as churches, synagogues and fraternal houses are selected because rents are generally less expensive at these locations. Meetings vary in length and type but the majority are open only to Gamblers Anonymous members. Occasionally, non-members such as journalists and doctors are allowed to attend. On these occasions it is made clear to visitors that they might be asked to leave the room, should any member desire to speak with confidentiality.

The meeting is conducted by a chairman, usually selected by the secretary of the group. Most often the meeting is chaired by a different person every week.

During a typical meeting members give therapy, and selections from the "Combo" Book, a small pamphlet which capsulizes the objectives and principles of Gamblers Anonymous, are read aloud. In addition, most of the following activities take place: new members are introduced, Fellowship-related announcements are made, voluntary contributions are collected from members only and necessary business is conducted.

A large portion of the meeting is devoted to therapy, during which the chairman calls upon individual members to talk about their gambling and related experiences. Persons giving therapy may talk about specific gambling incidents and how they started to gamble, came to Gamblers Anonymous, handle the urge to gamble, receive help through the Gamblers Anonymous program and deal with everyday life. At the conclusion of each therapy, members applaud to express their support and understanding for the person who has spoken.

Therapy serves both as a catharsis for the individual, and also as a means by which members share their experiences. It helps members solve everyday problems. Therapy also keeps memories of destructive behavior fresh. By remembering the problems, disillusion and anguish of their gambling lives, compulsive gamblers are less likely to become complacent and return to a life of gambling. In addition to the benefits gained by speaking, members also benefit from listening to and sharing from the experience of others.

A coffee break, along with the informal gathering that normally follows after the end of each meeting, are considered as important as the formal meeting itself. During these periods members are given a chance to interact with each other informally and share their knowledge and experience. Such interaction has been found to be important in promoting group solidarity and unity. This cohesiveness helps members stay with the program.

Once having seen the support given to each member, newcomers feel more comfortable to speak freely. The new member is asked to read and answer the Fellowship's Twenty Questions from the "Combo" Book and encouraged to give therapy. The Fellowship's standard procedure is to then ask the newcomer to make a commitment to the Gamblers Anonymous for at least ninety days.

At the conclusion of the meeting, all members stand and recite the Serenity Prayer:

> God grant me the serenity to accept
> The things I cannot change,
> Courage to change the things I can,
> And the wisdom to know the difference.

The Combination or "Combo" Book

At all Gamblers Anonymous meetings, the "Combo" Book is read, either in part or in whole. This book contains excerpts from a wide range of the Fellowship's literature, summarizing the most important parts of the program. This pamphlet is used more frequently than any other piece of Gamblers Anonymous literature, and it is continuously up-dated to reflect the Fellowship's evolution.

The following selection from the "Combo" Book outlines the principles and goals of Gamblers Anonymous, as well as summarizing the Fellowship's view of the compulsive gambler's plight:

Gamblers Anonymous is a fellowship of men and women who share their experience, strength and hope with each other that they may solve their common problem and help others to recover from a gambling problem.

The only requirement for membership is a desire to stop gambling. There are no dues or fees for Gamblers Anonymous membership; we are self-supporting through our own contributions. Gamblers Anonymous is not allied with any sect, denomination, politics, organization or institution; does not wish to engage in any controversy; neither endorses nor opposes any cause. Our primary purpose is to stop gambling and to help other compulsive gamblers do the same.

Most of us have been unwilling to admit we were real problem gamblers. No one likes to think they are different from their fellows. Therefore, it is not surprising that our gambling careers have been characterized by countless vain attempts to prove we could gamble like other people. The idea that somehow, some day, we will control our gambling is the great obsession of every compulsive gambler. The persistence of this illusion is astonishing. Many pursue it into the gates of insanity or death.

We learned we had to concede fully to our innermost selves that we are compulsive gamblers. This is the first step in our recovery. With reference to gambling, the delusion we are like other people, or presently may be, has to be smashed.

We have lost the ability to control our gambling. We know that no real compulsive gambler ever regains control. All of us felt at times we were regaining control, but such intervals — usually brief — were inevitably followed by still less control, which led in time to pitiful and incomprehensible demoralization. We are convinced that gamblers of our type are in the grip of a progressive illness. Over any considerable period of time we get worse, never better.

Therefore, in order to lead normal happy lives, we try to practice to the best of our ability, certain principles in our daily affairs.

The "Combo" Book also contains the Twenty Questions, devised by Gamblers Anonymous to define what it means to be a compulsive gambler. These questions are asked of every newcomer to Gamblers Anonymous. It is the Fellowship's experience that most compulsive gamblers will answer yes to at least seven of the Twenty Questions.

1. Did you ever lose time from work due to gambling?
2. Has gambling ever made your home life unhappy?
3. Did gambling affect your reputation?
4. Have you ever felt remorse after gambling?
5. Did you ever gamble to get money with which to pay debts or otherwise solve financial difficulties?
6. Did gambling cause a decrease in your ambition or efficiency?

7. After losing did you feel you must return as soon as possible and win back your losses?
8. After a win did you have a strong urge to return and win more?
9. Did you often gamble until your last dollar was gone?
10. Did you ever borrow to finance your gambling?
11. Have you ever sold any real or personal property to finance gambling?
12. Were you reluctant to use "gambling money" for normal expenditures?
13. Did gambling make you careless of the welfare of your family?
14. Did you ever gamble longer than you had planned?
15. Have you ever gambled to escape worry or trouble?
16. Have you ever committed, or considered committing, an illegal act to finance gambling?
17. Did gambling cause you to have difficulty in sleeping?
18. Do arguments, disappointments or frustrations create within you an urge to gamble?
19. Did you ever have an urge to celebrate any good fortune by a few hours of gambling?
20. Have you ever considered self destruction as a result of your gambling?

The "Combo" Book provides a brief history of Gamblers Anonymous, from its genesis as a simple idea shared by two men to the growth of the Fellowship around the world. Also in the pamphlet are twelve questions and answers on compulsive gambling and the Gamblers Anonymous Program. Some of the topics dealt with in this series concern the nature of compulsive gambling, the factors that cause a person to become a compulsive gambler, the dream world of the compulsive gambler and the way that compulsive gamblers can stop gambling and recover through the Gamblers Anonymous Program. The "Combo" Book ends with a section entitled "To All Gamblers Anonymous Members" which offers a number of practical suggestions to recovering compulsive gamblers.

The "Combo" Book often serves as a companion to the members of Gamblers Anonymous and is often referred to in times of stress. Many members feel that the following quotation captures the essence of this book, and of the Fellowship's program as a whole:

"Our Gamblers Anonymous experience seems to point to these alternatives: To gamble, risking progressive deterioration or not to gamble, and develop a better way of life."

The Gamblers Anonymous Way of Life

Far from being confined to the weekly group meeting, the Gamblers Anonymous program is a way of life. The recovery process generates an awareness of oneself that thoroughly permeates a member's life. Just as the diabetic needs insulin, the compulsive gambler needs a commitment to the Fellowship's program.

In addition to being a support group, Gamblers Anonymous becomes a family to many members. Love, empathy as well as support spring from the members' mutual understanding and desire to attain healthy, happy lives. The members accept each other regardless of their personal shortcomings. Acceptance provides the essential emotional security that many compulsive gamblers had lacked in their lives.

Those who come to Gamblers Anonymous are usually in despair. Often they look to the group for sympathy. What they get is empathy and understanding from a community of men and women ready to reach out and accept any individual who desires to be helped. The membership is fully aware that merely getting oneself to the meeting is a big step for a loner like the typical compulsive gambler.

Most compulsive gamblers believe that no one else's problems can be as severe as their own. Consequently, most newcomers to the group meeting are astounded to find that others have been in the same appalling situation. The simple discovery of common experience can bring enormous relief, and a bond with others can be formed on that basis alone. Compulsive gamblers are best understood by other compulsive gamblers; and it is with this knowledge that Gamblers Anonymous is able to provide guidance, friendship and recovery for many compulsive gamblers.

Newcomers learn that they are sick, but come to understand that though powerless while gambling, they have the ability to do something about their illness by following the principles of the Gamblers Anonymous Program. The Fellowship offers hope that instead of a bleak future of pain, life can be purposeful and joyous.

Giving personal therapy is a large part of the recovery program. By baring one's soul, the individual releases the feelings accumulated during a lifetime of compulsive gambling. Sharing the pain is a purgative process. While some find it difficult, others welcome the opportunity to speak freely. Often at the first meeting they speak of things that they may find too difficult to mention ever again.

Even though the therapy procedure is of undoubted importance, no one is ever pressured to speak. Hearing other members talk of their experiences creates a sense of trust and security. This allows even the most reserved members to share their experiences freely, in the knowledge that the confidentiality of their stories will be preserved.

It has been the experience of the fellowship that those who adhere to the program are also those who regularly participate in giving therapy. Members know that recovery depends on the openness and honesty with which one speaks during the meeting. Honesty is the absolute prerequisite of the Recovery Program. Successful Gamblers Anonymous members are fully aware of this and therefore make every effort not to accept dishonesty in themselves.

The person who cannot be honest in this way has little chance of recovering. Although it is possible for an individual to only passively attend meetings and yet to stop gambling, continuous abstinence inevitably requires full commitment to the program. A reversion to destructive behavior patterns is the unhappy and only alternative.

Most people coming to Gamblers Anonymous do so because it is their last resort. For some, the alternatives are jail or suicide. Others come because they need money, carrying with them the vain hope that the fellowship will provide funds. Still others turn to Gamblers Anonymous because a spouse has threatened divorce; whatever the reason may be, however, almost everyone coming to the Fellowship is desperate and emotionally spent. At group meetings newcomers learn that the desire to stop gambling is the only basis on which successful rehabilitation can begin.

Inevitably there are those who fail and who return to a life of compulsive gambling. Since pathological gambling is a progressive disease, the afflicted individual eventually destroys himself physically and psychologically through:

1) Irregular employment patterns leading to loss of steady income and loss of self-esteem
2) Dependence of drugs or alcohol
3) Committing crime to get money, which may lead to incarceration
4) Malnutrition
5) Dereliction
6) Broken marriages and family disintegration
7) Insanity/institutionalization
8) Attempted suicide
9) Severe illness or death from stress-related causes

Even if an individual attends Gamblers Anonymous meetings but continues to gamble, the disease will still progress. There may be an attachment to Gamblers Anonymous and an intellectual awareness that compulsive gambling is destructive, but there may be an insufficient emotional commitment to stop gambling. The individual in this situation may come to the meetings but still continue to gamble, feeling worse because he has not been able to grasp the program.

Success depends on adherence to the Twelve Steps of Recovery; laxity invariably results in backsliding. Even those holding back on so little as one point, such as not admitting a debt, eventually succomb to pressures that lead back to gambling.

Recovery takes much more work and self-discipline than that to which the compulsive gambler has been accustomed. Commitment to the Gamblers Anonymous way of life demands a complete reversal of both values and habits. Vigilance is substituted for complacency, for as we have said, anything other than assertive action leads to regression. To miss one meeting, for example, invites missing the second, and the third. Without question, this lack of discipline leads back to a life of gambling.

It is important to remember that the desire to stop gambling is usually a tremendous motivation to attend meetings and to adhere to the Recovery Program. Persons who define for themselves exactly what the program means, who underscore to themselves the importance of this goal, have a much easier time finding the necessary self-discipline.

Ultimately, Gamblers Anonymous represents a choice between freedom from or slavery to a debilitating illness. Some compulsive gamblers compare their recovery to that of a blind person gradually regaining sight. Such an analogy is particularly apt in that as the individual accepts the Fellowship's way of life, he gains an awareness of the many new options available in a life free from compulsive gambling. The recovering individual recognizes a whole new environment in which to function.

As the member makes progress in the program, the desire to gamble gradually subsides. The individual eventually reaches a point where a return to gambling is unconscionable. This is the stage also where many members begin to like themselves. A whole new personality emerges as the member strives toward growth and maturity.

Awareness of this progress encourages the person to try even harder for personal growth. Members tend to be kinder to themselves as they develop a capacity for self-love.

The emergence of self-esteem brings more of the same, in what might be thought of as a geometric emotional progression. As the sense of self-worth increases, the recovering individual is enabled to resolve problems in all areas of life, from marriage and family, to finance and employment. The satisfaction that comes with the successful resolution of these problems fosters a deeper feeling of self-respect.

Since rehabilitation does take time, it is important for the recovering individual to remember to be patient with himself, to take one day at a time. A better attitude toward oneself, however, can start almost immediately after the decision has been made to adopt Gamblers Anonymous as a way of life.

The Fellowship teaches its members to accept the compulsive gambler's behavior as an illness, and to make no other judgments concerning self or others. Such judgments only hinder the recovery process. Since compulsive gamblers tend to be negative thinkers, pessimists, Gamblers Anonymous works hard to help re-train members to see the world more positively. Instead of relentless self-criticism, the compulsive gambler learns to give himself credit for his successes. The ability to do this comes as a natural outgrowth of the development of self-esteem.

Since compulsive gamblers understand that they are not perfect, there is a tendency for them to punish themselves because of imperfections. The Fellowship helps recovering individuals to master this predilection for severe self criticism with the knowledge that imperfection is part of the human condition, and that character flaws can be constructively overcome. For the compulsive gambler, self-condemnation over one problem may facilitate a return to many others, including gambling. The operative belief is that all of life's problems, not just gambling, should be faced with confidence and faith in oneself.

Members come to practice the fellowship's principles in all aspects of life. While there are no guarantees that life will be perfect for each person, the principles of Gamblers Anonymous show an individual how to make choices and alternatives, how to handle things calmly and in stride.

Those who stay with the program eventually find that the Gamblers Anonymous way of life becomes automatic, second nature. Some members make the Fellowship the dominant social and philosophical pursuit of their lives, becoming exclusively involved in Gamblers Anonymous activities. Most, however, are content to attend weekly meetings and blend the fellowship program with many other interests. Many gain a new sense of "belonging," finding in the fellowship a spiritual fulfillment unattainable elsewhere. Regardless of the extent of involvement, being a part of this plan of helping others brings with it an incomparable feeling — the true essence of fellowship.

All Gamblers Anonymous members strive and grow together through the fellowship. Friendships deepen, understanding and empathy grow, bonds form and love for self and others abounds. The unity of the fellowship is so strong that any group meeting is home for the member, even though it might be filled with unknown faces. The bond is there because, in Gamblers Anonymous, there are no strangers, only brothers and sisters in fellowship.

Chapter IV

RECOVERY and UNITY
AN OVERVIEW

The Gamblers Anonymous Recovery Program is the foundation upon which those in the Fellowship are able to rebuild their lives. The Recovery Program is outlined in twelve steps and is a plan for a better way of living.

For compulsive gamblers to be fully productive members of society they must completely abstain from gambling. By practicing the Twelve Steps of Recovery, the individual is freed to fulfill his or her potential. This program also enables Gambers Anonymous members to lead ethical lives and attain self-respect.

Some of the twelve steps deal with the admission of powerlessness and/or wrongdoing. Other steps ask members to take the actions necessary to rebuild their lives. A third group of steps is spiritual in nature and is concerned with a power greater than the individual.

Each step is open to individual interpretation. Because the Recovery Program is designed to be adapted to personal needs, many different interpretations of the steps have arisen over the years. The commentary that follows is a basic overview of many different interpretations of the Twelve Steps of Recovery and can be considered as a starting point for more detailed discussion.

Step 1: WE ADMITTED WE WERE POWERLESS OVER GAMBLING — THAT OUR LIVES HAD BECOME UNMANAGEABLE.

In the first step of the Recovery Program members admit their powerlessness over gambling and learn to accept the truth about compulsive gambling — that it is an incurable progressive illness which only can be arrested through total abstinence from gambling. Members acknowledge that they were powerless to control their lives when gambling dominated their actions. Through this admission members gain the inner strength to deal with their problems and face responsibilities.

In Step One compulsive gamblers are asked to accept the fact that their lives had become unmanageable. Members acknowledge that the gambling illness disrupted their financial stability and many other aspects of their lives, including family, work and other personal relationships. The admission and acceptance that come with Step One are pre-requisite to controlling the destructive behavior caused by compulsive gambling.

The first step of the Recovery Program is just as important to someone who has abstained for a considerable period of time as it is to a newcomer. By regularly reviewing Step One, members are reminded of the past so that they will not repeat it.

Step 2: CAME TO BELIEVE THAT A POWER GREATER THAN OURSELVES COULD RESTORE US TO A NORMAL WAY OF THINKING AND LIVING.

Recognizing the nature of the compulsive gambling illness, members realize that *alone* they are powerless to establish a normal way of thinking and living. Therefore, compulsive gamblers understand that they need help from a power greater than themselves. In Step Two members are asked to believe in a Higher Power, which is a source of strength external to oneself and greater than one's self-will and self-determination. The Higher Power can be anything a member wants it to be, such as God or the psychological and emotional support from the Fellowship or the group. This step does not ask for belief in any organized religion but, more simply, a commitment to personal spirituality. Belief in a Higher Power enables the compulsive gambler to realize that a better way of thinking and living is possible than that offered by gambling.

Step 3: MADE A DECISION TO TURN OUR WILL AND OUR LIVES OVER TO THE CARE OF THIS POWER OF OUR OWN UNDERSTANDING.

Once members commit their lives to the care of a Higher Power, a great burden is lifted from their shoulders. Free from the limitations of ego, members try to live by the ideals of the power greater than themselves. Faith alone does not lead to a normal way of living, but faith coupled with the positive decision to commit oneself to the care of a higher Power leads the members toward recovery.

Step 4: MADE A SEARCHING AND FEARLESS MORAL AND FINANCIAL INVENTORY OF OURSELVES.

In order to attain a more meaningful life, the compulsive gambler must undergo a complete and thorough self-appraisal. Acceptance of one's shortcomings is a prerequisite to correcting them. Members strive to find the truth about themselves, for in truth is the freedom to choose the many alternatives and opportunities that life presents.

In order to make a complete moral inventory, members must examine to the best of their ability all aspects of their character. All negative characteristics should be examined, such as selfishness, greed, procrastination, anger, envy, pride, laziness, resentment, self-pity, jealousy, insincerity, self-deception, impatience, intolerance, pessimism, and dishonesty. Equally important, however, is the acknowledgement of all one's positive characteristics, such as friendliness, optimism, empathy, industriousness, humility, kindness, dignity, tolerance and honesty. Members are urged to make a written inventory; nothing should be withheld.

In Gamblers Anonymous, the financial inventory is as important as the moral inventory. Members make a list of all monies owed as a result of gambling activities, such as loans, bad checks, thefts and other debts. In addition, they itemize their financial assets and income.

The moral and financial inventories are as important to established members as they are to newcomers. By making these inventories an ongoing process, members continually assess their character. In this way, new defects can be recognized and growth can be measured. Because money is an integral part of gambling, the compulsive gambler must use the financial inventory, together with the moral inventory, to begin a true character change.

Step 5: ADMITTED TO OURSELVES AND TO ANOTHER HUMAN BEING THE EXACT NATURE OF OUR WRONGS.

In Step Five the member is truthful not only to himself, but to someone else, either on an individual or group basis. By revealing to another person the full extent of one's shortcomings, one gains an objectivity and perspective not otherwise available.

After making a thorough moral and financial inventory, it is imperative that the compulsive gambler share the findings with someone else. The admission of wrong-doing brings immense relief. Keeping the facts of the moral inventory locked inside oneself imposes a burden heavier than any person can bear. By sharing, pressure and anxiety are released.

Step 6: WERE ENTIRELY READY TO HAVE THESE DEFECTS OF CHARACTER REMOVED.

In this step members are asked only that they be ready and willing to have their character defects removed. This is a step of preparation in that it does not ask them to remove their character defects but simply to open their hearts and minds and to be ready for change.

Members are often reluctant to make necessary changes in their personality because of the security they experience from deeply ingrained character traits. In this step, the member is encouraged to be open to shedding his or her character defects, and to have faith that a new and better self will emerge.

Step 7: HUMBLY ASKED GOD (OF OUR UNDERSTANDING) TO REMOVE OUR SHORTCOMINGS.

In the same way that members of Gamblers Anonymous understand that they are powerless to control their gambling problem, they also realize that by themselves they are powerless to remove their defects of character. Once members are willing to have their character defects removed, the next logical step is to seek help.

Just as members come to accept a Higher Power, it follows that only that power can remove their shortcomings. Casting aside the pride that led them to believe that they could live exclusively by their own intellect, strength and will power, members come to learn true humility.

Humility before one's God means not only modesty but complete lack of wrongful pride in oneself. Members candidly admit all frailties, holding back nothing. Strength lies in the belief that it is possible to change our character with the help of the God of our own understanding.

Rather than an overnight remedy, the action of this step is an ongoing process of striving. Working toward change is most important. Members continue to let go of the old ways and allow the God of their understanding guide them toward peace and serenity.

Step 8: MADE A LIST OF ALL PERSONS WE HAD HARMED AND BECAME WILLING TO MAKE AMENDS TO THEM ALL.

Most compulsive gamblers are aware that they have financially damaged many people, but they are seldom aware of all the emotional harm they have caused. The extent of emotional and financial injury they have caused is made evident only by writing a complete list of those they have hurt. The success of Step Eight is in the individual's willingness to make amends to everybody on the list.

Step 9: MADE DIRECT AMENDS TO SUCH PEOPLE WHEREVER POSSIBLE, EXCEPT WHEN TO DO SO WOULD INJURE THEM OR OTHERS.

In this step, the member is asked to carry out the intention of the preceding step to the best of his or her ability. By making amends, members free themselves of the burden of wrongdoings. In this way the negative behavior of the past is transformed into the potential for acting positively in the future.

There are different ways of making amends. Some may be financial while others may be of a more complex and personal nature. Similarly, some amends may be made immediately while others may take a number of years. There are also cases where no amends can be made because to do so would be harmful to another person. Sometimes amends cannot be made because of the inability to communicate with the aggrieved person. Where amends cannot be made directly, an alternate method of restitution may be called for, such as an act of kindness or service to Gamblers Anonymous.

Common sense, the knowledge of when to act, and courage are essential for the successful execution of Step Nine. In any case, amends should be forthright and honest, no matter what the conditions surrounding them. A member should not avoid making amends by rationalizing that an amend will injure someone else if that decision is made to spare his or her own feelings.

Step 10: CONTINUED TO TAKE PERSONAL INVENTORY AND WHEN WE WERE WRONG, PROMPTLY ADMITTED IT.

Personal inventory is a continuing process of self-evaluation, encouraging the individual to make self-searching a habit, thereby increasing self-awareness. This personal inventory is a repeated assessment of one's attitudes and actions towards others as well as toward oneself. This should not be limited to an analysis of negative aspects of character but should include an appreciation of positive traits as well.

Step Ten calls for members to continuously evaluate themselves for wrongdoings that they commit. Once recognized, members find it beneficial to promptly admit to these wrongdoings. The timely acknowledgement of the wrongs that a member has committed leads to a catharsis of the anxiety, depression and sense of loneliness experienced prior to recognizing the wrongdoing.

In this step, members are enabled to make choices, find solutions to problems that arise, keep things in perspective, develop self-restraint, accept what they don't have, and take responsibility for their own actions. Practicing the tenth step of the Recovery Program helps change behavior patterns, discourages harboring negative emotions and encourages the development of self-esteem and other positive emotions. This ongoing process of self-appraisal promotes emotional health and maturation.

Step 11: SOUGHT THROUGH PRAYER AND MEDITATION TO IMPROVE OUR CONSCIOUS CONTACT WITH GOD AS WE UNDERSTAND HIM, PRAYING ONLY FOR KNOWLEDGE OF HIS WILL FOR US AND THE POWER TO CARRY THAT OUT.

Continuing contact with one's God, achieved through prayer and meditation, enables the member to grow personally and spiritually. One's God need not be a deity, therefore this step benefits not only those who believe in God but also those who are agnostic or atheistic. The Gamblers Anonymous program is based on personal spirituality, and as such gives members the freedom to choose by what means they contact the God of their own understanding. Whether by formal prayer or meditation, members are encouraged to make daily contact with their God. Through this continuing contact, members become more receptive to the potential experience of God's will for them and the strength to live accordingly.

Step 12: HAVING MADE AN EFFORT TO PRACTICE THESE PRINCIPLES IN ALL OUR AFFAIRS, WE TRIED TO CARRY THIS MESSAGE TO OTHER COMPULSIVE GAMBLERS.

The twelfth step is the culmination of the entire Recovery Program. The success of this step is determined by the effort of the members to practice these principles in their lives and in their efforts to convey to other compulsive gamblers that they can stop gambling through the practice of the Gamblers Anonymous program and thereby achieve self-respect, personal and spiritual growth. The emphasis here is not on the results, but on the effort a member makes.

The Unity Program

The Gamblers Anonymous Unity Program is a framework for the well-being of individual groups and the Fellowship as a whole. The Unity Program is outlined in twelve steps and is meant to insure the continuity and perpetuity of Gamblers Anonymous.

In order to maintain the Fellowship for present and future members, both individuals and groups follow the proven concepts upon which the Unity Program is based. The essence of this program is in the preservation of common welfare, members understand that what is best for the group is best for each individual.

The Unity Program serves to protect the Fellowship from disruption. Members work together under the principles of unity in order to preserve and perpetuate the opportunity for themselves and other compulsive gambers to recover and grow within the Fellowship.

Step 1: OUR COMMON WELFARE SHOULD COME FIRST; PERSONAL RECOVERY DEPENDS UPON GROUP UNITY.

The common aims, purposes and ideals of the Fellowship are of prime importance. These are maintained through the cohesiveness and unity of each chapter. Members work for whatever is needed to maintain their group in order that they and other compulsive gamblers might continue to give and receive help.

Step 2: OUR LEADERS ARE BUT TRUSTED SERVANTS; THEY DO NOT GOVERN.

Gamblers Anonymous relies primarily on group conscience to keep it functioning. Leaders within the Fellowship are entrusted to carry out the will and conscience of the group. They have assigned responsibilities but they act only within the authority granted to them by the group.

Step 3: THE ONLY REQUIREMENT FOR GAMBLERS ANONYMOUS MEMBERSHIP IS A DESIRE TO STOP GAMBLING.

Regardless of who a person is, or how grave their emotional, legal or financial complications may be, Gamblers Anonymous welcomes anyone who demonstrates a desire to stop gambling.

For membership it is not necessary that one pay dues or sign a pledge. Those who have returned to gambling are especially encouraged to attend meetings and get help because it is the desire to stop gambling — not the abstinence — that is required for membership.

Step 4: EACH GROUP SHOULD BE SELF-GOVERNING EXCEPT IN MATTERS AFFECTING OTHER GROUPS OR GAMBLERS ANONYMOUS AS A WHOLE.

Each Gamblers Anonymous group has great latitude to conduct its affairs within the framework of the Fellowship. This preserves the freedom of choice that is so important to the group conscience. The conduct of each group is limited only to the extent that its actions would conflict with the Guidance Code of Gamblers Anonymous.

Step 5: GAMBLERS ANONYMOUS HAS BUT ONE PRIMARY PURPOSE — TO CARRY ITS MESSAGE TO THE COMPULSIVE GAMBLER WHO STILL SUFFERS.

Reaching compulsive gamblers is a major goal around which the members of Gamblers Anonymous gather in unity. The perpetuation of the Fellowship depends on the practice of this principle.

The reason for this singleness of purpose is to maximize the efficiency of the Fellowship's efforts to carry its message to suffering compulsive gamblers, in or outside of the Fellowship. The gift of recovery works best when it is shared.

Step 6: GAMBLERS ANONYMOUS OUGHT NEVER ENDORSE, FINANCE OR LEND THE GAMBLERS ANONYMOUS NAME TO ANY RELATED FACILITY OR OUTSIDE ENTERPRISE, LEST PROBLEMS OF MONEY, PROPERTY AND PRESTIGE DIVERT US FROM OUR PRIMARY PURPOSE.

Gamblers Anonymous works in large part because the program is kept pure of outside interests. Energy, time and money would be wasted by supporting any outside cause or organization. Such support would also be detrimental to the public acceptance of individual groups or the Fellowship as a whole. Endorsement of anything outside of the Fellowship would also lead to internal disagreement. For these reasons, Gamblers Anonymous also takes no part in political causes or public issues.

Step 7: EVERY GAMBLERS ANONYMOUS GROUP OUGHT TO BE FULLY SELF-SUPPORTING, DECLINING OUTSIDE CONTRIBUTIONS.

In order to maintain the independence of the Fellowship as a whole as well as individual groups, Gamblers Anonymous does not accept outside contributions. This policy is sustained in order that no undue control can be exercised over Gamblers Anonymous, from without or within. By allowing outside contributions both groups and members would be deprived of exercising responsibility over their affairs and their obligation to the Fellowship.

Step 8: GAMBLERS ANONYMOUS SHOULD REMAIN FOREVER NON-PROFESSIONAL, BUT OUR SERVICE CENTERS MAY EMPLOY SPECIAL WORKERS.

Gamblers Anonymous operates on the principle that compulsive gamblers can best help each other recover without the use of outside professional services. Gamblers Anonymous members believe that they are the most qualified to conduct the Fellowship's affairs.

The validity of professional therapy is not in question. Gamblers Anonymous members are free to seek outside help, if they so choose. However, if professional therapists were to operate within the Fellowship, their views might conflict with Gamblers Anonymous principles. By remaining non-professional, Gamblers Anonymous avoids the controversies that would inevitably arise.

Gamblers Anonymous, however, may employ clerical personnel and other workers to assist in the operation of service centers, doing the jobs necessary to keep the Fellowship functioning smoothly and continuously.

Step 9: GAMBLERS ANONYMOUS, AS SUCH, OUGHT NEVER BE ORGANIZED; BUT WE MAY CREATE SERVICE BOARDS OR COMMITTEES DIRECTLY RESPONSIBLE TO THOSE THEY SERVE.

Gamblers Anonymous is run by the spirit of service and not be the force of vested authority. In order to avoid the problems inherent in the authority, Gamblers Anonymous is not organized in a formal hierarchy.

The Fellowship has no central autonomous leadership. The service boards that have been created have no formal veto power and are responsible to the will of the membership as a whole.

The National Service Office, the National Board of Regents and the National Board of Trustees have been set up by the membership of Gamblers Anonymous to administer and guide the Fellowship. These groups do not have power within themselves but they are responsible to each other, and to the entire membership.

Step 10: GAMBLERS ANONYMOUS HAS NO OPINION ON OUTSIDE ISSUES; HENCE THE GAMBLERS ANONYMOUS NAME OUGHT NEVER TO BE DRAWN INTO PUBLIC CONTROVERSY.

The survival and proliferation of Gamblers Anonymous is of far greater importance than taking positions on any issues outside the Fellowship. To make public pronouncements on non-Fellowship matters would inevitably split the group. Individuals naturally have differing opinions and eventually these differences could erode group solidarity. By engaging in outside issues, the Fellowship's concentration would be diverted from a therapeutic purpose, which is to aid in the recovery of compulsive gamblers. The association of the Fellowship's name with public controversy would unnecessarily antagonize some portion of the general public. By avoiding controversy, both individual groups and the Fellowship as a whole are able to concentrate on the aims and principles of Gamblers Anonymous.

Step 11: OUR PUBLIC RELATIONS POLICY IS BASED ON ATTRACTION RATHER THAN PROMOTION; WE NEED ALWAYS MAINTAIN PERSONAL ANONYMITY AT THE LEVEL OF PRESS, RADIO, FILMS AND TELEVISION.

Gamblers Anonymous does not compare itself to any other group, nor does it boast of its accomplishments and abilities to the public. However, Gamblers Anonymous does make itself available to anyone interested in the Fellowship or in the gambling problem.

In order to make the Fellowship visible, Gamblers Anonymous informs and educates the public about the problem of compulsive gambling and about the Fellowship itself. Personal stories of members in newspapers, magazines, on radio and television, as well as spot announcements all help to spread an awareness of Gamblers Anonymous. The Fellowship does not glorify the name of Gamblers Anonymous or its merits as a group rather, it works to encourage compulsive gamblers to attend the Fellowship's meetings.

Personal publicity is always shunned, and anonymity is carefully preserved because the Fellowship of Gamblers Anonymous is more important than any one member. By maintaining this policy, any problems that accrue to an individual member cannot harm the Fellowship. Similarly, any achievements attained by individuals working in the program benefit the group as a whole. This step is a constant and practical reminder that personal ambition has no place within the Fellowship's public relations program.

Step 12: ANONYMITY IS THE SPIRITUAL FOUNDATION OF THE GAMBLERS ANONYMOUS PROGRAM, EVER REMINDING US TO PLACE PRINCIPLES BEFORE PERSONALITIES.

The Twelve Steps of Unity repeatedly ask individuals to give up personal desires for the common good. Thus, the spirit of humility, which is the basis for anonymity, prevails. Members willingly sacrifice personal identity in order to preserve the collective reputation of the Fellowship and the group.

In Gamblers Anonymous, the principles of the Fellowship are placed before personalities, without exception. With the practice of anonymity, the principle of humility is truly at work, and it is this all-encompassing quality that permeates Gamblers Anonymous life everywhere.

Chapter V

SELF HELP — SERVICE TO OTHERS
"THE TOOLS"

The Gamblers Anonymous Recovery Program reaches into all areas of the member's life in order to help the individual achieve maturity through a growing sense of self-confidence and self-respect. To begin recovery a new member must first stop gambling. The first ninety days of abstinence from gambling are usually the most difficult of all for a newcomer in the Gamblers Anonymous Program. During this transitional period, new members who stop gambling begin to reverse their self-destructive habits. They work to change the selfish and immature behavior which characterizes the personality of compulsive gamblers.

Success in the program depends on the individual's desire to stop gambling and to return to a normal way of life. Yet, even for the most ardent it is no easy matter to accomplish a major change in character. Internal and external pressures on new members are immense: among these are legal difficulties, employment problems, marital friction and financial worries, all of which cause acute anxiety in the new member during this crucial introductory period.

Financial pressures are usually the most noticeable, and most new members come to Gamblers Anonymous burdened by debts. Most newcomers are in debt to creditors such as banks, finance companies, relatives, friends, employers, shylocks and bookmakers. Establishing a program of fiscal responsibility is imperative. The severity of these financial problems often leads to an assumption (made by gamblers and non-gamblers alike) that gambling is primarily an economic problem. It is not. Compulsive gambling is an emotional disease of which financial instability is only one symptom. Even if an individual were wealthy enough to pay all debts incurred through compulsive gambling, that person would inevitably lead a life of misery and despair. The illness would still wreak havoc in other areas of the compulsive gambler's life. Personal relationships would suffer and the level of self-esteem would decline to the point where torment and unhappiness would shatter the person's emotional stability.

As compulsive gambling progresses, losing is inevitable. An individual suffering from this illness could, theoretically, run up infinite amounts of debt, especially since he or she is likely to take greater risks as the disease progresses. Without Gamblers Anonymous, the compulsive gambler's destiny is to accumulate greater debts until struck down by some external force, such as physical illness, insanity, a prison sentence or even death, sometimes by suicide.

It is not surprising that most of those who come to Gamblers Anonymous are desperate. For this reason, many chapters of the Fellowship provide new members with sponsors to help them with the transition into abstinence and recovery. In sponsors, new members find others who have experienced similar problems and who are therefore able to care for and understand them in a special way. Often the relationships that arise between new members and sponsors develop into lasting friendships.

The Pressure Group Meeting

Whether or not they have sponsors, the Fellowship of Gamblers Anonymous has new members participate as soon as is practical in a Pressure Group Meeting (so called because its aim is to relieve the pressures affecting the member's life). The Pressure Group Meeting is not a "bail-out." Gamblers Anonymous does not lend money or arrange for loans, but rather shows members how to take the responsibility to pay all debts and meet all obligations. The Pressure Group Meeting is designed for the person who expresses a desire to stop gambling and who is willing to devote the time and effort to follow the Fellowship's program. This technique has been effective for thousands of people. Through it, recovering individuals are able to slowly and methodically put their lives in order.

Usually a new member will be given a Pressure Group Meeting after three to five weeks' attendance and abstinence from gambling. This allows the individual to begin putting his affairs in order, adjust to the program and prepare for the meeting.

Prior to the meeting, the new member is given literature that explains the purpose and aims of the Pressure Group Meeting, and which gives instructions on how to prepare for it. For example, the member is asked to compile a list of all debts, outstanding bills, personal living expenses, income and assets. Honesty and unsparing accuracy are crucial to the preparation of this list of assets and liabilities. Omissions of any kind are disastrous because they can eventually become an excuse to return to gambling. Moreover, calculations must be exact to ensure success. Without complete honesty and accuracy, the Pressure Group Meeting is useless.

Compulsive gamblers are fiscally irresponsible, and until they mature through the program and learn how to handle their monetary affairs, they are relieved of financial duties such as signing checks and handling money.

The problems discussed at a Pressure Group Meeting fall into four basic categories: legal, financial, career and personal. Over the years the Fellowship has developed an approach to dealing with each of these categories. Nevertheless, the problems of a new member may require flexible and creative solutions.

Legal problems typically concern the passing of bad checks, fraudulent loan applications, forgery and embezzlement. Legal problems are considered of paramount importance because they may lead to criminal prosecution. In some cases, the member may be advised to obtain legal counsel.

Financially the member faces two major responsibilities: to meet living expenses and to pay creditors. Taken together these obligations may seem to be overwhelming. In order to make this manageable, Gamblers Anonymous suggests that members first provide for their families, and then pay all debts.

Working from the financial statement submitted by the member, the Pressure Group committee prepares a schedule for the payment of all member's debts. Living expenses are provided for before creditor's repayment schedules are determined. A second job is often necessary in order to meet these financial commitments. For some members, the preparation of this schedule results in the immediate release of pressure; for others, relief begins with the implementation of the repayment schedule.

Compulsive gamblers often have problems at work which have been caused indirectly by their gambling; these may include malingering, absenteeism, borrowing from co-workers, theft or embezzlement. During the meeting, these problems are identified and solutions are formulated. The member is motivated by the enthusiasm, support and guidance from those on the Pressure Group Committee to behave responsibly at work.

Part of the Pressure Group Meeting is devoted to addressing the personal problems that most trouble the member, spouse or family. These include problems of personal habits, health and hygiene, as well as marital difficulties. The goal of the Pressure Group Meeting is to foster peace of mind, and hope, in both the individual and family. By demonstrating that seemingly insurmountable problems can be solved, the committee helps the compulsive gambler establish a purpose and a direction for a new life.

Initially, some members are reluctant to embark on the plan evolved from the Pressure Group Meeting because they fear rejection. However, it is the experience of Gamblers Anonymous that persevering in spite of fear results in success.

For the first time the compulsive gambler is learning to live with order and stability. Where life was once out of control, it now has a sense of structure and purpose. A review of the plan formulated in the Pressure Group Meeting is conducted by the committee to see how well the member has adhered to the plan and to adjust it to the changing circumstances in the member's life.

The 90-Day Plateau

After ninety days of abstinence from gambling the member is asked to assume certain responsibilities of service to Gamblers Anonymous. Since the Fellowship's primary purpose is to carry the message to those who still suffer, members must share the benefits that they have received. It is the belief of the Gamblers Anonymous Fellowship that after three months' abstinence from gambling along with regular attendance at meetings — a stage known as the *90-Day Plateau* — a member has demonstrated a desire to stop gambling and live a normal life. By this time the member will have been in the Fellowship long enough to have received significant benefits from the program. It is time for the member to reciprocate in kind and widen his participation in the Fellowship. There are many ways in which a member can serve.

Meeting Chairman: Chairing a meeting is considered both an honor and a privilege. Any individual who has abstained from gambling for three months and who has regularly attended meetings can serve as chairman.

Lifeliner: Even before the 90-Day Plateau, a member has the opportunity to be a Lifeliner. A Lifeliner assumes the responsibility, on a monthly basis, to help financially support the operation of the National Service Office (NSO) of Gamblers Anonymous. Every Gamblers Anonymous chapter has the responsibility to encourage support of the NSO through contributions by individual members.

Public Relations and Education: Gamblers Anonymous conducts a public relations program to let people know that compulsive gamblers have a place to turn to if they want to stop gambling. The Fellowship encourages its members to participate in this program by maintaining communications with the media and the public. Contact is also established with legal, medical and educational professionals to make them aware of the compulsive gambling problem and of the Fellowship.

Pressure Group Work: Because new members face a myriad of problems, concerned and active members of the Fellowship are sorely needed to suggest solutions and give advice at Pressure Group Meetings. As members gain strength through the Gamblers Anonymous Program, they are encouraged to serve on Pressure Group Committees. Members eligible to serve in this capacity are those who, by their own affirmation, have continuously abstained from gambling and who have adhered to the

Fellowship's program. These duties require sound judgement, common sense, and the ability to be both realistic and flexible within the context of what may seem to be an impossible situation. Effective members of the Pressure Group Committee are able to employ the experience gained from working on their own problems, the problems of others and from the knowledge that they have acquired practicing the Gamblers Anonymous Program.

Twelfth Step Work

The essence of Twelfth Step work is in giving without seeking personal reward. Each member is asked to put fellowship into practice by helping those who do not yet have the understanding and perspective that others have gained by progressing through the Recovery Program. Giving service to other compulsive gamblers perpetuates the Fellowship and strengthens each member's ability to live the Gamblers Anonymous way of life.

One important way that Twelfth Step work is carried out is through making a Twelfth Step Call. The purpose of a Twelfth Step Call is to reach out to a fellow compulsive gambler who has a desire to stop gambling. It is an encounter with a compulsive gambler who wants help, in which the person making the call shares his or her own experience. These contacts are made with both members and prospective members. The Fellowship has found the following guidelines to be helpful:

1) Members are urged to visit compulsive gamblers in need of help. Such personal contact is usually more effective than trying to explain the Gamblers Anonymous Program over the telephone or by letter, especially when prospective members are involved. The object of this visit is to get the compulsive gambler to attend a Gamblers Anonymous meeting.

2) Gamblers Anonymous members are urged to avoid trying to convince the individual they visit that he or she is sick. Frequently the person in question has already been the subject of numerous such diagnoses and is tired of hearing them.

3) It is suggested that the member making the call encourage the individual to talk about him or herself. Members are counseled to resist the urge to "sell" the program, but rather to share experiences.

4) The conversation should be simple. It is suggested that members give the individual concerned only as much information as can be absorbed.

5) Members should offer understanding of the individual's predicament but keep in mind that they are not professional counselors.

6) Most Twelfth Step conversations are held on a one-to-one basis. The presence of family members or friends often inhibits the individual seeking help from freely speaking his or her mind.

7) Gamblers Anonymous members making a Twelfth Step Call are reminded that they are not evangelists or reformers and therefore should not crusade or proselytize.

8) In the case of the newcomer, the goal of the Twelfth Step Call is to get that individual to attend the next Gamblers Anonymous meeting. Where other members are concerned, a goal is to encourage continued or renewed attendance at group meetings. Private discussions cannot take the place of meetings.

Although continued group and individual growth depends on members making Twelfth Step Calls, it is suggested that they should not undertake such efforts unless they have stopped gambling. A detailed understanding of the Gamblers Anonymous Program is not necessary to make a Twelfth Step Call. All that is really required is the ability to demonstrate that the program does work.

Sponsorship

Of all the ways that a member may be asked to help the Fellowship of Gamblers Anonymous, Sponsorship requires the most maturity. Any member undertaking Sponsorship begins with the awareness that individuals do not act alone; rather, they are extensions of the group as a whole.

Twelfth Step work is the beginning, but Sponsorship goes beyond the initial contacts made in the Twelfth Step because it calls for an on-going interest in the member. The member receiving help is assured that there is at least one person who empathizes with his or her problems, one to whom he or she can turn to without embarrassment. Sponsorship fulfills a human need to help others, strengthening the sponsor through sharing. Working with the member helps the sponsor to avoid complacency and keep continually aware of his or her own problems that have been caused by gambling. The sharing of personal experience between the sponsor and the member helps them both in pursuit of their recovery.

The duties of a sponsor are to do everything possible, within the limits of experience, capacity and prudence, to help other members continue their growth. Sponsors must let them know that they care and understand, that they can be counted on to help with any problems that arise. Sponsors are friends to their charges, and as good friends they are not afraid to tell them the truth, even if it is unpleasant. One of the most important duties of the sponsor is to make sure that the member attends Gamblers Anonymous meetings and adheres to the program. Part of this job is accomplished by introducing the sponsored person to other members, making him feel part of the group. Sponsors also introduce members to other local Gamblers Anonymous groups. In addition, the sponsor explains the Gamblers Anonymous Program to the member's family, mindful of the fact that family cooperation greatly increases the chances of recovery. In spite of these great responsibilities, sponsors must always remember that it is the Recovery Program, not their special talents or position that is important in helping the member recover and grow personally.

Each sponsor approaches this activity as his or her own personality and experience dictates. The most effective sponsors remain flexible and avoid dependence on any single approach. For example, while it is important to be firm, most members have come to realize that even the firmest of approaches should be tempered with understanding and care.

There are a number of pitfalls to sponsorship besides being too firm. Sponsors should avoid the tendency to become overprotective of a newcomer, thereby creating a dependence that does them both a disservice. This may result in the member developing an attachment to his or her sponsor, rather than to the program as a whole.

Another potential problem is that sponsors may take their roles too casually. If the member is timid or reserved by nature, an overly casual approach on the part of the sponsor may cause the member to drift away from the group. Sponsorship is an active form of participation, which requires continuing involvement.

Sponsors explain the Gamblers Anonymous program in ways that come most easily to them, and in terms of their own experience. It is important for sponsors to keep in mind that it is unrealistic to expect a member to absorb the Gamblers Anonymous program in its entirety during the first few months. Most sponsors at first stress a few important concepts, such as: the primary purpose of Gamblers Anonymous is to help compulsive gamblers stop gambling; the first step toward recovery is admitting that one is a compulsive gambler; and recognizing that life has become unmanageable and Gamblers Anonymous offers a practical program that works.

A sponsor may have to deal with a member who returns to gambling. If this happens, sponsors must not take it personally. Members who have relapsed by returning to gambling are usually discouraged and bewildered, and need that much more support. A lapse may be turned into a constructive opportunity for self-searching and honest analysis for both the sponsor and the member. Straying from the program in this way can be regarded as a learning experience and as a chance to start fresh.

Sponsors encourage members' families to give the gambler a chance to make good in the program, regardless of previous unsuccessful attempts to stop gambling. They stress that most members make the transition to a healthy life more easily when their families take an active interest in their recovery. Sponsors also inform the member's family about Gam-Anon, a separate Fellowship designed to work with the family and friends of compulsive gamblers.

By sharing the wisdom acquired through adherence to the Recovery Program, sponsors help guide members through a critical transitional period. Likewise, the sponsors themselves are strengthened through the experience. Through this program of mutual support, the Gamblers Anonymous Fellowship is sustained and perpetuated.

Chapter VI

FAMILY AND FRIENDS
GAM-ANON AND GAM-A-TEEN

Gam-Anon is a self-supporting fellowship of wives, husbands, relatives and close friends of compulsive gamblers. Gam-Anon is not affiliated with Gamblers Anonymous, but the two Fellowships cooperate closely in recognition of common goals.

Gam-Anon was started in New York City in 1960 when four wives of compulsive gamblers got together to talk about their common problem. A representative from Al-Anon was invited to discuss that group's approach to living with an alcoholic, and it was decided that the same principles could be applied to living with compulsive gamblers. In 1961 several Los Angeles Gam-Anon groups were started, and since then the Fellowship has grown steadily throughout the world.

The majority of Gam-Anon members are wives of compulsive gamblers, since most members of Gamblers Anonymous are married males. Typically, Gam-Anon meetings are held concurrently with Gamblers Anonymous meetings, at the same location in different rooms. In order to be a member of Gam-Anon, however, it is only necessary to have a friend, relative or be someone who has been affected by a gambling problem.

A number of people join Gam-Anon even though the compulsive gamblers they know are not affiliated with Gamblers Anonymous. Those who join Gam-Anon do so because they realize they too need help. When the family member or friend gains an understanding of the gambling problem and attends Gam-Anon regularly, the compulsive gambler may eventually attend Gamblers Anonymous meetings. However, Gam-Anon members are cautioned not to expect this result and that the reason for attending Gam-Anon is to find a new way of life for themselves.

The aim of the Gam-Anon program is to aid the individuals involved with a compulsive gambler to find help by changing their own lives. This is accomplished by the spiritual growth gained through living the Gam-Anon program, by giving support and understanding to compulsive gamblers and by providing comfort to their families.

Living or being associated with a compulsive gambler creates its own kind of hell. For most people, it is a devastating experience: family relationships become unbearably strained and the home is filled with bitterness, frustration and resentment. Emotionally, the stress takes its toll as the life of the Gam-Anon member seems to crumble and become unmanageable; tensions are aggravated because life, in material terms, is unstable. At any moment the house might be lost or the furniture repossessed. There may not be enough money to put food on the table or clothe the children.

Often those living with the compulsive gambler develop severe nervous problems. At times they are unable to think rationally; problems seem insurmountable and beyond understanding.

Gam-Anon's checklist of their thirteen questions follows:

Are You Living With A Compulsive Gambler?:

1. Do you find yourself haunted by bill collectors?
2. Is the person in question often away from home for long unexplained periods of time?
3. Do you feel that he or she cannot be trusted with money?
4. Does he or she promise faithfully to stop gambling; beg, plead for another chance, yet gamble again and again?
5. Does he or she borrow money to gamble with or to pay gambling debts?
6. Have you noticed a personality change in the gambler as his or her gambling progresses?
7. Have you comé to the point of hiding money needed for living expenses, knowing that you and the rest of the family may go without food and clothing if you do not?
8. Do you search the gambler's clothing or go through his wallet when the opportunity presents itself, or otherwise check on his or her activities?
9. Does the gambler hide his or her money?
10. Does the gambler lie sometimes compulsively, avoid any discussion of his or her debts, or refuse to face realities of the situation?
11. Does the gambler use guilt induction as a method of shifting responsibility for his or her gambling upon you?

12. Do you attempt to anticipate the gambler's moods, or try to control his or her life?
13. Do you feel that your life together is a nightmare?

The Gam-Anon Meeting

Gam-Anon meetings provide an opportunity for a strong bond to form between those affected by the problem of compulsive gambling. The meeting is opened with a moment of silent meditation and closed with the Serenity Prayer. During the meeting, members read sections of various pieces of literature published by the Gam-Anon International Service Office, Inc. Some of these pamphlets are entitled, "Living With The Gambling Problem," "The Gam-Anon Way Of Life," "Gam-Anon Guides," "Guideposts To Gam-Anon Procedures," "A Guide To Fourth Step Inventory" and "A Merry-Go-Round Named Denial."

Most of the meeting is devoted to members' therapies, during which Gam-Anon members speak of their problems or progress. There is a period of interchange between members, and those with problems are given suggestions from others who have lived through similar experiences. Members listen with open minds and in their responses attempt to help each other establish and then maintain a positive, healthy direction to their lives.

Financial problems are frequently discussed, since financial difficulty is endemic to the compulsive gambling disorder. Members work to regain a reasoned perspective on their family's financial problems and to help each other with suggestions on planning and budgeting.

Many who come to Gam-Anon feel that they are in some way responsible for the problems of their gambling spouses, relatives or friends. Members of Gam-Anon learn that they are not responsible for these problems and should feel no guilt because of them. Group discussions often serve to reinforce the important point that since compulsive gambling is the gambler's illness, it is beyond the control of the Gam-Anon member. Through group discussions, members help each other get rid of the undeserved burdens of guilt and remorse.

A significant function of the Gam-Anon group meetings is to provide spouses, relatives and friends of compulsive gamblers with the realization that they are not alone. For many members, the opportunity to share experiences with others is of invaluable benefit.

Members are urged to maintain communication between meetings. Telephone contact is especially important for members in distress and for all new members. The Fellowship also encourages the reading of all available Gam-Anon literature as another way for members to sustain themselves between meetings. Each of the pamphlets previously cited offers information, wisdom and help for a variety of circumstances.

There is perhaps no better way to present the Gam-Anon way of life than by setting forth appropriate selections from the following pamphlets:

Gam-Anon Guides

In response to the question, "Why do we have Gam-Anon?" this brochure answers: "Families of compulsive gamblers have found living with the gambling problem to be a devastating experience. Every one of us has faced the same problem you are facing. In Gam-Anon, we learn to cope with our problems through the practice of spiritual principles as a Group."

In order to accomplish its goals, Gam-Anon attempts to find solutions to the dilemmas that most frequently plague its members. Many Gam-Anon members need help in defining their roles as spouses of compulsive gamblers. Many wonder how they can be of the greatest help to the spouse, relative or friend who joins Gamblers Anonymous. Another problem concerns the question of how Gam-Anon members learn to live with or without the compulsive gambler. A major step in the recovery of Gam-Anon members is learning to have faith in a Higher Power.

"Gam-Anon Guides" is a pamphlet geared to the newcomer in the Fellowship. As such, it offers the following fifteen suggestions for new members:

1. Accept and learn to live with the fact that compulsive gambling is an illness.
2. To question or interrogate the gambler will serve no purpose. You are powerless over this situation. If he has something he wishes to hide, the truth cannot be forced from him. Why try?
3. To nag your husband about past losses or to talk of what might have been if he hadn't gambled will prove to be detrimental to his recovery as well as yours.
4. The past is gone and you will not find peace of mind until you can accept it without resentment.
5. The gambler, not his wife, should be responsible for calling his creditors to make restitution. Don't take this responsibility from him.
6. Experience has taught us that it is not helpful to borrow monies or co-sign notes to cover gambling debts, while the husband is gambling or when he comes into Gamblers Anonymous.
7. It is not recommended that the wife go to work specifically to cover gambling debts.
8. Prudence tells us that compulsive gamblers are seldom able to handle family finances. Perhaps this condition will be altered as he progresses toward recovery.
9. Discourage friends and relatives from lending the gambler money.
10. Gamblers Anonymous is a program for the compulsive gambler. Wives should not interfere.
11. It may be well to encourage the gambler to go to the first few meetings, however after this, his activities must be left to him. To

force the gambler to attend meetings is very apt to do more harm than good.

12. His gambling debts were not incurred over a short period of time, therefore don't be discouraged if he finds it necessary to pay back small amounts of monies over an extended period. Normal family expenses must come first.

13. Recovery is a very slow process for the gambler. Give him your encouragement and have faith.

14. Do take an honest inventory of YOUR character defects and work on them.

15. Come to Gam-Anon even though your husband may continue to gamble. We understand your problem and if you have an honest desire we can help you through our program.

"Gam-Anon Guides" offers a number of suggestions to members on how to keep emotionally healthy while affected by the gambling problem. They are encouraged to discuss their problems. By confiding in a member, stress can be relieved and perspective regained. Those living with a gambling problem are counseled to work off their anger. Rather than become obsessed with the idea of revenge, members are encouraged to release pent-up energy by working, practicing a hobby, in short, by doing whatever helps them calm down.

The strain of living with a gambling problem may also be diminished by escaping for a while, by separating oneself from the problem. By taking a brief respite, the Gam-Anon member may return in better condition to cope with the situation. Members are reminded that fun is as important as work and are encouraged to schedule definite times for recreational activities. They are urged not to drive themselves too hard, and to relax as often as they can.

"Gam-Anon Guides" suggests that it is good to give in occasionally, even if one is right about a particular point. Frequent quarreling leads to frustration for all concerned. By conceding an argument and refusing to carry it further, members may influence the compulsive gambler to do the same. Likewise, members are urged not to be overly critical. Rather, they are counseled to concentrate upon the good points in the personality and behavior of the compulsive gamblers in their lives.

Those close to someone with a gambling problem often develop the tendency to be too hard on themselves. To avoid the frustrations and disappointments that result from this approach, "Gam-Anon Guides" reminds members that since no one is perfect, they should be tolerant of their own shortcomings as well as those of others. Many times the spouses and friends of compulsive gamblers feel overwhelmed, even panicky. To cope with the chaos that results, members are encouraged to approach their problems one at a time, starting with the most urgent. Sometimes the behavior of a compulsive gambler is so disturbing and destructive that the person with whom they live withdraws from almost all social contacts:

To break this pattern Gam-Anon members are reminded that sometimes it is better to initiate communication with other people in order to create healthy relationships.

Living With The Gambling Problem

"Living With The Gambling Problem" further defines the Gam-Anon program and clarifies the issues of living or dealing with a compulsive gambler. This brochure addresses the problems introduced in "Gam-Anon Guides."

One of the questions discussed is, "What is my role as an individual involved with a compulsive gambler?" According to Gam-Anon, when one lives the Fellowship's way of life, one can be of great help to the problem gambler even if that person is a member of Gamblers Anonymous. "Living With The Gambling Problem" offers a number of suggestions to guide members in their efforts to help the compulsive gamblers in their lives.

Members are encouraged to make home life as pleasant as possible for the compulsive gambler. They are urged to make themselves attractive, both for the favorable effect on the compulsive gambler and for the therapeutic effect on themselves.

Many Gam-Anon members come to expect, or at least hope for, rapid recovery for the compulsive gambler. "Living With The Compulsive Gambler" cautions these members not to expect instant recovery. They are encouraged to have faith that the gambler is doing his or her best to arrest this illness. And if progress seems slow, the Fellowship reminds members to be thankful for whatever gains have been made.

Members sometimes become overly anxious for recovery to occur, and try to do for the gambler what the gambler must do for himself. Gam-Anon cautions members not to try to solve the gambling problem for the compulsive gambler.

Only when it is acceptable to the compulsive gamblers should their problems be discussed with others. The discovery that they have been the subject of gossip can be very detrimental to the compulsive gambler's recovery.

"If the gambler continues to gamble, how can I learn to live with this problem?" The Gam-Anon Fellowship concedes that to learn to live with a gambling problem takes almost superhuman patience for the spouse, relative or friend of a compulsive gambler. Realizing that pathological gambling is an emotional illness does help, as does the understanding that the gambler is not trying deliberately to hurt or destroy his or her family or friends. This knowledge, according to Gam-Anon, makes the problem a little easier to bear.

Because the only real happiness that one can be sure of comes from within, Gam-Anon encourages the member to build on his or her own inner core of spiritual strength and maturity as the best way to live with the gambling problem, rather than to depend solely on their gambling spouses for happiness.

The Fellowship believes that after years of living with a compulsive gambler, the Gam-Anon member is likely to have developed erratic or strange behavior. What is needed, therefore, is the desire to change. It is important to remember that because a member's character may change gradually through the years, one should not expect the trouble to end automatically even should the gambler stop gambling. Gam-Anon recognizes that unless members patiently unlearn the behavior patterns they have acquired over years of living with the gambling problem, their problems will persist for the remainder of their lives.

Thus, spouses, relatives and friends of compulsive gamblers must admit that they too have faults. Members must recognize this fact before they can help themselves through the Gam-Anon program.

The Fellowship's program fosters wisdom, serenity and courage, which leads to a better way of life. Through the growth that accompanies this understanding, the individual is able to meet old situations with strength and to face new ones with confidence.

New members of Gam-Anon are usually concerned with the recovery progress of the compulsive gambler in the Fellowship of Gamblers Anonymous. Gam-Anon advises members not to dwell on the compulsive gambler but instead to concentrate on their own needs. The Gam-Anon member learns that he or she is not responsible for the gambling problem or for its control. However, the Fellowship also encourages members not to give up hope that the gambler will accept the Gamblers Anonymous Recovery Program.

Gam-Anon members have found that examining every move and motive of the compulsive gambler results only in mutual degradation. Continual prying into the activities of the compulsive gambler leads to a loss of esteem for everyone involved. It is doubly important for them to accept the fact that nothing they say or do can change the compulsive gambler. Consequently, interrogation only serves to make the compulsive gambler more secretive and unreasonable, leading to further withdrawal.

Many have come into the Gam-Anon program after years of failure to change the behavior of a compulsive gambler. As the illness progresses, so does the anxiety and frustration of the people involved with the compulsive gambler. They do not understand the nature of compulsive gambling and often carry a deep burden of guilt that perhaps they were either a cause or contributing factor to the illness. Gam-Anon teaches members that due to the nature of the disease, guilt is unwarranted self-punishment. Gam-Anon members know that despite any of their efforts, compulsive gamblers would still pursue the same destructive behavior patterns.

The Gam-Anon Twelve Steps To Recovery

The Gam-Anon Fellowship has a Recovery Program consisting of Twelve Steps. This program is the foundation for the personal growth of Gam-Anon members. By following these twelve steps, members accomplish a positive character change as well as a greater understanding of the gambling problem. Eventually, members may reach *the serenity* that is the goal of the Fellowship.

1. WE ADMITTED WE WERE POWERLESS OVER THE PROBLEM IN OUR FAMILY.

To admit our powerlessness over the problems we face gives us a wonderful feeling of release. We learn we are not responsible for the gambler's problem. We cannot stop the gambling, no matter how we try. We also learned we are not to blame for the gambling. With this understanding of our powerlessness, we begin to feel free to concentrate on our own problems.

2. CAME TO BELIEVE THAT A POWER GREATER THAN OURSELVES COULD RESTORE US TO A NORMAL WAY OF THINKING AND LIVING.

After admitting the first step, we know that probably no human power can help us. A life made up of fears, worries and suspicions, such as ours, would need a Power greater than ourselves to restore us to what we call normal living.

Most of us think of the Power as God, as we each understand Him.

3. MADE A DECISION TO TURN OUR WILL AND OUR LIVES OVER TO THE CARE OF THIS POWER OF OUR OWN UNDERSTANDING.

Having come to believe in and accept a Higher Power we decide to turn our life over to this Power. In this way, with God at the reins, we are able to avoid worry. We are relieved of the heavy burdens we attempted to carry alone for many years.

4. MADE A SEARCHING AND FEARLESS MORAL INVENTORY OF OURSELVES.

We find that we had to become completely honest with ourselves. Most of us discover that we have many defects of character of which we were not aware. We find it helpful to take a moral inventory of ourselves. Among our faults we find self-pity, dishonesty, impatience, hate, false pride, envy, and negative thinking. Lest we become discouraged, it is also important to remember our assets as well as our liabilities.

5. ADMITTED TO OURSELVES AND TO ANOTHER HUMAN BEING THE EXACT NATURE OF OUR WRONGS.

It is very difficult to admit to ourselves that we are guilty of any wrong-doings, and much more so to admit this to another person. Once we are able to recognize our own wrong-doings and are able to talk about it, we have come a long way towards recovery. We may make excuses for ourselves or put the blame on something or someone else. We feel much better when we are able to be honest with ourselves. As we begin to talk over our problems with another person, the burden becomes lighter and the weight of it is removed from our shoulders. We learn to see ourselves as we really are.

6. WERE ENTIRELY READY TO HAVE THESE DEFECTS OF CHARACTER REMOVED.

Many of us find this step a very difficult one. When we accept the fact that serenity comes from within, our progress develops. Exploring further along this line, we gain insight. We see that with defects of character such as self-pity, self-justification, impatience and resentment, we will never find this peace of mind and serenity we seek. Having come this far in our thinking, we become willing to be rid of these stumbling blocks in our progress.

7. HUMBLY ASK GOD (OF OUR UNDERSTANDING) TO REMOVE OUR SHORTCOMINGS.

This step specifically concerns itself with humility and what the practice of it can mean to us. So with humility and without reservation, we ask Him to remove our shortcomings. We may find we want to hold tightly to some of our defects of character. We need to ask God for courage and patience in order to work this step daily. Day by day we discover new defects of character. Therefore, we need to ask Him daily for His help.

8. MADE A LIST OF ALL PERSONS WE HAD HARMED AND BECAME WILLING TO MAKE AMENDS TO THEM ALL.

We have allowed the gambling problem in our lives to twist our thinking. Many of us hit bottom mentally and morally. Because we were miserable, we made others miserable. We were unable to fulfill our obligations to give love and understanding. Instead of understanding and accepting the gambler's illness, we nagged and criticized. Now we feel the need to make amends. We may begin by making a list of those we have harmed. As we become increasingly honest with ourselves, we will feel the need to add to this list.

9. MADE DIRECT AMENDS TO SUCH PEOPLE WHENEVER POSSIBLE, EXCEPT WHEN TO DO SO WOULD INJURE THEM OR OTHERS.

By learning to live and work the steps, we can make amends to those we have hurt by showing love and kindness, interest in the welfare of those around us, and a general spirit of well-being.

10. CONTINUED TO TAKE PERSONAL INVENTORY AND WHEN WE WERE WRONG PROMPTLY ADMITTED IT.

The purpose of this step is to teach us vigilance. The defects of character we listed in step four may not have completely disappeared. Most of all, we need to guard daily against their reappearance. When we become aware of a new defect of character or one we have overlooked we can deal with it promptly. At this stage in our spiritual progress, we should not find it too difficult to promptly admit when we are wrong. With God's help and with humility, we work this step.

11. SOUGHT THROUGH PRAYER AND MEDITATION TO IMPROVE OUR CONSCIOUS CONTACT WITH GOD, AS WE UNDERSTOOD HIM, PRAYING ONLY FOR KNOWLEDGE OF HIS WILL FOR US, AND THE POWER TO CARRY THAT OUT.

We can take time out during the day for a quiet period of meditation and prayer. In doing so we become closer to God, asking in our prayers to be able to understand His will for us. When we have gained this strength, it will be easier to face truths each day. We can start each morning asking for renewed faith and courage to carry out His will.

12. HAVING MADE AN EFFORT TO PRACTICE THESE PRINCIPLES IN ALL OUR AFFAIRS, WE TRIED TO CARRY THIS MESSAGE TO OTHERS.

Having had some measure of success in working the other steps, we are now ready to help someone else who suffers. We wish to share with another, our wonderful new way of life. We know so well how miserable and unhappy those close to the gambler may be. We once traveled the same road ourselves. We realize that the more we give to the program, the more we receive. In the steps of recovery, we can find the answer to any problem.

The Gam-Anon Way of Life

The Gam-Anon Unity Program, along with other pertinent material, is presented in the publication entitled, "The Gam-Anon Way of Life." In this booklet, the official purposes of Gam-Anon are set forth.

A. To grow spiritually through living by the twelve steps of Gam-Anon.
B. To learn to live with the gambling problem.
C. To give encouragement and understanding to the compulsive gambler.
D. To welcome and give assistance and comfort to the families of compulsive gamblers.

Gam-Anon believes there is no limit to the spiritual growth and emotional maturity which can be experienced by those who participate in the Fellowship. This is because the process of recovery is continuous, without time limits and in which progress is measured one day at a time.

The Fellowship considers its program to be a psychological "house-cleaning" process. Part of this process, as noted, includes the taking of a moral inventory, as described in the Fourth Step of Recovery. "The Gam-Anon Way Of Life" includes a checklist to help members take this inventory.

Anonymity, a principle of great importance to the program, is also explained in "The Gam-Anon Way Of Life." Anonymity is the spiritual foundation of the Fellowship. Members are instructed never to violate anyone's anonymity including their own.

Before the public, members speak for the Fellowship as a whole. Therefore, members acting in this capacity confine their discussions to the program; the purpose is to spread Gam-Anon's message, not their own.

On the cover of the booklet "The Gam-Anon Way Of Life" a staircase is portrayed, at the top of which is a door marked "The Way To Serenity." Each stair symbolizes a plateau or point of growth on the way to that goal. In this metaphor, the first stair is acceptance, the second, hope. Then following, are faith, honesty, courage, willingness, humility, sincerity, action, vigilance, spirituality and sharing.

The official Gam-Anon symbol is a life preserver on which are printed the key words: serenity, wisdom, courage. A rope encircles the preserver, which has nine knots symbolizing the lessons learned from Gam-Anon, each representing a step toward a better life.

The first knot symbolizes admission by Gam-Anon members that they need help from the Higher Power and from the Fellowship. The second knot symbolizes the Higher Power and the need for belief in something greater than oneself. The third stands for help, that is, comfort and support for the compulsive gambler and for other Gam-Anon members. The fourth knot is for humility, for Gam-Anon members to realize that they too can be wrong. The fifth symbolizes detachment from the gambling problem. The sixth knot symbolizes living. It is a reminder for Gam-Anon members not to dwell on their anxieties but to allow themselves time for reflection, meditation and family fun. The seventh knot stands for thankfulness, reminding members to be grateful for the blessings they have received. The eighth is for happiness and for the fact that smiles can be contagious. The ninth knot symbolizes acceptance, reminding Gam-Anon members to take life as it comes and not to try to change that which should be let alone.

"The Gam-Anon Way Of Life" booklet also presents the twelve-step Unity Program of the Fellowship. These steps serve as a guide for the common welfare of individual groups, and the Fellowship as a whole. By working to preserve group unity, Gam-Anon members are able to continue receiving the help they need through participation in the Fellowship's Recovery Program. The collective experience of Gam-Anon members has shown that adherence to the Unity Program is crucial not only to the survival of the group, but to the survival of each member as well.

The Gam-Anon Unity Program

In order to maintain unity our experience has shown that:

1. Our common welfare should come first; personal serenity depends on Gam-Anon unity.
2. Our leaders are but trusted servants; they do not govern.
3. The only requirement for Gam-Anon membership is that there be a gambling problem in the family.
4. Each group should be self-governing except in matters affecting other groups or Gam-Anon as a whole.
5. Gam-Anon has but one primary purpose — to carry its message to the family of the compulsive gambler.
6. Gam-Anon ought never endorse, finance or lend the Gam-Anon name to any related facility or outside enterprise, lest problems of money, property and prestige divert us from our primary purpose.
7. Every Gam-Anon group ought to be fully self-supporting, declining outside contributions.
8. Gam-Anon should remain forever non-professional, but our service centers may employ special workers.
9. Gam-Anon, as such, ought never be organized; but we may create service boards or committees directly responsible to those they serve.
10. Gam-Anon has no opinion on outside issues; hence the Gam-Anon name ought never be drawn into public controversy.
11. Our public relations policy is based on attraction rather than promotion; we need always maintain personal anonymity at the level of press, radio, films and television.
12. Anonymity is the spiritual foundation of the Gam-Anon program, ever reminding us to place principles before personalities.

In order to preserve unity, Gam-Anon offers suggestions on how groups can recognize and avoid "three deadly enemies" that can destroy the group.

The first of these three enemies is the discussion of religious denominations and beliefs. The Gam-Anon program is designed to help members regardless of their religious beliefs.

The second "deadly enemy" is gossip. Discussion of the personal affairs of others, including the gambler, can polarize and eventually destroy the group.

Gam-Anon describes the third "deadly enemy" as dictatorship. Since there are no dominating authorities of governing leaders in the Fellowship, members should remember that any attempts to impose a hierarchy can jeopardize the survival of the group.

"The Gam-Anon Way Of Life" booklet is used at all of the Fellowship's meetings. Many members look to it every day for help and strength and depend on its wisdom to see them through times of distress.

Gam-Anon's Approach to Finances

Most people who come to Gam-Anon have been through financial crisis as a result of living with a compulsive gambler. The experience of living with or being related to a compulsive gambler is particularly frustrating because family generosity does not result in any change in the gambler's behavior. Nevertheless it is difficult for most parents to refuse to assist even a wayward son or daughter, though money only serves to temporarily retard the symptoms of a continuing and destructive disease.

For the non-working wife, the economic pressures of living with a compulsive gambler can be exceptionally difficult because she may have no control over family income or expenditures. In fact, the money may be squandered before it ever reaches the family. So intense is the compulsive gambler's desire to obtain money for gambling and gambling debts that even wives with independent resources find it difficult to keep money from their husbands.

Furthermore, these wives often try subconsciously to make things right by allowing their husbands to have control over family finances. Many women cannot break out of the societal mold that places the man at the head of the family, and, of course, many women allow themselves to be financially and emotionally ruined because they love their husbands and believe that love requires unconditional support. Some even fear losing their husbands if they do not comply.

In Gam-Anon members come to understand that compulsive gamblers cannot be trusted with money. Members realize that they must assume the responsibility for supervising family finances. The Fellowship helps its members to understand how to handle these responsibilities, by following a budget. Gam-Anon emphasizes that family needs come first.

Gam-Anon does not advocate that a woman work to help her husband pay off his gambling debts. Similarly, the Fellowship strongly suggests that no one finance, sign for or consolidate a gambler's obligations. Wives who choose to work or who are already working are told not to use the money earned to extricate the compulsive gambler from his debts.

Gam-A-Teen

Gam-A-Teen is a self-help group for the children of compulsive gamblers, whether or not their parents are members of Gamblers Anonymous or Gam-Anon. Gam-A-Teen acknowledges the fact that children of compulsive gamblers are frustrated and confused by conditions in their family life. Thus, the purpose of Gam-A-Teen is to show young members how to cope with the gambling problem in their family. Members are helped to become individuals in their own right and to find peace of mind from within.

Gam-A-Teen also emphasizes the fact that compulsive gambling is not hereditary. The group seeks to help youngsters who may want to escape from their problems in whatever way, including gambling, by encouraging them to face reality rather than run away. The group demonstrates that although the child should have love, respect and understanding for both parents, "Yours is the only life over which you have any control."

No matter how difficult a child's home life might be, he or she can build a better life by following the Gam-A-Teen program. The group has both a Recovery Program and a Unity Program. Meetings are run according to the group therapy principle. Gam-A-Teen is independent of both Gamblers Anonymous and Gam-Anon, in recognition of the fact that only children of compulsive gamblers can truly understand the problems of the children of other compulsive gamblers.

Gam-A-Teen groups are run by their own members and are self-governing. They do, however, have sponsors from Gamblers Anonymous, Gam-Anon or both. Sponsors attend the meetings, but do not run them or preside in any way. They act as arbiters in any situation where necessary and answer questions that may arise. Gam-A-Teen sponsors strictly preserve the confidentiality of the meetings.

Summary

Throughout the Gam-Anon literature, reference is made to the fact that the Fellowship's program is run in the spirit of self-help. No one is compelled to participate; coercion of any kind violates the fundamental tenets of the Fellowship.

Nevertheless, as the collective expression of many years of experience, Gam-Anon has learned that those who want to succeed in the recovery program would do well to follow the Fellowship's guidelines. New members come to see that following the Gam-Anon program is the best way toward peace of mind and well being.

It is obvious from reading this chapter that Gam-Anon and Gamblers Anonymous use many similar words, concepts and strategies. It is also apparent that underlying the recovery programs of both Fellowships are similar assumptions about behaviorist psychology, the value of belief in God or in other expressions of personal faith, the importance of the Group in the recovery process, personal anonymity, etc. But these parallels do not make the two fellowships identical in goals, membership or structure. Each fellowship must be understood as an independent, voluntary, self-supporting association of men and women who seek recovery from their own unique experience with the compulsive gambling problem.

Gamblers Anonymous, Gam-Anon and Gam-A-Teen are the best programs designed to help those whose lives are afflicted by compulsive gambling. The most effective way to get help is in the therapeutic process of sharing experiences with others who have lived with the compulsive gambling problem. The energy of minds together in a common purpose is extremely powerful and healing. This is the spiritual essence of Gam-Anon and Gam-A-Teen.

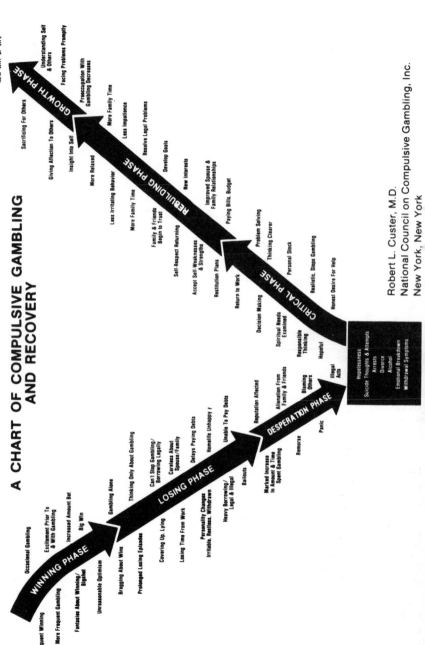

A CHART OF COMPULSIVE GAMBLING AND RECOVERY

WINNING PHASE

- Occasional Gambling
- Frequent Winning
- Excitement Prior To & With Gambling
- More Frequent Gambling
- Increased Amount Bet
- Fantasies About Winning/Bigshot
- Big Win
- Unreasonable Optimism
- Gambling Alone
- Bragging About Wins
- Thinking Only About Gambling
- Prolonged Losing Episodes

LOSING PHASE

- Can't Stop Gambling/Borrowing Legally
- Covering Up, Lying
- Losing Time From Work
- Careless About Spouse/Family
- Personality Changes Irritable, Restless, Withdrawn
- Delays Paying Debts
- Homelife Unhappy
- Heavy Borrowing/Legal & Illegal
- Unable To Pay Debts
- Bailouts
- Reputation Affected
- Marked Increase In Amount & Time Spent Gambling
- Alienation From Family & Friends
- Remorse
- Blaming Others
- Panic
- Illegal Acts

DESPERATION PHASE

- Hopelessness
- Suicide Thoughts & Attempts
- Arrests
- Divorce
- Alcohol
- Emotional Breakdown
- Withdrawal Symptoms

CRITICAL PHASE

- Honest Desire For Help
- Hopeful
- Responsible Thinking
- Spiritual Needs Examined
- Decision Making
- Return to Work
- Restitution Plans
- Accept Self-Weaknesses & Strengths
- Self-Respect Returning
- Realistic, Stops Gambling
- Personal Stock
- Thinking Clearer
- Problem Solving

REBUILDING PHASE

- Paying Bills, Budget
- Improved Spouse & Family Relationships
- New Interest
- Develop Goals
- Family & Friends Begin to Trust
- More Family Time
- Resolve Legal Problems
- Less Irritating Behavior
- Less Impatience
- More Family Time
- Insight Into Self
- More Relaxed
- Giving Affection To Others
- Sacrificing For Others

GROWTH PHASE

- Preoccupation With Gambling Decreases
- Facing Problems Promptly
- Understanding Self & Others

NEW WAY OF LIFE

Robert L. Custer, M.D.
National Council on Compulsive Gambling, Inc.
New York, New York

100

Chapter VII

TREATMENT, RESEARCH & EDUCATION
THE PROFESSIONALS

Compulsive gambling is a serious and growing social problem. But until recently, there has been little understanding of this disorder by most members of the professional community. Consequently, one of the goals of Gamblers Anonymous has been to inform psychiatrists, psychologists, physicians, social workers, clergy, judges, law enforcement officials and all others who encounter compulsive gamblers as to the nature and treatment of this disease. The need for the dissemination of this information is quite significant, in as much as many professionals who have been contacted by the Fellowship had not considered compulsive gambling an illness.

An understanding of the nature of pathological gambling enables the professional to direct the sufferer to Gamblers Anonymous, which conducts the most successful therapy for this disorder. Other treatment is more successful when used in conjunction with the group therapy that the Fellowship provides.

Realizing the value of research and treatment, Gamblers Anonymous cooperates with a number of agencies involved in the treatment or study of pathological gambling, such as the National Council on Compulsive Gambling, the National Foundation on Compulsive Gambling, the Johns Hopkins Compulsive Gambling Counseling Center and other treatment centers. This chapter will be devoted to the work of some of the specialists in the field of pathological gambling.

THE WORK OF ROBERT L. CUSTER, M.D.

Dr. Robert L. Custer is recognized today as the foremost expert in the study and treatment of compulsive gambling. He is Chief of the Treatment Services Division of the Mental Health and Behavioral Sciences Service of the Veterans Administration and is also associated with most of the agencies which treat and study compulsive gambling. Dr. Custer cooperates closely with Gamblers Anonymous to help individuals who suffer from pathological gambling.

Due largely to Dr. Custer's efforts, in 1980 the American Psychiatric Association officially recognized pathological gambling as a behavioral disorder. Since this recognition, awareness has spread among mental health professionals concerning the course and treatment of the disease.

In its *Diagnostic Statistical Manual III*, the American Psychiatric Association notes that pathological gambling and alcoholism usually begin in adolescence. The disorder is apparently more common in males than females, according to the APA, and is more common "in the fathers of males and in the mothers of females with the disorder than in the general population."

The DSM III also lists several factors that increase the likelihood of compulsive gambling in an individual. These include the loss of a parent by death, separation, divorce or desertion before the child is fifteen years of age. Also contributing to the likelihood of the disorder is parental absence or inappropriate discipline such as inconsistency or harshness. Other factors that contribute to the compulsive gambling disorder are an adolescent's exposure to gambling activities, a high family value placed on material and financial symbols, and lack of family emphasis on saving, planning and budgeting.

The 1978 Custer Survey of Recovering Compulsive Gamblers

Working with Gamblers Anonymous in 1977, Dr. Custer along with Lillian F. Custer, R.N., conducted a preliminary study at a National Gamblers Anonymous Conference to establish data on recovering compulsive gamblers. The sample group of 150 members was taken from Gamblers Anonymous groups throughout the United States and Canada. To increase the likelihood that respondents were actually recovering from the disorder, those surveyed had been in the Fellowship for an average of over seven years. The findings are not meant to represent the compulsive gambling population, or even the Gamblers Anonymous membership as a whole. The findings, however, are germane to the understanding of the recovery process.

The survey suggests that 96% of the members of Gamblers Anonymous are male. Dr. Custer notes that while this finding agrees with the observations of many of those who have attended meetings, it does not accurately reflect the incidence of female compulsive gambling in the United States.

Dr. Custer speculates that the small number of female members in Gamblers Anonymous may be caused by their preference for private therapy. Another possible reason for this low level of membership is the lack of support female compulsive gamblers receive from their husbands, both in terms of general encouragement to seek help and, more specifically, by their husbands' failure to attend Gam-Anon meetings.

Other demographic highlights of this survey include the high incidence of Gamblers Anonymous members who are married, well-educated, employed, and of the Jewish faith. Dr. Custer points out that further study is needed to determine whether these characteristics hold true for compulsive gamblers as a whole, or for the membership of Gamblers Anonymous.

Dr. Custer's survey also examined the recovering gamblers' relationship to the Gamblers Anonymous program as well as to related Fellowships. The overriding finding of this portion of the study was that the surveyed members are strong supporters of Gamblers Anonymous, Gam-Anon and Gam-A-Teen. They attend Gamblers Anonymous meetings regularly and have good spouse support at Gam-Anon. It should be noted that most of the sample group members had ready access to Fellowship meetings, a situation that is not true for compulsive gamblers living in some areas.

This portion of the Custer survey also uncovered the fact that almost six in ten (58%) of those surveyed had had one or more relapses while attending the program. Dr. Custer emphasizes the importance of recognizing that since the sample group is made up of successful Gamblers Anonymous members, relapses, therefore, do not necessarily indicate an inability to grow and recover within the Fellowship's program.

The study also found that some 40% of those surveyed had seen a mental health professional before going to Gamblers Anonymous. Dr. Custer speculates that help was sought but not forthcoming, due to a general lack of knowledge about compulsive gambling. The fact that mental health professionals may not have known about Gamblers Anonymous leads Dr. Custer to conclude that these professionals must learn more about compulsive gambling the Gamblers Anonymous program and the treatment of compulsive gamblers.

Also included in Dr. Custer's survey were the Twenty Questions asked of each new member upon entering Gamblers Anonymous. While the Fellowship believes that most compulsive gamblers will give the answer "yes" to at least seven of the twenty questions, Custer's survey found a much higher proportion of "yes" answers — an average of 18 among those surveyed. Fully one-third of those responding answered "yes" to all twenty questions.

Fourteen of the twenty questions were answered affirmatively over 90% of the time and three received "yes" answers in 99.5% of the responses. These three questions asked whether gambling was making home life unhappy, if money was borrowed to gamble and if remorse was felt after gambling. These findings prompted Dr. Custer to speculate that remorse may be a crucial factor motivating an individual to seek out Gamblers Anonymous.

The 1977 study also examined several behavioral patterns and character traits among the members. Respondents to the survey tended to be competitive, athletic and with high energy levels, according to their own descriptions. Somewhat surprisingly, there was a lower incidence of drinking and smoking than one might have expected from the group.

Dr. Custer compared the data collected from the survey on the character traits of compulsive gamblers to observations made at various compulsive gambling treatment centers around the country. Upon comparison, he found that most of the traits that compulsive gamblers indicated as characteristic were present before gambling started. Custer concluded that these were lifelong traits, starting in adolescence or earlier and continuing through recovery. Of concern to Custer, however, was the finding that there is a tendency for the amount of drinking by compulsive gamblers to increase after gambling was discontinued.

The portion of Dr. Custer's study concerning childhood and family history indicated significant parental deprivation during the members' formative years. Whether by the absence of a parent (21%), physical abuse (13%) or illness in a parent (36%), at least half of the members surveyed had undergone a significant disturbance in the parent relationship during childhood. Because of this, Custer believes, compulsive gamblers tend to enter adolescence with a lowered sense of self-esteem, and therefore take risks such as gambling, to prove self-worth and gain acceptance.

Dr. Custer notes that alcoholics, depressives and suicidal patients have similar backgrounds to the compulsive gamblers who were surveyed. The significant incidence of suicides and alcoholism among close relatives suggest that further study be directed toward looking for manic-depressive disease in the family.

The Custer study was also designed to find out more about the history of gambling behavior among the respondents. It was found that gambling behavior, as well as the first significant bet (defined here as $20 or more) begins mostly in adolescence. There was a high frequency of an early "big win," which Dr. Custer believes to be a strong reinforcing factor. He indicates that further study should examine the "big win" more closely, with considerations taken for age, income, social level and date.

The study also found that the mean age for the onset of gambling was 17 years, and the mean age for first attending Gamblers Anonymous was 39.7 years. From this gap, Dr. Custer concludes that compulsive gambling is most definitely a chronic disorder.

Other findings from this study reveal a high percentage of Gamblers Anonymous members who described gambling as an ego-building activity. Most also admitted the urge to gamble even though they had not returned to gambling. Dr. Custer finds this to be a tribute to the Gamblers Anonymous program, and to the importance of a philosophy of the Fellowship of "taking it one day at a time."

The Custer study also examined the compulsive gambler's problems as they relate to their families and to the community at large. Even more striking than the high incidence of financial, family and employment problems encountered by those surveyed is the finding that almost one-fifth (18%) had attempted suicide. This illustrates the effect of chronic severe stress, the impact of losses and the degree of despair to which compulsive gambling leads.

The final part of Dr. Custer's study evaluated the progress members had made since joining Gamblers Anonymous. The results were impressive. More than eight in ten (84%) said that they had developed healthy substitutes for gambling. More than seven in ten (74%) felt that they had made a good adjustment since joining the program.

Other findings reinforced the success of the Gamblers Anonymous program. Almost all (99.5%) of those surveyed indicated that they were behaving more responsibly. Similarly, 98% indicated that they have made or are making restitution, and 96% reported that they had stopped gambling completely. Dr. Custer concludes that "this constitutes the essence of successful treatment for the compulsive gambler, namely, stopping gambling; making restitution and seeking treatment."

Dr. Custer recommends that studies be undertaken to learn more about the importance of the availability of gambling, and what he calls the "addictogenic" qualities of different types of gambling and their relationship to treatment, if any. He also believes that further study is needed to evaluate the damage done by compulsive gamblers to their families, employers, the banking and loan institutions they deal with and the judicial system.

The complete survey and findings of the Custer study are included in Appendix II at the end of this book.

1979 Custer Study of the Phases of Compulsive Gambling

Over the course of his extensive research on compulsive gambling, Custer has come to identify the three major stages of the compulsive gambling disorder: *the winning phase, the losing phase* and *the desperation phase*. The following is excerpted from "An Overview of Compulsive Gambling," a research paper prepared by Dr. Custer and delivered at South Oaks Hospital, Amityville, Long Island, in April, 1979:

The course of the compulsive gambler can be roughly divided into three phases: in the early phase (or *winning phase*), the individual gambler frequently has a history of a substantial win initially or very early in their gambling career. This usually occurs prior to the legal age in a legal gambling facility. They continue to win frequently and become enthused and excited prior to and with gambling. The amount bet is steadily increased, but huge increases are atypical during this phase. Gradually, they begin to bet more frequently. They are pleased with their winnings and tend to splurge or squander this added money to impress others. During this phase, winning continues as knowledge of gambling, odds and risks are quickly developed. At this point, the gambler is a skilled gambler, can stop and still has control but does not want to stop what is so enjoyable and profitable. There is rare borrowing at this stage since winnings are usually adequate. This phase may continue from months to several years, and typically, ends with a substantial big win which approaches an amount nearly equal to or exceeding their annual salary at *that* time. The winning and particularly the big win establishes in the mind of the compulsive gambler that it can happen — could happen again, and could be even larger. They also see this as the solution to any financial problems. Also, it is enjoyable and requires little planning or effort.

This winning episode heralds the end of the first phase and the beginning of the second phase (the *losing phase*) when an attitude of optimism about winning has become a classical part of their style. They brag frequently about their wins and gambling is always on their mind. At this time, their gambling behavior begins to lose more and more of the social context, and they begin to gamble alone. After the big win, the amount of money bet significantly escalates with anticipation of still larger wins. Then, they encounter a losing streak which is difficult to tolerate. Their winnings pool is quickly depleted since they are betting much more heavily. They draw upon sources of money they may have earned, saved or invested in order to get even. Losing is intolerable, they must get their money back. They begin to chase. Chasing is betting more in order to recoup losses. It is a pattern which wise gamblers consider the cardinal sin of gambling. The compulsive gambler who has developed an irrational optimism disregards this principle. He bets heavier, and more frequently, and with a sense of urgency which seems to diminish his betting skills. This in turn leads to more losses. The search for money intensifies, and bond cashing, cashing in insurance policies and legal borrowing begins. Borrowing is a new experience for the compulsive gambler. It has for them the quality of a gambling win; money promptly available with no effort required. The future payments required are thought to be no problem, since gambling will provide the money. Again at this point of heavy borrowing, there is a substantial increase in the amount gambled. The once skilled gambler is now a much less skilled gambler who is betting more. The intent is to repay the loans as quickly as possible in order to prevent the family from knowing. Covering-up and lying about gambling behavior becomes increasingly more important. The gambler becomes very ingenious at giving excuses to his spouse and employer. But he "knows": a winning streak is inevitable and only the next bet away. At this point, the compulsive gambler begins to produce toxic effects on those around him. They begin to lose time from work, and their productivity diminishes. The family sees less and less of them, and when they are at home, their attention to family needs and problems is not forthcoming. As the inattention (pre-occupation) increases, family and work problems increase. The relationship with the spouse deteriorates markedly once lying is exposed. Wins do occur periodically through this phase, but the winnings usually represent less than what has been borrowed. At these moments, only the most urgent debts are paid, but most cash must be held in reserve to insure prompt return to gambling activity. Although there are ups and downs, the compulsive gambler continues to lose ground. The fervent wish of the gambler is to have even larger wins, to pay off debts, and to have a large money reserve to avoid borrowing again and thus allow for uninterrupted gambling.

The pressure of the creditors increases and threatens the secrecy and safety of the compulsive gambler. Bills must be intercepted or explained. The family deprivation of basic needs leads to alienation from spouse and parents and children. As legal borrowing resources are exhausted, the risk of illegal borrowing emerges. This usually begins first with the bookie, later with the loan shark. Eventually, these pressures lead to a critically dangerous financial state in which the gambler must have a large sum of money or be in danger of injury, death, loss of jobs, divorce or imprisonment. At this point, the gambler gives at least a partial confession and pleads for money from parents, spouse or in-laws. Invariably, this money is provided in order to bail the gambler out of his predicament. With the bailout, there is either an open or tacit agreement to stop gambling. The bailout seems to be particularly damaging since it does not allow the compulsive gambler to assume responsibility for his/her own behavior. It is similar to the big win which again encourages unreasonable optimism, and it creates an illusion that nothing bad can ever happen to them. Any cessation of gambling is short-lived. The first bailout marks the end of the losing phase and the beginning of the third phase, or *desperation phase*. Several bailouts are likely to occur during the third phase with a steady erosion of genuine concern, which progresses to alienation as those family members loaning the money see no repayment *and* continued gambling behavior. The characteristic of this phase is another marked increase in the amount of time and money spent gambling. There appears to be a state of panic caused by the knowledge of large amounts of money owed, the desire to repay promptly; the alienation from family and friends; the disgrace in the community; and a nostalgic desire to quickly recapture the early days of winning. Thus, the gambling increases at a frenzied pace with the belief that a huge win would repair all of these problems. The optimism that this will occur continues but is beginning to wane. The striking characteristics of this phase are the consuming intensity of gambling, and apparent disregard for family, friends and employment. Under this pressure, the once skilled gambler's expertise completely breaks down. Losses of available money without credit for loans leads to increased risk of further illegal loans and non-violent crime to obtain money for gambling. A few are much more likely to also become involved in a dishonest maneuver (scam) to obtain money from other naive and unsuspecting gamblers. Bad check writing becomes the chief technique to obtain funds. They rationalize this illegal behavior on the basis of full intent to repay what they have taken. They are stimulated by the image of repaying their skeptical creditors. Surprisingly, a few compulsive gamblers are able to continue their employment or business throughout this phase. They seem to have the energy to pursue two full careers simultaneously. The compulsive gambler is never a relaxed person, but the restlessness, irritability, and hypersensitivity at this stage increases to the point that sleep is disturbed, eating is erratic and life has little pleasure; the gambling itself is by this time providing virtually no pleasure. Even in this late stage, there are still occasional significant wins, but this only leads to heavier gambling and heavier losses. Then the world of the compulsive gambler comes crashing down. They are physically and psychologically exhausted with a feeling of hopelessness and helplessness. They are heavily in debt, alienated from everyone, on the verge of divorce, and welcome nowhere. One-fourth of them are about to be arrested. Depression and suicidal thoughts and attempts are fairly common at this time. It is not known how many complete suicide. It is at this time they see only four options: suicide, imprisonment (others controlling), running or seeking help. They still have the urge to gamble.

Custer's 1981 Study of "The Soft Signs of Pathological Gambling"

In 1981 Dr. Custer, along with Lillian F. Custer, R.N., presented the findings of a study they had conducted on the "soft signs" of pathological gambling. According to Dr. Custer, the soft signs of a particular behavioral disorder are considered to be "those signs which are not diagnostic but are seen to be, at times, associated with the disorder." Hard diagnostic signs, by contrast, are those fundamental elements of personal history, character and behavior consistently associated with a particular disorder.

The soft signs associated with a disorder such as pathological gambling are considered to be supplementary information to the hard diagnostic signs of that disorder. Custer points out that soft signs lend credibility to a diagnosis, enabling the diagnostician to be more confident in recommending a course of treatment. Soft signs are also important in distinguishing the pathological individual — in this case the pathological gambler — from the antisocial personality who gambles. Custer adds that it is crucial that this distinction be made before determining an approach to treatment. The study of soft signs is also important because some may be identified as hard signs of the gambling disorder.

The Custer study identified a number of personal characteristics as soft signs of pathological gambling. One of the most striking of these is the characteristic of superior intelligence; pathological gamblers have an average I.Q. of over 120, compared to the median score of 100. Custer notes that the anti-social personality who gambles is likely to have below average intelligence. Compulsive gamblers are also likely to describe themselves as having a high energy level, and are also somewhat intolerant of those with less energy. They often have a history of excellence in athletics and also good academic performance in school, unless disrupted by gambling. Pathological gamblers tend to be "workaholics" and are not likely to have any hobbies.

The study found that the personalities of pathological gamblers were marked by interesting contrasts: they try hard to avoid conflict, through lies, exaggeration and distortion if necessary. However, they also tend to be highly critical of their spouses; friends and family. Compulsive gamblers also tend to describe themselves in extreme terms: as perfectionists, as very generous *or* very stingy.

Gambling dominates the activities of pathological gamblers, to the exclusion of others. They tend, for example, to honeymoon where gambling is available. Rarely do they take drugs or alcohol to augment the gambling high. Custer also found that compulsive gamblers are attracted to people who gamble and take risks; they themselves are likely to be risk-takers in business ventures. Even their sleep is interrupted by insomnia or nightmares about gambling.

The Custer study also identified a number of communication patterns that can be considered as soft signs of pathological gambling, such as the use of the telephone to the extent that it disrupts social or business activities. These individuals also tend to become bored easily in social situations, and their attempts to feign interest are usually only half-hearted at best. Custer found that compulsive gamblers tend to be good organizers but poor participants. They like to initiate projects but they rarely see them through to completion.

Not surprisingly, Dr. Custer found that pathological gamblers are far from fastidious in their handling of money matters. Few of them were found to have had savings accounts as children and, as adults, most operate with the belief that money is to be spent, not saved. The study also found that compulsive gamblers rarely borrow or steal when they have money to bet. However, when they do borrow from legal lending institutions, they tend to do so in increasing amounts and frequency. Compulsive gamblers are likely to borrow against or discontinue life insurance policies, and to pawn their own or their spouses' jewelry when money is needed. The incidence of bankruptcy for compulsive gamblers before joining Gamblers Anonymous is one in five, which is much higher than that for the general population. Pathological gamblers are likely to be big tippers and big spenders but, according to the Custer study, they are not likely to be ostentatious when they spend their money. Most prefer to carry their money in cash, rather than as checks.

The Custer study also examined the gambling characteristics of pathological gamblers. Gambling is the most pleasant, exciting and relaxing experience for these individuals, but over time these feelings gradually diminish. Although winning is a pleasant experience as well, this pleasure too diminishes with time. Losing, however, is agonizing, relieved only by a return to the next bet. Most pathological gamblers clearly remember a big winning episode, during which their winnings amounted to more than six months' salary at the time.

The study also found that compulsive gamblers usually have a sophisticated knowledge of the probabilities in the forms of gambling they most frequently pursue. Most also possess an "unusual loyalty" to their bookmakers, not through fear but instead by regarding them as friends or business partners. However, pathological gamblers are likely to distrust the gambling industry as a whole.

According to Dr. Custer, compulsive gamblers usually do not keep a record of wins or losses. They may pay debts from gambling winnings, but they usually keep a reserve fund for gambling. The high priority placed by these individuals on gambling extends beyond money, and most regard gambling as more important than other social activities.

Dr. Custer's Treatment Approach

Compulsive gamblers who seek help through Dr. Custer are treated at first with intensive counseling to get them through the "desperation phase." After this initial period of two to three weeks, Dr. Custer suggests the gambler and therapist make an agreement in which the patient promises to do everything in his or her power to avoid gambling. The gambler's family is often brought in to reinforce this commitment. The next step in Custer's therapeutic approach is to involve the patient in the Gamblers Anonymous program. There a plan is formulated with the compulsive gambler to make full restitution of debts and also guide the individual toward the resolution of any legal or marital problems. Finally, the gambler is encouraged to participate in activities that provide substitutes for gambling and which help to re-establish meaningful life goals. A "V" chart designed by Dr. Custer, tracing the course of compulsive gambling and recovery, appears on page 100.

Dr. Custer is strongly in favor of group therapy sessions for compulsive gamblers, because chronic manipulative and deceptive behavior is more easily recognized in the group situation. The rationalizations used by compulsive gamblers to justify their behavior are more readily exposed when confronted by people who have used the same ploys and excuses.

Dr. Custer estimates that his treatment program, which includes Gamblers Anonymous membership, is effective for about half the cases treated.

Dr. Julian Taber's Study of the Treatment of Compulsive Gamblers

In an attempt to further understand the relationship between compulsive gamblers and those who treat them, Dr. Taber developed a study of the disease and its treatment. In his capacity as head of the Brecksville Unit of the Cleveland VA Hospital, Taber composed a questionnaire and then circulated it among four discrete groups: recovering compulsive gamblers in the Gamblers Anonymous program, treatment experts, psychologists and psychiatrists.

Group I
Recovering Compulsive Gamblers

Forty-four members of Gamblers Anonymous from chapters in Cleveland, Detroit, Pittsburgh and New York comprised the sample group of recovering compulsive gamblers. The individuals participating in the study had attended meetings regularly in the month preceding distribution of the questionnaire. Almost four in ten (39%) of the recovering compulsive gamblers responding had returned to gambling at least once during their association with Gamblers Anonymous.

Group II
Treatment Experts

The sample group of treatment experts was made up of twenty-nine individuals who were highly motivated to learn about and help pathological gamblers. Dr. Taber's criteria for selecting the sample group were their experience in the clinical treatment of gamblers and with the problems that pathological gambling creates for the family. Most of the members of this group were also members of the National Council on Compulsive Gambling.

The treatment experts participating in Taber's study had an average of 11.6 years of professional experience. Twenty-eight of the twenty-nine experts stated they had worked with compulsive gamblers who wanted help with the gambling problem. A majority of the sample group worked in the psychological, psychiatric or social work fields, and twenty-two of the twenty-nine also had experience in general addiction counseling.

Group III
Psychologists

Twenty-six psychologists, all holding the Ph.D. degree, comprised the third group polled. This group was drawn from the Cleveland Psychological Association, whose membership is made up of clinical workers.

The group of psychologists had an average of 17.7 years of professional experience. Eight of the psychologists polled stated they had worked with compulsive gamblers who had requested help for the gambling problem, and eighteen had no such experience. However, twenty reported significant experience with addiction counseling.

Group IV
Psychiatrists

This group in Dr. Taber's study consisted of thirty-two psychiatrists who were members of the Cleveland Psychiatric Association. While the group had an average of 18.2 years of professional experience, only six had worked with compulsive gamblers seeking treatment. However, 13 of the remaining 26 psychiatrists reported experience with other addiction counseling.

Findings of Taber's Survey

Dr. Taber's questionnaire consisted of 59 questions on compulsive gambling, its causes and treatment. Respondents were asked to agree, disagree or register "no opinion" with the statements presented.

Overall, the response patterns of gamblers and treatment experts were found to be alike, as were the patterns of psychiatrists and psychologists. The study also found considerable dissimilarity between the psychology/psychiatry group and the recovering gambler/treatment expert combination.

Taber found that, in general, recovering gamblers and treatment experts were more willing to take a position (register an opinion) than the psychologists or psychiatrists, and that both of the latter groups seemed much less sure of their opinions. Only on questions dealing with social problems and policy did recovering gamblers show significant uncertainty. Dr. Taber points out that since it is a principle of Gamblers Anonymous that it takes no position on controversial or political issues, members identifying closely with the Fellowship's philosophy would naturally find it difficult to violate this precept.

A series of questions on theoretical issues brought some interesting results. Virtually all experts were convinced that excessive gambling is a symptom of some deeper problems. Both gamblers and treatment experts were certain that compulsive gambling is an illness, while the members of the traditional psychiatric and psychological professions seemed less certain of this. Most respondents agreed with the notion that compulsive gambling is not just a habit, although as a group, psychologists were not quite as convinced.

Treatment experts generally thought that compulsive gambling clouds good judgment and agreed with the notion that gambling is an *addiction* that produces some kind of "high." Similarly, the experts agreed that the addiction develops most readily from character defects, but they differed sharply and evenly on the question of whether or not a character disorder is related to compulsive gambling. Dr. Taber points out that members of self-help groups such as Gamblers Anonymous have a very different concept of character than do mental health professionals. Most all respondents agreed that a mood change takes place during periods of gambling. All groups rejected the idea that self-punishment motivates the compulsive gambler.

All groups agreed that emotional immaturity is characteristic of the pathological gambler. With a few differences, each of the four groups seemed to feel that the compulsive gamblers are likely to have had enduring relationships with their families, jobs or communities at some point in their lives. The two groups most familiar with compulsive gambling — compulsive gamblers and treatment experts — agreed that cross-addictions are likely in pathological gamblers, while psychologists and psychiatrists seemed uncertain. Taber adds that from his own experience, nearly all compulsive gamblers have additional major or minor addictions. The pursuit of money was rejected by all groups as a motive for gambling.

Taber's study also included a series of questions on treatment technique. In general, everyone agreed that compulsive gambling could be treated successfully. Although the psychological and psychiatric professionals were not as sure as the others, all groups tended to favor the use of group therapy. A majority of all four groups, with the exception of some psychiatrists expressing uncertainty, placed a high priority in treatment on the development of self-discipline and self-control. Insight into the causes of gambling, as a goal of therapy, was largely rejected by recovering gamblers and treatment experts. Psychiatrists favored this goal, while psychologists were evenly divided on the question. Learning how to resist the urge to gamble was a goal favored by all.

When asked whether or not they thought compulsive gamblers tended to have stress-related illnesses, recovering gamblers and treatment experts responded affirmatively, while psychologists and psychiatrists tended to express no opinion. Taber adds that research on the frequency of stress-related illness in compulsive gamblers is sorely needed. The study also found that recovering gamblers tend to distrust both hospitalization and professional help as means to recovery. Half of the recovering gamblers agreed that participation in Gamblers Anonymous was sufficient, but majorities of the three other groups surveyed disagreed.

Recovering gamblers were alone in the belief that they could be understood only by other compulsive gamblers. Taber adds that this belief is one of the most damaging myths of any self-help group, and aside from bolstering a faltering ego, serves no useful purpose. All groups, however, seemed to believe firmly in the usefulness of self-help groups. Simple self-control techniques were unanimously rejected as inadequate to the compulsive gambling problem. However, despite some uncertainty among psychologists and psychiatrists, all expected compulsive gamblers to assume responsibility for themselves. Only the psychologists seemed prone to try behavior modification techniques such as electric shock therapy, assertiveness training and covert sensitization (a technique where the subject is taught to hate the thought of gambling). Here Dr. Taber adds his own opinion that his experience has found most behavior modification of little use in working with compulsive gamblers. All groups generally agreed that if professionals are to treat compulsive gamblers they should receive specialized training in the problems of compulsive gambling.

The study also included a number of questions on the objectives of treating the compulsive gambling disorder. Taber found an interesting division of opinion over the question of substituting hard work for gambling. Recovering gamblers and treatment experts seemed to favor work as an alternative to gambling, while those in the traditional mental health professions did not favor the substitution. Taber indicates that his personal bias is against this alternative, and toward teaching serenity and relaxation skills to encourage a more relaxed lifestyle. He notes, however, that this alternative is also strongly endorsed by those same groups who favored a substitution of work for gambling.

All groups surveyed in Taber's study favored total abstinence from gambling as a treatment goal, although the psychologists were less certain of this. All agreed, though with some uncertainty on the part of the psychologists, that attendance at Gamblers Anonymous meetings should be encouraged as a life long commitment.

Dr. Taber offers the opinion that social policy toward gamblers and gambling strongly influences both the number of compulsive gamblers and the effectiveness of treatment efforts. He adds "No issues are more controversial than those of social policy."

Recovering gamblers were the only respondents in favor of using the plea "innocent by reason of insanity" as an explanation of gambling-related crimes. All groups favored restitution of monies taken unlawfully. Taber adds the hope that the judicial system should eventually come to see restitution as a preferred alternative to incarceration.

Dr. Taber found all groups to be "shockingly free" of opinions as to where the profits of legal gambling should go. Further, the study found that all three groups of therapists felt that legalized gambling is harmless to the vast majority of the population, while a slight majority of recovering gamblers disagreed with this. Taber warns that "the general population will pay a price for legal gambling beyond their own wagers." The study also found that recovering gamblers, treatment experts and some psychologists favored regulation of the gambling industry in order to minimize the chances of addiction, while psychiatrists disagreed with this. All groups agreed that the plight of the compulsive gambler should not be ignored.

Psychiatrists were found to be heavily in favor of legalized gambling, while only the recovering gamblers, by a slight majority, would outlaw gambling. All respondents rejected the idea of licensing gamblers to allow "only the responsible" to gamble, and all but recovering gamblers were in favor of letting teenagers gamble for money. No professional groups wanted to take public positions on legalized gambling. Nevertheless, Taber's study found considerable disagreement over the question of whether or not the spread of legal gambling will create new compulsive gamblers. Only the group of psychiatrists favored the idea of a state raising money through gambling, but all groups favored a role for the government in regulating the gambling industry. Regarding the question of whether the spread of legal gambling will cause new problems, the psychologists and psychiatrists did not feel that the proliferation of legalized gambling will cause new problems, while treatment experts expressed alarm at the prospect. Not surprisingly, Dr. Taber adds his opinion on the side of the latter group.

Taber concludes that, on most issues, the traditional professions of psychology and psychiatry seem supportive of the treatment of compulsive gambling, and that there seem to be few theoretical or technical differences in regard to compulsive gambling between the professions. He feels that Gamblers Anonymous members generally distrust professionals but also is of the opinion that there exists a mutual respect and a latent willingness to work together. However, Taber expresses concern over the fact that none of the groups seem willing to take stands on social policy, adding that gambling policy, like the treatment of compulsive gambling, is too important to leave to the politicians.

Dr. Taber says that the mental health profession, as a whole, has been slow to meet the challenge of compulsive gambling and of addiction in general. He observes that psychologists, in particular, have been hesitant to take firm stands on many of the issues posed by the survey. He believes that psychology can only prove viable if psychologists, himself among them "define the profession as a service profession and learn the ethic of service."

A complete copy of Dr. Taber's questionnaire and its results follows in Appendix III at the end of this book.

Dr. Julie Moravec's Study of the Personality of the Compulsive Gambler

The extensive testing done at the Miami VA Center has provided some interesting insights into the personalities of compulsive gamblers. According to the tests conducted by Dr. Moravec, pathological gamblers tend to spend more time thinking about the past and the future than about the present. Results indicate that the compulsive gambler's present is burdened by guilt, regret and resentment from the past, and with over-idealistic goals for the future.

The study indicates that compulsive gamblers tend to be dependent, seeking support and acceptance from others. Pleasing others is a common form of manipulation, and constantly obtaining acceptance becomes the primary method by which compulsive gamblers relate.

According to the Miami study, compulsive gamblers tend:
1) to be unable to accept weaknesses in themselves
2) to see the nature of man as essentially evil
3) to see opposing sides in life as antagonistic
4) to deny feelings of anger or aggression
5) to have difficulty establishing and maintaining warm personal relationships.

Test data also indicate that the pathological gambler tends to be a loner who chooses not to seek advice from others and who has a strong need to achieve. There is a general reluctance to follow instructions, to praise others, to accept the leadership of others, and to conform.

The Moravec study also found that most compulsive gamblers are not neat and organized with work and details, and that they do not make plans before starting on difficult tasks.

Not surprisingly, these tests also indicated that most pathological gamblers tend to desire independence and freedom, wish to come and go as they please, speak their minds as they choose and make decisions on their own. Compulsive gamblers tend to do things without regard to what others may think, criticize those in positions of authority and avoid responsibilities and obligations.

Results from the testing conducted at the Miami VA Medical Center indicate that compulsive gamblers are likely to argue for their own point of view. They tend to be leaders in groups to which they belong, persuade others to do their bidding and tell others how to do their jobs.

One very striking finding of the Moravec study is that typical compulsive gamblers have a high level of intelligence, especially when compared to the educational levels they had attained; few had any post-secondary education.

A conclusion from the Miami study is that compulsive gamblers, in spite of the possible paradox of their aggressive behavior, tend to have strong fears and anxieties about being unaccepted and unloved. These fears are gradually transformed into an obsessive, insatiable need for

116

affection and reassurance of being loved. Such obsessions are thought to be at the core of the maladaptive compulsive gambling behavior.

The research conducted at the Miami compulsive gambling treatment center was aimed at discovering the combination of pathological variables of personality which may indicate the presence or potential of the compulsive gambling disorder. The operative theory behind this study is that by better understanding the behavior of compulsive gamblers, both prevention and treatment of the disorder may be better coordinated.

Other studies have been conducted by Dr. Michael Ferriolo and Dr. Anthony R. Ciminero to analyze the link between compulsive gambling and addictive behaviors. At the Miami Center, pathological gamblers are treated in the same unit as drug and alcoholic abusers, in part because compulsive gamblers and those who suffer from these addictions are plagued by many of the same "core issues" such as lack of self-disclosure; inability to trust people; depression; poor self-esteem; lack of assertiveness; inability to handle stress; inability to identify and affectively deal with feelings; marital, financial and legal problems. Most importantly, all addictive personalities resort to the addictive behavior as an effective short term mechanism to cope with these core issues, in the same way that compulsive gamblers resort to gambling.

Dr. Durand F. Jacobs Study of Traits Leading to Compulsive Gambling

Dr. Durand F. Jacobs, Chief of the Psychology Service of the Jerry L. Pettis Memorial Veterans Hospital in Loma Linda, California has been conducting research on compulsive gamblers for a number of years. A major purpose of this research has been to develop a theoretical model of the addictive personality, and of treatments for addictive disorders.

Dr. Jacobs defines addiction as "a dependent state acquired over time in an attempt to correct a chronic stress condition." (Jacobs, 1982). Jacobs has proposed that there are two sets of factors, one physiological and one psychological, that increase the likelihood of a person acquiring an addictive behavior pattern.

The set of physiological factors is described by Dr. Jacobs as "a life-long...resting state of over or under-mobilization." Jacobs believes that a significant proportion of addicts, including compulsive gamblers, are either chronically hypotensive or chronically hypertensive. Hypotensive individuals find life to be dull and empty. For them, the excitement of gambling replaces their depression and boredom with exhilaration and the feeling of being "acutely alive." Conversely, Dr. Jacobs also believes that a substantial proportion of addicts and potential addicts are physiologically hypertensive, that they are agitated and anxious most of the time. These individuals relieve their anxiety through the use of alcohol, narcotics and other experiences that produce what Jacobs calls a "mellow low."

117

The second set of factors that predispose individuals to addictive behavior patterns are psychological in nature. According to Jacobs, a particular psychological profile may be common to all types of addictions. Persons likely to become addicts are those who "since early childhood have come to perceive themselves as inferior, unwanted and rejected by parents and significant others." This psychological torment that characterizes their lives is not only relieved by addictive substances or experiences, but replaced by fantasies of power and esteem. Thus the addictive behavior patterns are perpetuated. Whether the addictive substance or experience produces a physiologic "high" or mellow "low," the end result is the same: those indulging become less critical of themselves, often engaging instead in self-complimentary daydreams. Such experiences are, therefore, characterized by dissociation from reality. In extreme cases, those with addictive personalities "cross over" into alternate lifestyles and assume altered personalities. Dr. Jacobs points out that this desire to alter identity distinguishes the "true addict" from the simple abuser. Abusers seek only to reduce stress while retaining their identity and continuing in their social role.

In 1982, Dr. Jacobs set out to test his model of the addictive personality by conducting a survey among members of Gamblers Anonymous. Eighty-three members filled out questionnaires, over the period 1981 to 1982. Dr. Jacobs cautions that the findings are preliminary and are not necessarily representative of all compulsive gamblers or even of Gamblers Anonymous members. Dr. Jacobs found that the members of the survey group had a strong tendency to deal with the stresses and frustrations of childhood "through a combination of denial and wish-fulfilling fantasy." This tendency manifested itself in adult life as the compulsive return to gambling for experiences that provide escape and fulfillment similar to those of childhood.

In childhood, fantasies of taking on another identity are considered no more than the products of a healthy imagination. Among adults, however, this tendency is considered pathological if it recurs on a regular basis. Dr. Jacobs' study examined the tendency of compulsive gamblers to dissociate (live another life) while gambling. He found that almost all of those surveyed had experienced a dissociative state to some degree, with almost four in ten feeling that they took on another identity all the time they gambled. Most Gamblers Anonymous members also reported that at some point in their gambling careers they had felt as though they had been in a trance while gambling; over one third reported feeling this way frequently.

The Jacobs study delved even more deeply into the nature of the dissociative state experienced by compulsive gamblers while "in action." Over two-thirds of the respondents reported that at some time while gambling they felt as though they were outside of themselves, watching themselves gamble. Almost a quarter of them reported feeling this way frequently. Similarly, over half of those surveyed reported that they had experienced "memory blackouts" when they had been gambling.

Dissociative states such as those described above have been noted in psychological studies of alcoholics and drug addicts. This study, according to Dr. Jacobs, was the first one to systematically verify such experiences among compulsive gamblers. An interesting question is raised by this finding. The dissociative states experienced by those addicted to drugs or alcohol may have been attributed to the presence of toxins in these substances. However, the high incidence of dissociation among compulsive gamblers belies this explanation, since less than half of all gamblers reported using drugs or alcohol in the years when they were gambling. It must be pointed out that the Jacobs' study did not investigate the question of whether drugs or alcohol were used while actually gambling. It is the psychologist's opinion, however, that the high frequency of dissociative behavior among compulsive gamblers cannot be explained simply by their use of drugs or alcohol.

Few of the compulsive gamblers surveyed believed themselves to have suffered from an underlying hypotensive state. Dr. Jacobs speculates that in many cases it was not until these individuals began gambling that they first learned of their deep need for physical excitement. He asks, "Is it possible that they did not appreciate how deprived they were until they experienced the sharp contrast that gambling produced in their usual emotional state?" Supporting Dr. Jacobs' implied hypothesis are the reasons most frequently given by compulsive gamblers for gambling: 1) to escape their own unhappiness, boredom and stress and 2) to find stimulation. These are precisely the motivations that might be inspired in those who suffer from an underlying hypotensive resting state, i.e. those whose lives are boring and empty.

Most of the Gamblers Anonymous members responding to Dr. Jacobs' questionnaire had known for years that their gambling was out of control. Despite this understanding, their resistance to stopping gambling actually increased over time and was strongest just before quitting. Time away from gambling meant "falling back into 'the pits' of their physical, social and psychological reality."

One of the most heartening findings of the Jacobs study is "the virtual disappearance of their complaints about experiencing chronic hypotensive states once they were able to maintain abstinence from gambling." Gamblers Anonymous members have found alternatives to gambling that lead to stimulating and rewarding lives, according to Jacobs.

Family life was found to be the greatest source of gratification for the Gamblers Anonymous members surveyed. Correspondingly, threats to family stability were cited by the survey group as the most important reminders that gambling was out of control. Family and friends were credited second only to Gamblers Anonymous as the influence most helpful to their abstinence. Dr. Jacobs states that the importance of marriage and family ties cannot be overstressed, and concludes that treatment programs for compulsive gamblers should help those recovering rebuild relationships with family and friends.

The goal of Dr. Jacobs' research is to identify those teenagers or young adults who are likely to develop addictions such as alcoholism and compulsive gambling, and to intervene effectively before the self-destructive behavior patterns begin. Hence the study of factors predisposing to compulsive gambling has a dual purpose: to aid in the recovery of those currently suffering from the disorder and to reduce "the likelihood that succeeding generations will have to endure the same tragic, costly and often losing battle against the ravages of compulsive gambling and other addictions."

Chapter VIII

MEMORIES OF SICKNESS, EXPERIENCE WITH RECOVERY

Section I: The Gambling Years

Gamblers Anonymous members recount their gambling experiences to enlighten others and also to bolster their own resolve to abstain. The simple act of telling, referred to by the Fellowship as "giving therapy," is itself a recovery process — powerful in proportion to the honesty and depth with which these stories are told. Many of the memoirs that follow may be startling, even shocking to those not familiar with the Fellowship; for the tellers, such candor is not only painful, but healing.

The tales related in this section range from childhood misdeeds to major crimes, including violence and suicide attempts. In virtually all of these stories, persons other than the compulsive gambler were harmed, with spouses abused and children neglected or abandoned. The plight worsens, past the point of the sufferer's endurance until, as more than one compulsive gambler describes, the choice was either Gamblers Anonymous or death.

These are members' stories and, as such, most have happy endings. Most have survived to achieve normal, productive lives. But the stories of the millions of compulsive gamblers who still suffer, though mostly unrecorded, are of unthinkable degradation. Yet they can include recovery and a healthy way of life if they include Gamblers Anonymous as well.

No story here is complete. No matter what the unpleasant experiences recounted, every story is a mere synopsis of the pain and humiliation inflicted by compulsive gamblers upon themselves and their families.

So that we may understand the suffering of the families of compulsive gamblers we have included stories from their point of view.

Early Retirement

The paving of my path to GA started very early in life when in elementary school I stopped at the candy store to spend my one cent to try to find the single pink caramel chocolate covered candy amongst the many white ones in the display box...finding the pink one meant I would win a prize. Stealing pennies to pursue this need to find "pinkie" soon became part of my schoolday routine. Playing cigar box marble games, flipping for Topps Bubble Gum Baseball Cards, and spending nickels and dimes on pickboards were my next steps down the road.

My interest in the New York Yankees (while living in Brooklyn through the 1940's when the Dodgers were the love of nearly all Brooklynites) led me to bet for them (and against the Dodgers) before I was fourteen years old. Bookmakers were readily available to my gambling friends and myself, either at the poolroom where I could watch the Ticker Tape or at the candy store hangout where I could look at the newspaper and discuss the upcoming "action." My friends and I played a good amount of baseball, softball, paddleball and stickball — for money. I was an onlooker and "bettor" of the one-on-one basketball games, and the handball games — set up for "big money" at the Ave. P. Park. During the winter, we played poker, black jack, gin rummy, red dog, Monopoly and other games almost every day. My parents, who both worked, were pleased to see their youngest son involved in his non-school hours with his "friends" playing ping-pong and Monopoly — not knowing the stakes involved.

Once a day became five times a day and more. During my early high school days, the gambling was supported by my part time delivery job at a dry cleaners and a dainty store on 65th St. My interest in the stock market started to sprout before my sixteenth birthday with my purchase (through my older brother's account) of a speculative Cuban sugar stock. With this addition, I had many areas of excitement in what I considered a most fulfilling, active teenager's life: involved in sports betting, card games, dice games sporadically thrown in, and, established every Sunday morning with my Italian friends, pickboards, raffles, Irish Sweepstakes, contests from magazines, newspapers, and the stock market. Gradually I even got involved in the then highly speculative penny stock craze, and the Canadian Market. Oh, how exciting I thought my life was.

Shortly after my seventeenth birthday I was winning $500-$750 wagers on the Yankees in the World Series. This reinforced my belief that gambling was better than the stock market to accomplish my goal of retirement by thirty-five years of age. High school, junior college, finding employment, marrying, having children, and adding to my destruction were all in front of me...as was my crossing paths with Gamblers Anonymous, over twenty-five years later.

Daily sports betting started with that World Series win, and came to be interspersed with regular crap games, card games, an occasional ride to the racetracks, both flats and trotters. The dreams of big wins and thirty-five year age retirement grew with each passing week, month and year of furious gambling activity. Accomplishment of this retirement dream, unbeknownst to me, was becoming more farfetched as each new loan took place. My parents, brothers, employer, bank A, Finance company A., etc., were among the many dozens of loan sources that I was able to tap. My position of responsibility in purchasing and management in the graphic arts business enabled me to obtain additional illegal resources of funds through outright stealing and payoffs. I rationalized these crimes as fair reimbursements for my efforts, and as just recompense for the profits I made for my employers.

Marriage at twenty one, fatherhood at twenty-three and twice more, were only happenings along the way in my twenty-three plus years of active compulsive gambling.

Honesty with my employer, bookmaker, friends, wife, children, and other family members, or even casual acquaintances no longer existed. Eventually I found out that I deceived no one, and knew deep inside that my troubles were getting more severe. I responded by gambling with even greater intensity, so that I could still cling to hopes of the big bet that would resolve everything. On several occasions my winnings were huge, only to be followed by a spiral of losses that left greater depths of misery and monthly debts.

The maturation of my three children passed unnoticed by me, never to be recaptured. Instead I gambled with the thought of my doing it for my family.

Days were consumed with the study of the Sports Eye, NY Post, Newark Star Ledger, Basketball Digest, Sporting News, Football Focus, etc. All the studying culminated in the evening phone calls to place any bets and then following the results into the wee hours of the morning. How difficult it was to start the next day unless I could look forward to that very same gambling activity of the day before. Time was passing me by, and my world was closing in. Disappointment to me was the possibility of cancellation of games that I could bet on, such as when President Kennedy was assassinated, the loss of bookmakers and betting sources shut down by police raids, or my inability to make good on losses and thus being shut out of betting activity by a particular bookmaker.

In my mid-thirties (when my dream of retirement was supposed to have been achieved) I was paying at least one creditor every day of the month. At thirty-eight I had a heart attack which curtailed my wagering for about a week while I was at the coronary care unit. Betting continued as usual during the balance (an additional 2 1/2 weeks) of my hospital stay. I nearly died, yet I continued in the pursuit of killing myself.

Around my 41st birthday, after actively gambling for almost 24 years, I went to my first meeting of Gamblers Anonymous. Most people have set their life's foundation by the time they are forty, but I was just starting work on giving direction to my life — without gambling.

Gamblers Anonymous has always shown me the way, so I may accomplish a life of honesty, value, happiness, security, employment and awareness. Without gambling, my life is open to living, not just to continual escape.

Gamblers Anonymous has led me to the sunshine and I never want to let those clouds of gambling enter my life again.

Thief

I started my gambling career when I was thirteen years old. I come from a middle-class family. Both my parents worked very hard to give us every advantage possible. From the time I was thirteen years old, I started hanging around bowling alleys, bowling for small amounts of money. Then when the alleys were filled, or it was raining, we would bet on raindrops falling down window panes. If the sun was shining, we would go through the cemetery behind the bowling alley and we would play acy-deucy on top of tombstones. We would gamble behind the temples and the churches, any place that we could find a place to gamble. We would gamble, on anything and everything, including racing, insects, raindrops and snowfalls, and license plates. You name it and we did it.

Now, I was an average kid who came from a middle-class family. Why did I gamble? I didn't know at this point why I gambled. All I know is that the destruction that I caused while I was growing up will have to remain with me for the rest of my life, because by the time I was sixteen years old, I was bowling and being backed by people, and I got paid to bowl whether I won or lost. If I won, I could win a lot of money and if I lost — I got paid $50 to bowl whether I won or lost, and if I won, I got paid 35% of whatever I won.

I also would climb out my bedroom window at twelve o'clock at night on a Friday night because my parents did not know that I was gambling. I would go to the bowling alley, and bowl in pot games until ten o'clock in the morning, go back home, climb back through my bedroom window, get in bed, and when my parents came in to wake me, it was like I was never gone. I did a lot of that type of gambling, and I won a lot of money bowling. I won an awful lot of money bowling. But, as a compulsive gambler, that was not enough. It just wasn't enough action.

By the time I was sixteen years old I hit my first shylock, and I was into shylocks from sixteen until twenty-five when I came into Gamblers Anonymous. At seventeen years old, when I graduated high school, I caused by father to sell his business to pay off over $80,000 in gambling debts that my brother and I had incurred. Because of that, my father was never able to retire, and when he died at age 74, he still had to work just to be able to live. I went to college and my father worked two jobs to send my brother, my sister and I to college all at the same time. And, all I did in college was spend my time in the game room, playing cards. That is all I did. Eventually I flunked out of school and went into the service.

I went into the service to improve my life, to get my education. I was going to get a new start. Within 11 months I was court-martialed twice for breaking into lockers and stealing money with which to gamble. I was thrown out of the Air Force with a general discharge. I was very lucky to get a general discharge, because I was court-martialed twice for stealing money to gamble. When I got out of the service, I moved back to my parents' house, and I used to crawl into my parents' bedroom, while my parents were asleep, and put my hand in my father's pockets and take whatever money I could find. I took a gold coin collection that he had, and I sold it. I stole his cameras; I stole my mother's jewelry; I stole my mother's silverware, and I sold it. I stole from relatives. I borrowed. I cashed bad checks. I used to go to every single A & S Department store, buy a blender, and return it to every other store I could possibly find. I bought 26 blenders, at $46 each, and all on my A & S charge card. And I returned it for cash, just to get the money to gamble. I went to Gertz Department Store in Jamaica and four weeks in a row I cashed a $50 check. Finally, I got caught. The times I got caught were unbelievable but I always managed to get a bail-out. Now, a bail-out was when I would go to my parents and say, "Mom, I need $1,000 or the shylock is going to kill me. Don't tell Dad." And then I would go to my father and say, "Dad, I need $1,000." I wound up with $2,000, because my parents would hock their souls to protect their children, and I played on that, and took advantage of it.

I met a girl who was going to Bridgeport University and she graduated college when she was eighteen years old. She was teaching when she was eighteen and had her Master's degree when she was twenty; we were married when she was twenty, and by the time she was twenty-one she was a total neurotic. We were married fifteen months, and I turned my wife into a piece of garbage, because I lied to her constantly and there was never any money. If a check had to be made out, I was the doctor, the lawyer, the butcher, and I was the candlestick maker. I was anybody you could possibly imagine. I was the rent. We were married fifteen months, and we were evicted from our apartment.

I stole from my wife's parents; I stole from my wife's grandmother, and I just did everything to destroy my wife. A week after we got married, we got home from our honeymoon, and I took every single check that we got from the honeymoon and paid off shylocks. I stole a diamond watch that my parents had given my wife and I hocked it. I convinced her she lost it at a friend's wedding. These are all things that I did before I came to Gamblers Anonymous. Anything that I could get my hands on to raise any kind of money I would do.

When I came into GA, I was making $95 a week, and I was paying shylocks $350 a week. I had 17 judgments against me. I owed three finance companies. I owed 32 people money, and I used to call myself a minus zero, because of this. It took me a long time to pay everyone of these people, but through the GA program, every single person that I owed money to was paid back. It was slow; it was painful; but, I had to do it, and that was the GA way. Through this program I have developed from a degenerate to a normal human being with one exception. I cannot gamble.

Now, I go to the GA meetings on a regular basis. If a doctor told me that I had cancer, and if I went for cobalt treatment once a week for three hours, it would be fine, I would go. Compulsive gambling is a cancer, and it is a cancer that starts in childhood. It happened to me, and it happened to my twin brother. The only difference between myself and my twin brother is that my brother is still a compulsive gambler who is in action. I am a compulsive gambler whose disease is arrested. My disease will never be cured. It can only be arrested. And, it can only be arrested if I can continue to go to a GA program.

The Prize Fighter's Story

I came into the world in 1909, in a tough section of Lynn, Massachusetts, known as the Brickyard. In this neighborhood you had to fight your way through life. I think I was born with clenched fists, indicating that I was to be a natural fighter. I believe I was also born to be a crapshooter.

At the age of twelve I did become a fighter and in my 189 fights I made a total of $50,000. When I quit boxing I didn't have a dime left. At the age of twenty-four I had to start all over again.

For my first amateur bout I received a gold watch and fifty cents for expenses. The watch I gave to my Dad, but with the fifty cents I walked down the street and on the corner stood a tall, gawky kid called Skippy. He had a pair of dice in his hand and told me I could double my fifty cents. For the next forty years I was chasing that half dollar. During all those years I guess my gambling losses must surely have been in the 100,000 dollar class.

I can recall the checks my father used to write every Saturday night. As he saw me come in the house he would get out his check book and say, "How much?" This was my crutch until he passed away.

The only check I ever forged was one for twelve dollars with my Dad's name. The licking he gave me was worse than any I had in the ring and that stopped me in the check business. Once I stole fifty cents from my Dad's pocket to go to the movies, but he knew his finances. When he found the fifty cents missing he gave me another licking. That really cured me.

For forty years I have been paying finance companies and banks. You can imagine the thousands I borrowed and the interest I paid — enough to retire. But I never realized that I was sick.

I can truthfully say that the first thirteen years of my married life were the worst I ever had, but since joining G.A. eighteen months ago, it has been a thousand per cent better. G.A. has taught me to do things I should have done forty years ago. I never realized how sick I was, and it seems there was no way of arresting this ailment until G.A. was born.

Abe W.
New York

Jerry And I

One of the reasons I came into Gambers Anonymous is because of the story of Jerry, a gambling partner and a dear friend I mourn.

Jerry was my neighbor, with the qualifications for true friendship: interest in horses and sports. He was a quiet, gentle guy. He was married but there were no children in Jerry's life. Jerry gambled and his wife prayed. This was their way of life.

We had a merry time for years. There was evening harness racing on weekends and then regularly during the week. As we both worked normal hours, Saturday often became the time of the double-header: attending two racetracks on the same day. Our wives did not complain. After all we were only at the track.

I do not recall at what point football came into our lives. For years Jerry used a local bookie to place action on college and pro football. He was successful with football. At the end of a season he usually showed a profit. I joined him.

Football, the handicapping, the talk, the games (morning, afternoon and evening) soon dominated five months of our lives. If we were winners on a Saturday, our night would be spent at the racetrack. An afternoon disaster forced us to stay home.

As the years progressed we progressed to more dependable bookies. This was necessary as our friends were playing through our contacts. We learned to "lay off" and "shave" bets. The telephones burned with action through an entire weekend. The talk and the action soon became a way of life. College and professional basketball came next. Our houses were filled with newspapers, selection papers, sports sheets, records and charts. The telephone, television and radio were going all the time.

This ten month sports season seemed perfect in every respect — it left the summer free for Belmont and Saratoga. Card games peppered the horse and sports action. Vacations were arranged and spent near race tracks. Trips were taken to San Juan when funds were plentiful. Friends and family who chose to visit were usually quarter poker players. All was well. My children were growing up and seemed satisfied. Jerry's house was being paid off. We never questioned the true condition of each others bank account. We were having a ball.

Then Jerry moved away in an attempt to control his gambling. After many seasons our gambling was completely out of hand. This curtailed our trips to the race track, but the sports season could not be eliminated, and by the first summer in the new house, Jerry had lost badly. There was only one recourse — get involved with a pastime. What were his interests? He could not afford a football team, so he bought a horse. A horse seemed the lesser evil than gambling, and as an added incentive the horse might return a profit. The one horse might turn into a stable or a farm!

We traveled paddocks from good tracks to bad and finally arrived at the end of the line. The horse was being drugged to stand up and one day returned from a race completely destroyed. He was shipped to a farm for a rest and then brought back, but Jerry could not maintain him. The horse was sold at a loss, but Jerry's house was sold with a profit. He moved into an apartment in the next town and talked about adopting a child. If one spends $10,000 on a horse, one will surely invest $10,000 on a child. Perhaps this would calm the situation. The adoption came to pass and now Jerry had a good job, a new baby and a wife. But Jerry's gambling grew worse. Now the players were many. The telephone rang incessantly. We silenced it for the neightbor's benefit. When the click-click became unbearable we hooked up a small lightbulb. We struggled through the football season. By February, Jerry was looking for a second job to cover his losses. He found part-time work as a maitre d' at the stadium, and Jerry informed me that all was well. He did not tell me about the parties after the events, or the Friday card games. There was also a new escape — pills.

I did not hear from Jerry for some time. No track. No calls. I became suspicious. I had recently scored big and bought a new car so I took the opportunity to pop by on a Sunday and display my success.

All was great with Jerry. The stadium sent the pay check home. Jerry was giving up horses and football. He was playing safe. His money was invested. The stocks were doing great. Jerry's success in a five-month period was astronomical. His money was invested in a casino stock and Atlantic City just opened.

We spoke infrequently during this period. I called for his action when football season started and he refused. I called for tickets to football games and arrangements were made. The baby was fine. The stocks were fine. Everyone was drinking champagne. His original investment had tripled but he weakened and called in a bundle on the Dodgers in the World Series. He lost.

Then in late October in San Juan I got a telephone message which read: "It's me, Jerry. I am here."

He was alone. His wife and baby were home. I did not understand. We talked. The new stock was a disaster. He had sold everything and bought a loser. His wife wanted a separation. He wanted scores. We played the tables together and on the plane home we played knock-rummy.

In December, two weeks before Christmas, Jerry sat in my living room, very high on pills. He was now living alone in a small room around the corner. The situation was hopeless. His wife no longer loved him. She did not like his gambling.

As a gesture I called for information about the nearest Gamblers Anonymous meeting. I volunteered to go with him, but he found excuses not to go. Jerry started betting football. He struggled through the playoffs with limited action. During this period he swore not to start betting horses when the racetrack reopened, but on January 12th he came to my house and said he wanted to go to Yonkers.

This night marked the beginning of regular play at the races. We did not have to call each other to go to the track now. We crossed paths or sat together as a routine. Jerry was at the track every night. Eventually, my invitations to sit down met with his refusal. He said he would sit upstairs with the boys and stop by later. The boys thought he was sitting with me.

The last time I saw Jerry was an hour and a half before the first race of an evening card. He seemed lost, standing alone in the middle of the empty clubhouse, gazing at the vacant starting gate. We talked a minute and we parted and that was all.

My wife called me at work on the following Tuesday. She was hysterical. Jerry had been found dead, in bed, with a note on the table next to his pills and an empty bottle of Scotch. I left work to console my wife and finally broke down that evening. We cried and buried him.

It was not until I came into Gamblers Anonymous that I saw the reality of Jerry's disaster. He never understood that he was truly sick.

I returned to Jerry's grave during my fourth week in Gamblers Anonymous. I prayed for his soul and then calculated the years of his life engraved on the stone. He was only thirty-four.

Hal T.
Bloomfield, N.J.

From Another Member of Gamblers Anonymous

My wife was in the hospital having our daughter and I was home listening to the ball game on the radio — I had a bet on it. After the ball game was over, I went to the hospital. My mother-in-law was outside and she said: "Congratulations." sarcastically. I asked what about? It had taken my wife 20 hours to deliver our son and I expected the same thing to happen this time, but she delivered in two hours, and I wasn't there, because I had to listen to the game.

When I visited her I barely paid attention. I was watching sports on TV. I was an animal who had no regard for my wife and children. I didn't even know they existed.

From the Story of Larry R.

Inevitably, during each binge, the time would come when I could no longer completely conceal everything. My wife would have to be told. The scenes were always the same.

I would arrive home at 3:30 or 4:00 a.m. I dreaded the sight of the light burning in the kitchen, for I hoped this time she might be asleep. But she would still be awake, drinking coffee or tea, waiting and wondering. She would tell me first about dinner. It had long since gone the way of so many dinners before it — down the garbage disposal — while my wife invented excuses as to my whereabouts for our children or for friends who called or dropped in. She would wonder aloud why I had phoned at 4:30 p.m. saying I would be home in thirty minutes, and why I had not called again for twelve agonizing hours.

It is difficult to say whether the gambler or his wife is the more physically, mentally and emotionally damaged by the ravages of a gambling binge. For the wife can only wait and wonder. Her husband may be in jail, in a wreck, in another country, alive, dead or broke. She can usually be quite sure he is broke. She imagines all these things, including infidelity, and she tries to fight back with every weapon at her disposal. She may love, plead, cajole, threaten, nag or "talk things out" until she is blue. If she is married to a compulsive gambler, it will be in vain, for his is a progressive illness and over any considerable period of time he gets worse, never better.

In each of these scenes, a familiar pattern would repeat itself. My wife would drag the facts out of me, one at a time, like pulling teeth. One by one, as we talked, lie after lie and debt after debt would be revealed. To my wife, each bad check — each forged signature of her name at a finance company — each dividend check or freelance script check I had intercepted at the mail box — each new loan on the insurance policy or pink slip I had smuggled from the house — each new bank account I had opened — was a bitter blow to her pride, trust and love.

Sitting in the kitchen, we would watch the sun come up, wondering how we could face this or any other new day. Lack of sleep, physical, mental, and emotional exhaustion, and the overwhelming list of added debts would somehow have to be concealed from our children, our friends, and our neighbors. Of course I would then promise, and mean it with all my heart, never to gamble again for as long as I lived.

But I had no answers for her unending demands for an explanation. I could not explain my reasons for gambling. For each "why," there was an unfathomable drive buried deep in my subconscious which I could not begin to explain.

I thought my problems were financial. I know now that they were emotional. I tried to find answers through psychiatry. I tried religion. I tried going to every place in the city where I had ever cashed a check to make arrangements for them not to let me do so again. We wrote letters to these people. My wife took complete charge of the family finances, giving me, at my request, only enough money to get through one day at a time. We put pink slips, deeds of trust and all other securities in her name. We stopped my charge accounts. And still I found ways to obtain money with which to gamble. I sponged from friends, and then from nodding acquaintances. I actually borrowed money from my 67-year-old mother, a widow with only $67.00 per month income from a pension. And with each fresh "taw" my hope would spring anew. "Just once more." "This time...this time for sure, I'll win enough to pay everything off. Then when I finally get out of this mess, I'll never gamble again." These were my thoughts. These seem to be the twisted thoughts of every compulsive gambler.

At least five different times my wife and I sat down to a list like that, hoping each time for a new start. We had as many trial separations, usually immediately following the confessional. The first few times, I took my belongings downtown to my club. They finally threw me out for not paying my bills. On our last trial separation, I had to be content with a cheap hotel room near Skid Row. Actually, these cooling-off periods were essential to my wife's sanity. After a few days, I would return to attempt still another reconciliation. Each time we would agree to try again for the sake of the children. Surely, our love for each other was still great enough to overcome this compulsion. Surely, rather than ruin the children's lives along with ours, I would come to my senses in time to avoid complete disaster.

After ten years of this madness, my wife at last gave in. I came home from work one night to find a letter explaining that she had taken a plane to Los Angeles. She had sold our car to get enough money to sustain her and the children until I could make arrangements to sell the house and send her more. She loved me and no other man. She could never love anyone else. She forgave me completely. But she had simply reached the end of her endurance. All this was stated in the letter.

My reaction was spontaneous. After reading it through several times, I tore up the letter, dialed the airport, and asked for take-off time of the next plane to Reno. I had $150.00 in my pocket, from a fresh-cashed paycheck. But would the airlines accept a personal check for the round-trip fare to Reno? They would, so long as I had a driver's license and my name was listed in the local phone directory.

Thus it is always so very easy for the compulsive gambler to raise ready cash to feed his ulcer. I wanted all the $150.00 cash for the proposed Reno binge. Rather than use any of this "sacred money" that I had in my pocket, I deliberately wrote a worthless check for my plane fare, telling myself, as always, I would make it good when I won. Twenty-five minutes after finding my wife's letter, I was airborne for Reno.

From the Story of Beatrice L.

When my husband was gambling I thought he was making payments on the house. One day men from the bank came and they were going to foreclose. I didn't know what was going on and I was petrified. They were going in and out of the rooms. I asked them: "What are you doing here?" and they answered: "Well, you haven't made a mortgage payment in six months." I died a thousand deaths. I didn't know what to do. I couldn't wait for those men to leave because as soon as they did I called my husband at work and asked him if he had been making the payments. "Sure I have, hon," he said. "Don't worry."

I told him the bank men had just been here. I was so nervous and upset. I asked him to bring the payment book home that night — I wanted to see with my own eyes. He came home without the book. I attacked him when he walked in the door. "Where's the book? I asked. He said, "Don't worry." That's all he could say, "Don't worry." Finally, I saw the book and I almost died. He hadn't paid. I'd been giving him the money and it was all going for gambling. I was hysterical and all he would say was, "Don't worry."

From Another Member of Gamblers Anonymous

I conned, passed bad checks. I would do anything to gamble. I would travel 50 miles to the track, lose all my money. Travel the 50 miles back home again, beg for more money and turn right around and go back the 50 miles and lose again. I didn't care about anything or anybody — just gambling. I was like a crazy person. One day I did go nuts. I was home and something snapped. I began throwing furniture and threatening to kill my wife and kids.

The police came and I spent six days in the county jail. My wife filed charges against me: I was someone she didn't know any more. I couldn't raise the $266 for my bail bond. My bail was $2,500. When my cellmate heard this he laughed. He was in for bank robbery and his bail was $50,000. When he stopped laughing he said to me: "What would you do if your life depended on that $266?" Those words hit me. It started me thinking and it was the first time in my life that I realized what I was doing, because if I had to depend on that $266 I'd be dead. I sat in my cell for the next six days and I thought and I began to see what I was doing.

From the Story of Tony B.

My wife and I were no longer talking. My life and all my time was preoccupied with gambling. From the moment my eyes would open in the morning until the last scores came in after midnight, I thought of nothing but gambling. I can remember one Christmas I had a bad week gambling and my wife and daughter were excited about Christmas. I always made life miserable for them around this time because my wife would always spend money for gifts which meant I had to come up with money for gambling from some place else. The argument I started had nothing to do with my wife or daughter. It was totally related to my gambling but I made her believe it was because of her. One thing led to another and she packed her bags and called her father to come and get her. I thought it was all over. All the frustration and desperation I was experiencing I took out on them in the cruelest and most insane thing I have ever done. In front of my daughter I went totally berserk. I knocked down the Christmas tree that my wife and daughter had so enjoyed decorating just hours before. I smashed all the ornaments on the tree. I threw my wife's suitcase right through the wall, smashing the plaster board. I punched walls, ripped doors off the hinges. This continued for about an hour until her father arrived and just like that it was over. As I sat on the bed with tears rolling down my cheeks I could hear my daughter's screams, "Please, daddy, stop." "Please, daddy, stop." I felt so alone and desperate as I turned on the radio to find out I had lost again. You're right! Gambling was leading me to the gates of insanity...or DEATH.

From the Story of Another Gamblers Anonymous Member

You have started your employment and are progressing nicely. It's fall and you are enrolled in a major university majoring in finance, attending classes two evenings a week. You enjoy the business world and tolerate school. Your family life is pulling at you with too many bosses at home. Mom, working full time, is divorced since you and your brother were kids. The three of you live in a small apartment with your grandparents. Five people on each others' nerves. You view your parents' failure to continue a marriage as part of your composition; you will also fail. You must find something to succeed at, to let the world know that you are number one.

You find an escape, inching your way with your sharp mind and some money. Gambling, an accepted pastime, a way to have fun, relax and easily accessible. In your office someone passes out football tickets and you try one. You bet a friend $5 on a Sunday game, you learn about lines, home fields, spreads and all the lingo associated with your new "toy."

In the spring you find the race track, and then find the trotters. Shangri la, Utopia, a new world all wrapped into one.

From the Story of Another Gamblers Anonymous Member

You may ask, how can you get hurt playing Bingo at churches and social clubs? But they took a lot of time and money from me. I went from Bingo game to Bingo game and sometimes from Bingo games straight to Reno — and of course, I lost every cent. I also did all kinds of things to gamble. It got to the point where my husband absolutely forbade me to play any more but I would sneak out when he wouldn't miss me and gamble. I borrowed the money because I never had money in my bag.

I would even play blackjack with my kids and have them ask their grandmother for money. I guess that was my bottom — conning my own children.

From the Story of Bill B.

In those days they had counter checks at the bank and I'd walk in and pick one up, fill it out — it didn't make any difference what name I'd put on it — I had an honest face. I took many banks for many checks, and motels, hotels, drugstores, too; it didn't make any difference. I got letters from banks: "Enclosed find check for amount of X. We don't wish to have your account in our bank any longer." I was bouncing too many checks.

I didn't trust other people to kite checks, so I would kite checks with myself. I used to float them back from one account to the other. I had to, plus, it was exciting. It was something more than the games: how was I going to get the money? I ended up in lots of difficulty legally and otherwise. I bought an interest in a local crap game and I paid off more cops with more money. They must have had gold-plated revolvers with the money I gave them. All the money I made in the crap games and everything else I just poured back in. I was my own best player.

Then I appeared before the grand jury and a Senate Investigation Committee and it got kind of sticky. I came to Gamblers Anonymous simply because my wife found out about my gambling the second or third time I'd taken all the money from the savings account. When she went to make a deposit where she thought there were many thousands of dollars, there was nothing. She ended up dragging me to Gamblers Anonymous and to Gamblers Anonymous I went. I wasn't interested in stopping gambling at the time; I was just interested in getting her off my back, and I did.

Instant Gratification

I used to think that "bankers and brokers" games and marbles were my earliest gambling experiences, but after a few years of Gamblers Anonymous therapy I realized my compulsive personality was formed before that. I always wanted things right away with no forethought. If it was a pair of roller skates or an ice cream I wanted it now. If it was baseball cards, I had to beat everybody on the block for all of them. Gradually this trait became my way of life. Every urge had to be instantly gratified.

I thought the easiest and fastest way for me to attain everything I wanted was to gamble. By the age of fifteen my gambling was becoming a daily habit. I started making small bets on the Yankees and Knicks as well as running football and baseball pools. I was also able to start borrowing from shylocks at this age. I went out on some dates but I was always more interested in gambling results than the girl I was with at the time.

After failing to establish any relationships I gave up and gambling filled all my waking hours either by actually betting or by just lying in bed dreaming about perfect poker hands or photo finishes with my horse winning. I neglected my obligations to my parents and I stole from them whenever the opportunity presented itself. My late teens were spent in race tracks and card rooms. I lived between Roosevelt, Yonkers, Belmont and Aqueduct race tracks, and I could get to at least one track each day. Gambling now took up all of my days, and my greatest thrills were at the races. Twin doubles, large exactas, and triples were my dreams even though most times I left the track without money for the toll bridge or even a pretzel. If I won I was happy until my next losing day.

Then I got married and my personality changed radically. Things that happened to me before marriage because of gambling I could accept and sometimes laugh at; being asked to leave the seminary I was studying at because of gambling was not traumatic because I wanted to gamble more than I wanted to be a priest. Yet after 15 years of gambling I decided to get married but I never accepted the responsibility. I wanted a wife in name only. I did not want to accept the companionship which marriage offered. I had a complete breakdown in my mental outlook on life. I had to lie to a person who knew my 24-hour schedule: why I would not be home for dinner; why I had to go for the paper in the evening and come home four hours later; why there was never enough money in the checking account to pay our bills.

There was also a financial burden I never had when I was single, which increased after our first child was born and my wife had to leave her job. I had no real peace of mind to share with either my wife or son. Within five years we had three children and my responsibilities were increasing. I entered into bookmaking and then illegal business ventures to "provide" for these obligations. In actuality I was searching for more money to cover my increased wagering style. I was now gambling at least 17 to 18 hours a day and lying in bed the other seven hours wondering where I was going to get money for my gambling debts.

Life at home became a nightmare. After gambling all day I had to go home to a rejected woman and children who did not understand my non-caring attitude. I became so tense that in order to eat dinner, I would drink a six-pack of beer just to calm my nerves. Eventually, that became a habit to just relax myself even during the day. My conscience was in battle with the real me. I had a very religious upbringing and my gambling lifestyle was in complete contradiction to this early training. I had become a nervous, conniving, cheating, immoral individual.

At work I embezzled equipment which I sold to customers. I had access to stolen goods which I resold at a profit. I had become a bookmaker at work, only to lose whatever I won to my bookmakers at night. I had also become a drinker and suffered blackouts. I carried a gun because I had fears of being mugged and yet the only time I used the gun was when I was drunk and shot at street lights. The person who had entertained thoughts of becoming a priest was now a menace to society and yet, when I associated with compulsive gamblers I felt I was normal.

Besides the mental strain I suffered from physical ailments because of neglect. I had bad teeth and would only go to dentists if the tooth abscessed. I had serious bleeding hermorrhoids which I neglected because of the "cost" of a doctor's visit. My blood pressure was in the danger zone and because I drank I had dizzy spells and heart palpitations throughout the day, living with the daily fear of a stroke or heart attack.

After seven years of almost non-stop gambling I contemplated suicide to free myself from my daily grind. I could not cope with reality. I wanted so much to win at the game of life but gambling kept taking me away from that goal. Finally I found my way to the Gamblers Anonymous program and I thank God for it daily.

John C.
Bronx, N.Y.

Torture Events

When I was gambling I used to go to Madison Square Garden. I think now of the lobby, and of the thousands of bodies without faces, people not human, just bodies and always the action. When it was the Universtiy of Utah versus the University of Pittsburgh, I'm sure there were a 150 from Utah, 200 from Pittsburgh, and 17,000 compulsive gamblers sitting in the Garden watching basketball.

Those of us who went to the Garden had a need to see the action and live through this torture — for me it was a torture event, not a sporting event. The game wasn't decided until four minutes before the end, so in those last four minutes my heart went from one end of my side to the other. This is also true of baseball, which is a slower torture.

Today I have no desire to set foot in another stadium at all. It brings back awful memories. Once I could name all the ball players — this was a great accomplishment. Today, I think: so what? And I have no desire to follow sports, so I come to Gamblers Anonymous to remind myself that these are the unimportant things in life.

A Pomona Wife's Story

When Bill and I were married in 1954, I knew that he had done some gambling and a few things to get money that weren't quite honest. But I didn't realize then what a terrible illness he had. I believed he would stop gambling after we were married. I wouldn't listen to the many people who tried to warn me. I was convinced I could change him. It didn't take long to find out how wrong I was.

Soon after we were married he went on a gambling spree. I remember how shocked I was to find out he had lost what little money we had. This was the beginning of many worries and heartaches.

That first spree of his was followed by another and another. Each time he came home he would just sit and hang his head, saying he didn't know why he had done it, and promising never to do it again. I wanted to believe him. We always had to sit down and figure out a way to survive until the next payday. I had to face the bill collectors with lies. I hated this. I could feel they knew I was lying to them. I quit answering the door or the phone. I told my mother that when she called to let the phone ring twice, hang up, and call back. I would not answer otherwise.

When I found out that Bill had written two checks that he knew we couldn't cover, I got really scared. I think that's when I realized there was something terribly wrong with my husband. I tried many times to talk to him about it, but we just never could.

I woke up one night after midnight to find Bill gone. He had gotten out of bed and gone to a card club after I had fallen asleep. In anger, I called my father to come and get me, but the next day I returned when Bill promised never to do it again. After that, however, I found it very hard to go to sleep, fearing he would sneak out again.

When I became pregnant with our first child, I thought surely this would make him stop gambling. Instead, he got worse. I used to think he couldn't possibly love me and treat me like this. I planned to stick around until the baby was born, figuring that if he wouldn't stop gambling for me, he might stop for the baby. I worked for the first six months of my pregnancy, but had to quit because of the strain. My paychecks were going for his gambling anyway, so why work?

After our baby girl was born, I arranged to get out of the hospital a day early because we were short of money. I called my husband's place of employment to tell him to come and get me. When I was told he hadn't come in that day, my heart sank clear to the floor. There was nothing else to do but call his folks to come for me. They were the only ones I knew who had the money to get me out of the hospital. They were very kind to me.

This experience left me bitterly confused. I felt I should leave him and then I feared that if I did he would really get into trouble and end up in prison. So I stayed.

Looking back, I don't know how I stood it. I spent so many nights alone. I sat by the window waiting for him to come home, hoping and praying. I cried my eyes out. I tried calling every card club I knew of, ready to have them tell Bill it was an "emergency" call, but it did no good. Even if he heard his name called, he wouldn't come to the phone. When he finally did come home, I'd scream and holler at him. This just wasn't me at all. The names I'd call him were awful. He'd just sit there with his head lowered not saying a word. After I'd calmed down a bit, we'd try to talk things out. It wasn't easy. Everything I said he would twist around, making me feel I was to blame for his gambling. I'd usually end up saying: "O.K. — we'll try it your way," and I'd get my hopes all built up again, only to have them smashed the next day if he was able to borrow some money.

I was afraid to leave the house during the day because he might come home while I was out and sell or pawn everything he could lay his hands on. When I had gone to visit my mother one day, he sold our dining room set and pawned our radio and silverware. After that, I couldn't trust him at all. If he said he was going to get a haircut, I found an excuse to go with him because I no longer believed anything he told me. He had let me down too many times.

I became suspicious of everything he did. If he was a little bit late getting home from work, I'd accuse him of gambling. When I discovered that I'd been wrong, I thought to myself: "He probably will gamble now just to get back at me."

I also became very sneaky. I had to hide what money came into my hands. When he was asleep, I'd go through his wallet to see if he had been holding out on me. I could usually sense when he was going to gamble or had been, but I got so I hated to accuse him of it when I was not sure.

There was a time when he let some traffic citations pile up, having gambled away the money with which he should have paid the fines. A police officer came out one afternoon to pick him up. I was so scared I didn't know what to do or where to turn. His parents were on vacation and we already owed everyone else I could think of. There was nothing to do but let him sit it out in jail. This hurt me terribly, but at the same time I thought it might make him see the light. During that period our furniture was repossessed and I had to move in with my folks because we were so far behind in our rent. It was a hard struggle, but I had hopes now that, after being jailed, he would straighten out. I thought he could see where his gambling would lead him.

After he got out, we lived with my parents for two and a half months, for Bill had lost his job. He decided to go to work for his dad, and we moved in with his folks. They were building a new chicken ranch out on the desert. Bill worked hard at the ranch and seemed pretty happy. It wasn't an easy life for us, but he wasn't gambling and that was the main thing. My worries began again when he started building up a commercial egg route. I found out he was using the money gained from this route for gambling. I hated him for it. I couldn't understand anyone stealing from his own folks.

After much heartbreak, we decided it would be best if we left the ranch. Bill got a good job with an insurance company but it didn't take long for them to find out he had lost a previous job due to gambling, so they let him go. I was very upset over this, but once again I thought: he's got to see what the gambling bug is doing to him. I imagined that losing that good job would help him see the light. He was able to get another good job as a salesman and things went sailing along beautifully for about three months. At that time, I can say I was happy and had gotten back my trust in him. We were able to pay off old bills. Once again I trusted him with the money, trusted him to leave the house for work or for a haircut, and I didn't feel I had to go with him any more.

Then came that terrible day when he went to pay back his sister some money he had borrowed, and from her place went to a card club. I recall that I just didn't want to believe it. We had been so happy. He just couldn't go back to that miserable life again. But he did.

We thought perhaps a psychiatrist could help him, for I couldn't stand it anymore. I was taking most of my feelings out on my three little children. They didn't know what was going on. They asked where daddy was and why was I crying. I don't know what I told them — anything but the truth probably, just so they wouldn't bother me.

Bill went to a psychiatrist for about two months and ended up one day slipping off to a card club instead of keeping his appointment with the doctor. I remember how sick I was at finding out that apparently psychiatry couldn't help him either.

I went along for another couple of months not knowing what to do, then on our daughter's birthday, he gambled again. I was numb with despair. That was all I could stand. I think I was ready for a mental institution. I knew something had to be done. I kept thinking about the children. If something happened to me, who would take care of them?

The next day Bill went to the State Hospital to see if they could help him. They said they couldn't, but referred him to Gamblers Anonymous. When he got home, he called G.A. right away. They told him someone would come out to see us that evening, and the promsie was kept. A young couple visited us. I was amazed as they told us their story. I had always thought we were the only ones in the world with a problem like this. They sat there telling "our" story.

Bill went to his first meeting on February 7, 1962. I was very skeptical at first. Bill's gambling problem seemed so bad to me I couldn't see how this would help him. But then again, the man from G.A. who had come to our home had stopped, and his story was our story. Still, I was a little afraid of getting my hopes built up too much. I didn't want to be let down again.

I was worried when Bill came home from that first meeting. He didn't have much to say. All he said was that he thought it was okay, and told me how the meeting was conducted. I didn't think he was overly impressed with what he had seen and heard, but he kept going to the meetings and I with him when I was able to. I had been fooled by what I thought was his negative first reaction to G.A. Apparently it had really gotten through to

139

him, for he became deeply interested in G.A. and everybody in it.

To me, G.A. is a miracle. Bill hasn't made a bet of any kind in almost fourteen months.

Through an organization called Gam-Anon I have learned that I am not so perfect either. These meetings are really helping me to become a better person.

Bill and I still have our problems, as in any marriage, but there is no more gambling and we are able to sit down and really talk to each other. We love and respect each other now and I wouldn't trade it for anything.

Margie M.
Pomona, California

Gambling Sickness

As I climbed upon the rocks above the sea I felt the sharp pain of my broken ribs. I stood and looked out over the misty ocean and watched the roaring waves crash against the rocks. I knew that death waited below and I wanted to die. Irresistibly, my mind carried me back to the time of my youth.

I thought of the times I climbed great mountains and stood upon high peaks. The rugged canyons plunged downward and swept into long green valleys. The blue waters of the Snake River wound among the gorges, cut across the lowlands and disappeared into the distant horizon. I turned and scanned the towering mountains to the north, and I came to understand, in some part, the vastness of creation. Lying upon my back, I searched the blue sky and became aware of the phenomenon of endless space. A growing hunger to know God rose within me.

Later, I stood upon our porch in the winter and came to understand the miracle of a white world of drifting snow. The excited cries of my brothers and sisters penetrated my being as they expressed the joyous wonder of the coming of spring. They scrambled among the wild sage in search of a tiny flower or any form of the new life that springs like magic from the first splotches of bare ground in the wake of the melting snow. I felt the enchantment of the warm chinook wind that pressed against my cheek. It blew across the hills and valleys, turning the carpet of snow into torrents of water that rushed toward the swelling creek below. I saw the pale green of budding willows that grew en masse upon its banks. My heart filled with joy as I heard, close by, the clear and piercing song of the meadowlark, for this bird with its grey body and soft yellow breast was the symbol that winter was in full retreat. At home I heard the clear voice of our mother raised in song. She, too, was filled with the joys of spring, and because she lived close to God she gave expression in the words of the melody. They fell softly upon my ears, "Count your many blessings, name them one by one, and it will surprise you what the Lord hath done."

Another time, I stood in a meadow and felt the warmth of the brilliant sunlight as it brought to life the wildflowers that bloomed at my feet. Their vivid colors flooded the meadow, spilling over into the pale green of the fields, and scattered among the blue sage that covered the gentle slope of the foothills; and I became aware of the miracle of beauty in creation. I stood beside the fence in the fall, and felt the wind pull at my clothes as it rippled across the fields of golden wheat; and I came to understand the miracle of productivity of the soil.

There was a time when I stood in the desert and dropped to my knees to inspect a tiny flower, perfect in pattern, color and fragrance, blooming within the shadow of a tall cactus. I rose to my feet in wonder, that the power behind the sun, the moon, the stars, the seasons, and the great earth with its masses of life, had within its nature that which could conceive this tiny flower scarcely larger than the head of a pin.

I met my true love. We stood before the minister as he pronounced us man and wife, and in the first years of that sacred union I came to understand the blessings of the tender, understanding love which only a woman brings into the world. In due time I held in my arms, for the first time, my infant son. Humbleness welled up in my heart. I looked down at the face of my wife who had been the channel of this unfoldment of life. The smile on her lips, and the light in her eyes, told me that we thought as one.

Then came that black day when I entered Santa Anita race track, in Arcadia California. I stood in front of the paddocks entranced by the sleek thoroughbreds as the grooms lashed the tiny saddles upon their backs. I sensed the excitement of the crowd as it surged around me. We moved toward the grandstand. I bounded up the high stairs two steps at a time. My body felt as if it were devoid of gravity, and then I turned and looked out at the beautiful spread below. My eyes followed the contour of the track as it swept around in a great oval. Then I beheld the masses of color that covered the infield. The clear-cut pattern of the vivid flowers formed a design as though it were stamped there by the hand of God, and beyond this I saw the gentle rise of the oak covered knolls as they swept toward the base of the rugged mountains silhouetted against the blue sky to the north.

The horses were on the track and the starter lined them up in the iron stalls. My hand gripped the tickets that I had bought on the horse of my choice. The faint ring of the bell, the lunge of the horses and riders, and the race was under way. I jumped to my feet, searching for my horse among the pack that moved swiftly up the back stretch. The roar of the crowd was deafening. I was frantic, for I could not see my number among the leaders as they moved into the far turn. Suddenly the voice of the announcer penetrated the din..."on the out side — here comes Captain Cal — it is Captain Cal now taking command." A tremendous exhilaration swelled within me. A wild shout burst from my lips. People turned and stared at me, but I rushed to join the winning line that formed in front of the cashier's window.

I walked toward my parked car. My step was light and I felt as one who had been reborn. How could I know that among the beauty of the flowers, the enchantment of the noble thoroughbreds thundering around the track, there were the seeds of an all-consuming passion that was to become my way of life.

In the weeks and months that followed, the gambling fever took possession of me. I was carried on the crest of a great wave that engulfed my every waking moment. There was no room for doubts, no hint of the evil that would hurt my loved ones, for it offered fabulous sums of money which I would shower upon them as an expression of my love. Like a man under dope, I was carried far beyond the realm of reality. For a time I knew a happiness I had never known before. I could do no wrong. The money poured in. But the time came when my luck changed. As I continued to lose, doubts began to rise. My conscience came to life, bringing confusion and gloom. I was heartsick. One night I awoke and a flash of reality cleared my mind. I vowed with all my heart that I would never gamble again. With this resolution came peace of mind. I drifted into tranquil sleep.

The next day my vow was broken, and in the months that followed I left behind a long trail of broken promises that brought me face to face with the sickening realization that I could not stop gambling. As the sickness grew, I sacrificed one by one the principles I had learned to live by. There was suffering in my home. The wife who had given me her love, and placed into my keeping her hope for happiness, lived in poverty, humiliation, loneliness, and heartbreak. My children, whom I loved dearly, lived in want and insecurity, without the companionship or guidance of their father, and many beautiful things in life passed them by.

How quickly the years passed. My mind became a battlefield for terrible guilt and the obsession to gamble.

Little by little, I retreated into a hideous, lonely world. Gambling no longer brought visions of large sums of money, but was simply a dark monster that shadowed my every move.

A day came when I stood at the foot of a white bed in St. Luke's Hospital in Pasadena, California, gazing at my dying father. Helpless grief made my head swim, and a wave of nausea swept through me at the thought of my failure as a son. There was a terrible hurt in my heart. I closed my eyes and whispered a few words of prayer for my beloved dad. When I again looked at him, he had lifted his head and was frantically searching the room. Then his eyes came to rest upon my face. Slowly his head dropped back to his pillow. A faint smile crossed his lips and I saw again the look of affection he had for me always. I moved softly to the head of the bed and picked up the limp hand and pressed it to my body. Never again would I hear his voice or feel the touch of his kindly hand

142

upon my shoulder. I dropped to my knees and put my head against the still-warm body and the sounds of my grief passed into the silence of the still room.

I sat beside the casket in the mortuary and the only sound in the dim light was the beating of my own heart. I dwelt on my wasted life. A shiver of cold fear moved in to haunt me. A thousand times I had promised or swore that I would never gamble again, but always it was there to claim me, and each time a little of me died with my broken promise. Rising I moved to the casket and looked down upon the quiet face. This was my last chance. If only in this great loss could I find the strength! The sounds of my whispered words seemed to fill the silent room. "I promise you, Dad, that I will never gamble again, so help me God!"

We laid his body to rest beneath a sturdy pine in the Rose Hills Cemetery. In the days that followed, like a man in a dream I moved quietly about my work, fearful that any sudden movement might break the spell and chase away the peace and serenity that, like a timid dove, had come to rest in my mind. The terrible churning of my gambling compulsion was stilled, but I lived with a feeling of unreality. If only I could find again the feeling of God around me. Each day I lived with a prayer in my heart.

In January I was driving toward my job in the Whittier Hills. The sun was just rising and a sense of well-being surged within me. My mind and heart opened to the fresh wonders of the new day. My nostrils were filled with the smells of the dew-laden foliage that covered the countryside. Suddenly I am possessed with the thought that something wonderful is coming into my life this day. Then, without warning, it is there — the vision of the crowded grandstands at the racetrack. I could see the thoroughbreds streaking around the track, and the piles of money seemed so close I could touch them. It was all there for the taking. It seemed the answer to all my problems and the fulfillment of the secret hopes that poured into my mind again. Like a cyclone, my obsession swept all before it. Turning the truck around, I drove hurriedly back toward town.

Evening came. I vaguely sensed the vast area of the race track parking lot that surrounded me. The crowds were long since gone, but still I sat there staring into the darkness. A parade of thoughts, born of the sickness in my soul, poured through my mind. My conscience felt like a bloody mass. A world of desolation closed in on me. "Oh, God," I whispered, "Was I born for this? Why will you not break the shackles and set me free? Why, dear God, why?"

I stand by the rail in a gambling club in Gardena, having once again made the long trip from Santa Barbara and spend endless hours at the gambling tables. Impending doom has placed a clutching hand upon my heart. With heavy eyes I scan the faces of the suffering humanity around me. The flushed white faces, the shaking hands and the cries of resentment speak of the hell they live in. Close by is a young woman heavy with child. She smokes nervously on a cigarette held between twitching fingers. I realized that even the unborn infant cannot escape the stigma of this terrible sickness. I moved through the door out into the cold, crisp night. My hands and feet are heavy as I reach my car and start the long drive home. My car increases its speed when I think of my wife. The awful guilt that has become such a painful living part of my world up through the years spawns, as always, a haunting urgency that I must get to her at all cost, and now the car moves faster and the road becomes a blur before my tired eyes. Then for a moment I cease to be and my head slumps upon my chest only to jerk up at some invisible warning. I am rushing toward a mass of street equipment and red lights in the middle of the highway. I jerk the steering wheel toward the open road and then I am tumbling. I hear dimly the screeching of metal as the car slides on its side and comes to a halt. I cannot move and I feel numbly that this is the end. Sounds of glass sliding from its mooring and clattering upon the pavement drift to my dulled ears.

I am lying in the hospital and the pain in my soul far overshadows the hurt in my body, for I have come to the sickening realization that, added to all my other sins, I am now a menace upon the highways. I cannot understand the miracle that I still live. I watch, and wait through the long night and then she is standing by my side. I cringe as I steel myself to face her. The pallor of her cheeks matches the grey gloom of the approaching dawn that seeps through the windows. She bends over me and gently kisses my face. I close my eyes tightly to hold back the rush of tears. A thousand words of endearment rush to my lips, but I cannot speak.

I hear the voice of a man. I open my eyes and see the dim outline of my son standing at the foot of the bed and I am deeply humble that he has not forsaken me ...

Again I am making the long drive home from Gardena. My mind and body are numb from the nightmare of the past few hours, for I have made my last great struggle to win the money without which I tell myself I cannot survive, but now my last shred of hope is gone and I do not have the strength nor the will to go on.

I pass again the scene of my wreck and it rises to haunt me. Now the highway joins the seashore and I slowly bring my car to a halt and climb upon the rocks above the sea. Now — this is the end.

The pale moon passes behind the clouds and in the darkness my body stood rigid. In one last effort at self-preservation I strained into the future, hoping for a small ray of light that could sustain me, but there was none. I was a man who lived without hope. I searched my past, hoping to capture a pleasant memory that would hold back the darkness. But I saw only my more than fifty years strewn along a dark pathway. I took my last deep breath and leaned toward the swirling mass below where I must find peace. "God forgive me." I did not hear the sound of my own voice. I could not move, for the face of my wife appeared before me. How could I

144

kill myself, knowing that she still cared for me? I can understand the words that I have heard, "It sometimes takes greater courage to live than it does to die."

I reached home and stood for a moment looking upon the dim light in the window that awaited my return always. I climbed the stairs, and like a wounded animal crawled into the sanctuary beside her and I knew she was crying. I stared into the darkness. Suddenly my mind began to whirl. It became a thing that shrieked through the endless darkness of hell. It swelled into a bulging mass of stark fear, and with the speed of light it plunged in all directions, but...there...was...no...escape. And then the quivering mass was stilled, and I seemed to be floating up from the depths of a chasm, and again my mind came into focus. My body was chilled from sweat and I knew that my sanity hung by a tiny thread. What was I to do now? Where could I turn for help? *Was* there any help — anywhere?

Sitting on the davenport, I watched intently the face of a man who had traveled a hundred and twenty miles by bus to bring into my home the message about something called Gamblers Anonymous. I was stirred to the depths, for he was describing in every detail the pattern of my own miserable life. I struggled for self-control as I recognized the same sickness in this man that I had. His voice penetrated the confusion of my mind. He spoke of the founders of a new movement. Then he said the words I so desperately wanted to hear; that other men like me were living in freedom from all forms of gambling, and were finding a new life.

He took his leave and I gratefully promised to be at the next meeting. As I closed the door behind him, I whispered a prayer of thanks to my God, for in my heart I felt the stir of something without which man cannot live. My friend had brought me hope.

The following Friday evening my wife and I were at the meeting in Los Angeles. Our friend was there to greet us and we were welcomed with warm handshakes. I sat quietly beside my wife. Slowly I scanned the faces of the men around me. "How can they help me?" I wondered. I remembered all the words of advice given me through the years. I remembered the pain and deep suffering I had caused others. I remembered that my children had grown up in the cruel grip of insecurity to face their worlds in timidity and uncertainty and that they would carry its scars the rest of their lives. In the time of my own deep suffering and despair, my soul had cried out to comprehend the mystery of life, but the only certainty I could understand was that I live for a short time, in the very center of an eternity that had already passed, and an eternity that would never end. How could a man cast away his chance to share, with those he loved, this miracle of life, in the full expression of love, hope, peace, joy and beauty, living upon the earth? Yet still — I COULD NOT STOP GAMBLING. If only they could give me medicine, or a doctor could open my body and cut away the awful obsession and set me free.

My hands were limp and damp as I became aware that a man, standing in front of the group, was speaking. His voice was filled with humbleness as he talked of his wasted life, a broken home, the loss of his family, of heartbreak and loneliness, and finally the desire to end his life. He told of being unable to break the yoke of his compulsion to gamble.

The hours passed like moments and I hung onto every word from the men who rose to speak, for they were telling my story. As their stories unfolded, I knew they were men of my own kind. I came to realize with great sadness that the wives and innocent children bore the cruel brunt of this desolation. I felt a surge of compassion toward them, such as I had never before known for anyone. I yearned to help them. But what could I do? Then the last speaker rose to his feet. In his face was the same compassion that filled my own heart. As though he could read my thoughts, he spoke the words that were to sink deep into my soul and taking root, open a secret door to a hidden power that was to change my whole life. "If you would help your fellow compulsive gamblers in this room and this fellowship to carry its message to those millions who still suffer, the greatest contribution you can make is to stay away from the first bet."

Reluctantly I saw the meeting come to a close. I wanted it to last forever, that I might keep the strange and wonderful feeling that gave peace and rest to my soul. I felt the touch of my wife's hand upon my own. I turned and looked into her face, and I saw a new light in her eyes. She was beginning to understand my compulsion for gambling as a terrible sickness. A wave of love and intense tenderness swelled in my heart for her. Through thirty-one years of marriage she had not faltered in giving me loyalty, love, and devotion — far beyond the duty of any wife. I knew that without her my life would have ended years ago, for she had been the one solid thing that I held to in my struggle to survive.

Every week in the months that followed, together we made that two hundred mile drive to our G.A. meetings. In those months I came to understand the power in the simple spiritual principles of this wonderful fellowship, when put into practice by each individual. I learned the strength in the bonds of understanding, friendship and compassion. I found an inexhaustible inspiration and hope in the lives of the old pioneer members, in their proven freedom from their obsession, and the new life they had found. I learned the living truth of a great principle; he who, with compassion, seeks to help another, must always help himself in the process. Never once has the beautiful miracle that was awakened in my soul on the night of my first meeting grown dim; it has continued to grow. Now, standing squarely between me and my obsession, IT HAS SET ME FREE!

Always, as I walk through the open door of the meetingplace, a feeling of humble gratitude sweeps over me, and I return the smiles and words of friendly greeting extended me from the people in all walks of life. For this hideous compulsion to gamble is no respector of persons; it will strike anyone who is emotionally susceptible to its curse. Some still wear the pallor of the sickness. There are the new members seeking help. As always, my wonder grows when I contemplate the miracles that have taken place in the lives of people here in this room, in the two years I have been coming here. For within this humble fellowship I have seen broken lives put back together again. I have come to realize that, in all the dark history of this baffling affliction, here is the first real help. Many of us have passed through the courts of our land with no one to understand the cause of our crimes. I think of the hundreds of thousands of homes scattered across our beloved America that are filled with desolation and misery from gambling sickness. I know that there are millions of little children, and other millions yet unborn, who must look to Gamblers Anonymous if they are to have the fruits of their golden years.

I climb upon the rocks above the sea and look out over the great ocean and its waves crash against the rocks below. Once a symbol of death, it has now become a thing of beauty, for at long last I have found peace in freedom from my obsession. I now walk in dignity and usefulness among my fellow men. There is love, trust and harmony in my home.

Because of the cross I have borne these many long years, I strive to have an understanding heart. And because I have searched for God, my deep and new life is rising within me. The growing light of my spirit reaches out to join the brilliance of the sun that shines above me. It carries my spirit high above the earth and I feel the presence of God in the misty, billowing clouds, in the swells of the boundless ocean whose incessant waves march toward the shore. I see Him in the silence of the great mountains, standing like sentinels against the far horizon, and in the quiet reaches of the desert wastelands. I see Him in all life that springs from the earth — in the songs of the birds, or the squirrel that scrambles among the branches of the tall trees. I see Him in the beauty of the wildflowers that bloom in the spring, and in the love of a mother, or the innocent, trusting face of her child. Even though I face eternity in the very center of infinity, I have no fear, for I have come to live with a deep conviction that I no longer walk alone.

Anonymous

Section II: Gamblers Anonymous And Recovery

If there is a theme that recurs through the stories that Gamblers Anonymous members tell us when first coming to the Fellowship, it is of the relief that they felt upon discovering that they were not alone. Until that first group meeting, most had believed themselves to be the only ones who suffered from the gambling sickness; the only ones who had been driven to destroy their finances; family life, health and hope for the future by the desperate need to "stay in action." A major hope, then, that accompanies this second set of personal stories is that compulsive gamblers who have not yet come to the Fellowship may learn that there is a place to go where others have learned to control this insidious affliction.

In contrast to the first set of personal stories, which deal mostly with the ravages of compulsive gambling, the remembrances that follow are of introduction to Gamblers Anonymous, recovery and personal growth. However, one aspect of the Gamblers Anonymous recovery process, in which members help other compulsive gamblers who still suffer, is severely under-represented in the stories that follow. While thousands of members render innumerable hours of such assistance each year, few were willing to tell of these experiences out of respect for the Fellowship's spirit of humility. Let the reader be aware, therefore, that most of the stories that follow have unwritten endings, in which members of Gamblers Anonymous help other compulsive gamblers conquer the gambling problem, thereby assuring the continuation of their own personal growth.

I Couldn't Stop

I made my last bet on November 21, 1964 and three days later my wife and I went to our first meeting of Gamblers Anonymous. That was the first time I ever heard of the Fellowship. I didn't know what to expect and I had no idea how they could help. I did know, however, that I was a very sick person with an addiction for gambling.

My gambling experiences are as fresh in my mind today as they were then. It is most important to me that I never forget the misery and unhappiness I inflicted upon my wife and children. I'm not great on direct quotes but "to forget your past misdeeds could cause you to repeat them."

My gambling started at age 15, playing poker with friends every Friday night. I think I owed money from the first day I gambled and the pressures of having to pay back began very early in my life. Only after coming to Gamblers Anonymous could I face up to just what I had made of myself from my mid-teens on. I was considered a joke by most of my gambling friends. I constantly tried to freeload as I never held onto money long enough to even pay for a late evening snack after the poker game. I always made myself available to run errands for my older gambling friends with the hope that some day I would be accepted into their gambling fraternity. In retrospect, I certainly earned no one's respect nor could I respect myself.

I quit High School after 2 years because I wanted to gamble full time. I tried to convince myself that I wanted to help support my mother, but this was all nonsense. I never really had a normal social life, opting to devote all my time to gambling. My weekly card game continued but I added sports and horse betting to my life. Even though I gambled constantly during these years my debts never skyrocketed as my earnings were comparatively low and I had not established credit.

My most vivid recollections during my gambling years were unhappiness and depression. I can remember leaving a racetrack with tears in my eyes, praying to God to cure my affliction.

In 1952 I was drafted and I gambled at every opportunity. Two years later I was discharged and then proceeded to gamble, without thought of getting a job, for an entire year. My mother asked the Veterans Administration to help me, and as a result, I received a High School Equivalency diploma and eventually graduated college. I continued to gamble during this period — striving to complete my education so that I could earn larger sums and gamble for larger stakes.

I met and married my wife in June of 1956. I never made her a part of my gambling, and for the most part, tried to hide it from her. Soon after my marriage, I started a new career and my income increased rapidly. My gambling also accelerated and my need for money far exceeded my capacity to earn it. In order to feed my ever increasing gambling habit, and maintain some semblance of financial stability at home, I literally begged, borrowed and stole from everyone around me. I owed banks, finance companies, bookmakers, family and friends. In addition, I began to embezzle money from my employer giving no thought to how or when I could get the funds back to where they belonged. My debts increased steadily and my situation was out of control.

I telephoned bookmakers, betting thousands of dollars each day, without having more than the dime to make the call. Before coming to Gamblers Anonymous my life had become completely unmanageable. I constantly lied and conned in order to continue gambling. I knew at this time that I was a very sick man but I didn't know how to stop gambling. I can recall going to the local Veterans Administration office and talking to different veterans' group representatives. I pleaded for help but they could offer no assistance except to suggest that I sign myself into a VA hospital. I tried this but was informed that there were no beds available for the mentally ill.

Just prior to attending my first Gamblers Anonymous meeting I found myself at a personal low in my life. My debts were enormous and I was awaiting discovery of my stealing. In addition, the pressures exerted on all other segments of my life were becoming too much to bear. I was destroyed emotionally with a negative outlook for my future. I could no longer dream of the day when I would win all the money I could ever need. I saw myself as hopeless, born a sick gambler and condemned to die that way.

My sister-in-law heard of Gamblers Anonymous and she made the initial call to the Fellowship. She spoke with Irv L. and was told that there was a meeting that night. The information was passed on to my wife, who asked if I would go that night. I jumped at the chance to attend as I would have done anything in order to stop gambling. As I would learn later, I had two things going for me even then. I knew I was very sick and I had a sincere desire to stop gambling.

My first Gamblers Anonymous meeting was an absolute revelation to me. First, there were others in the room like me. I was burdened with so much guilt, having such a low opinion of myself, that I couldn't conceive that there were others as sick as I. It was reassuring to see and hear men with the same sickness. I was able to communicate with people who understood my problem and to accept their help willingly. Secondly, there were men in the room who had stopped gambling, from periods of one week to 6 years. What I saw that night ignited a flicker of hope in my heart. I kept asking myself "if these men could stop gambling and begin a better way of life, why can't I?"

During my early weeks in the program I sought advice constantly. My problems didn't evaporate overnight but I was told how to handle them, one day at a time. Every man in the room helped me, either by sharing their gambling experiences during the therapy portion of the meeting, telephoning me between meetings or answering my questions during the coffee break. And most important, I sensed that they really cared about me — a relative stranger.

My financial problems did not disappear but I was told by experienced members how to face them and minimize the pressures they created. I was told specifically how to talk to my creditors; to solicit their understanding and assistance so that I could help myself. I had to get a part-time job in order to pay my monthly living expenses and have something left over for creditors. I listened very attentively to what these men had to say and I invariably followed their advice.

I liked being part of Gamblers Anonymous and tried to emulate the strengths of those members I admired and respected. I soon became involved in the Gamblers Anonymous program as I wanted to help someone else as all those others had helped me.

I've been coming regularly to Gamblers Anonymous meetings, and have not gambled, for 19 years and 1 month. My family and I have benefited materially and spiritually, and I have noticed other changes in myself. I have reached a point where I like and respect myself. I consider myself a worthwhile part of the human race, capable of sharing what I have acquired from the Gamblers Anonymous program.

I owe my life to Gamblers Anonymous and could never repay the Fellowship for what has been done for me.

Never Too Old To Change

I was a World War II war bride and arrived in New York City in 1949. Prior to coming to the U.S. I had not engaged in gambling, although my father had gambled away an import business and my mother had to work as a professional cook to feed and clothe eight children.

My husband was an easy-going, kind, generous man who gave me a free license to do pretty much as I pleased in my spare time. He worked a night shift and I had a day job in a law office. For a year or two I led a pretty routine life but one day I went to the New York racetrack instead of going to the office — I believe it was simply out of boredom. I enjoyed the noise and the excitement in the clubhouse and somehow managed to pick one or two winners. The following Saturday I went back to the same racetrack, but lost all my previous winnings plus an entire week's paycheck. By then I could no longer live the routine life. Spontaneous visits to the racetracks were followed by visits to Las Vegas; sometimes I would take a taxi to the airport and fly out to Vegas when I should have been at the office working.

I must have visited Las Vegas about four times a year for several years. I had established excellent credit at the casinos and would write markers for 1 to 5 thousand dollars on a visit which I would make good on my return to New York by withdrawing from our savings account. During these years my husband never checked our account nor did he question my need to make these trips out west.

Shortly after my husband's death in 1966 I decided to move to Las Vegas and make it my home. Since I had won money on one or two previous visits I figured I could live on my gambling winnings without having to pay the expensive airfare back and forth to New York. In 1972 my net financial worth was $36,000. I thought I was good at playing 21 and played the game at the big strip casinos as if money were going out of style. I gave no thought to my future, my health, my living conditions or anything else. The game was the thing and when I would drop a thousand dollars or so I always knew there was more in the bank. After about five years of gambling steadily I discovered to my horror one day that my bank account was down to $500. I was living in a motel on a weekly basis and decided to find an apartment so that I'd have a roof over my head for a month. Then I hoped to find work. I found a place to live and placed a deposit on it but went out for one "final" shot at winning back some of the money I had lost. I lost all the money I had left and could not move into

151

the apartment. Now I was forced to stay three nights at the Salvation Army hostel and walk all over town seeking work. I could not find an office job because I was in my sixties and was forced to move in with a family and take care of three children and keep house for a working mother. It was not easy to clean six rooms, to cook, to get up at seven a.m. to get the kids off to school. I finally was given housing under a seniors project and received my social security widow's pension amounting now to $350 a month. Up until four months ago I would still gamble with my pension check and usually end up without sufficient funds to buy food, ride a bus or sometimes pay the light bill. Four months ago I heard a dealer in a casino tell her 'relief' dealer that I would be broke pretty soon. Up until that time I had about fifty dollars in chips on the table. She was right. I sat at the table until all the chips were gone. I got up and left the casino, sick at heart and suddenly I recalled what the dealer had said and I said to myself, "How stupid you have been — with all the money you have given to gambling they look down on you and even laugh at you." It was then I decided 'this is it' and I reached for a telephone and called Gamblers Anonymous. There was a message record playing and I left my home number. The next day I was called and someone picked me up and brought me to a meeting. I couldn't believe there were other people with the same problem. Even though I had contemplated suicide at one time previous to this visit, I still hadn't thought of Gamblers Anonymous. Now I have been clean for four months — my personality is changing for the better. I am working as a senior companion four hours a day at a convalescent home. I am learning to survive on a small pension. I have put the past behind me — no use looking back. With the help of G.A. and my Higher Power I hope to live a useful, sensible life and one day at a time, stay away from gambling. I know now you are never too old to change. I have repaid most of my personal debts and am finding love where before there was scorn.

Sandi L
Las Vegas

A Casual Visit To The Racetrack

Every Thursday evening at the Hotel Lenox in Boston a group of men gather around a table and as each one rises to speak he begins by saying "My name is Bill, (or Joe, or Bob, or Jim) — I am a compulsive gambler." This is a meeting of Gamblers Anonymous, and these men from every walk of life, teachers, lawyers, salesmen, taxi drivers, businessmen, are baring their souls to gain the strength, experience and hope necessary to effect a recovery from the insidious illness of compulsive gambling.

On the evening of August 24, 1960, I found myself at the Hotel Lenox for the first meeting of Gamblers Anonymous in Boston. I was frightened and embarrassed, and had circled the hotel several times before I got up enough courage to walk into Room 101. As I listened to the many stories of heartache, despair and hope of those who wanted to lead a new and different life, my own life swept before me. It took me back twenty years to when I was 24, married, and held an excellent position with a nationally known organization. Who could have imagined that this fine job, as well as my family and friends, were destined to be thrust aside by my obsession with gambling?

It all started in perfect innocence with a casual visit to the racetrack with a friend. While my friend could take it or leave it, I became "hooked" from the very start. The pageantry and the color of the track fascinated me and my early losses did not dull my interest in the slightest. At first I went once a week on Saturdays, but soon that wasn't enough. I found myself hurrying through my work on many days so that I could get to the track. In six months I was sadly neglecting my job as a salesman and received a stiff warning from my employer. It had little effect, for I was so obsessed with the urge to gamble that everything else had become secondary. For the next six months I did little or no work and was at last dismissed from my position. I obtained evening employment so that my days would be free. The racetrack was the only important thing in my life.

All during this period I continually borrowed money, first from family and friends, then from banks, finance companies and credit unions and finally, as a last resort, from the "shylocks" whose interest rates alone took a large part of my earnings. It was inconceivable that a person like myself, with so limited an income, could incur such tremendous debts.

For many years my family could not understand what motivated my actions. I was brought up in an atmosphere of honesty and kindliness. Although of very modest means, my family constantly came to my rescue, hoping against hope that each time would be the last. Even after they had exhausted all available funds I continued to pressure them to borrow money for me. I systematically bled every member of my family, always promising that the new loan would be the last. I often thought of robbery, many times of suicide.

From time to time I enjoyed a lucky day or a lucky streak which served to whet my appetite for more and more. I had now reached a point at which it was no longer a case of winning or losing, but simply of *having* a bet. Not being able to gamble on certain days was a torture I didn't think I could endure. The racetrack had become my escape, not just from the ring of the telephone or the knock at the door but from all my inadequacies.

The anticipation of going to the races, the planning, the conniving, the false hope, were all part of the game. I was on a merry-go-round and I didn't want the ride to stop. Actually, it was a toboggan slide, iced fresh every day. The ride to the bottom was inevitable, and I seemed not to care. My friends were friends only if they loaned me money. A new friend was quickly evaluated as to what size "touch" he could stand. My thinking had become so distorted that I shunned anything that held a semblance of normalcy.

It was not uncommon for me at the end of a day's races to drive ninety or a hundred miles to another track where there was night racing. Many times, while driving across the country, I would notice the sun settling behind the hills and wonder if this was the sunset of my life. I was always rushing, always deep in a frenzy, helpless against the insidious thing that kept driving me on and on. I would console myself with the knowledge that if I lost again there would be an "ace in the hole" the next day: I had conceived a new plan for borrowing money, or found a new loan shark. I would definitely allow a waiting period to elapse so that the shark wouldn't think I was too anxious. I felt that by playing it "cool" I could make him think I was a better risk.

On other occasions the only way I could raise funds was to disappear for two or three days; my wife would become panic-stricken, thinking that some harm had befallen me. Then I would make that long distance phone call and the voice on the other would say, "All is forgiven. Please come home. We'll help you just once more." Again the borrowing of a large sum of money, once again a fresh start, and a return to gambling with more recklessness than before.

I was filled with remorse and self-pity. I became frightened at the thought of what I might do next. I realized that getting money from my family in this way was a form of blackmail. I began to feel that I was an incurable misfit, incapable of ever coping with the normal demands of society.

Of all the people close to me, my sister was the one who had begun to realize what was happening. She saw that I was "sick" and unable to help myself. She suggested psychiatry to me and I did consider looking for professional help, but always at the last minute I found some excuse. I was not ready or willing to "give up."

It was in April, 1960, that I first heard of G.A. My sister had read an article about it in a Boston paper and passed on the information to me. I wrote to G.A. headquarters in California and shortly afterward received a letter and a brochure on how to start a group in the Boston area. This had no effect on me and I continued on my merry way. It appeared that I was bent on destroying myself. I became a physical and mental wreck from lack of sleep, from working by night and clinging to the daily ritual of form sheets and parimutuel tickets which in most cases were torn into confetti. In the late stages I gambled at the lowest possible level, often being without funds after two or three races and then depending on my track acquaintances for "touches" to keep me in "action."

It was on Sunday morning, August 20, 1960, that I got my first big break. A man who introduced himself only as "Jay" called me on the telephone. He told me he was organizing a Gamblers Anonymous chapter in Boston and before I could start my negative thinking he went on to tell me some facts about his own life. I was flabbergasted; it was as though I was speaking about myself through his lips. Reluctantly, I agreed to attend the first meeting the following Thursday evening.

I am ever grateful to my wife and my sister for encouraging and prodding me into going to that meeting. Room 101 of the Hotel Lenox was buzzing with excitement when I walked into it. It was the first meeting of its kind in New England. A man who had attended meetings in New York greeted me at the door and tried to put me at ease, but my heart was pumping. I sat down in one of the rear seats and shortly afterward the meeting began.

I heard three men from the New York group speak. They had flown into Boston for this meeting at their own expense. One of them told of having earned in excess of $25,000 per year for the past fifteen years. He had lived on less than $5,000 of his annual salary, the rest going for gambling. He had not gambled for four months and to me that seemed like a very long time.

At that meeting I did not get up to speak but I heard many people tell their stories and it gave me a tremendous amount of relief. I was no longer alone. At the close of the meeting, the men and their wives chatted over coffee. One man from New York who hadn't gambled in ten months named every Kentucky Derby winner since the inception of the big race; he had gambled for thirty-five years before coming to G.A. I admired him and was suddenly filled with a new kind of hope. I could visualize for the first time the possibility of a life without gambling. The first effects of G.A. had started to work. When I walked out into the street from that meeting I had to restrain my elation. I wanted to run and shout the good news. I kept repeating to myself "There is hope! There is hope! There is hope!"

I knew that this was going to be a fight to the finish. I was convinced that if I didn't succeed at G.A. I would never again have an opportunity to live a normal and peaceful existence. My first step was to see all of my creditors and lay my cards on the table. I made no false promises. I fought for and got reduced payments on many of the bills. In some instances I had to stagger the payments but everyone saw something coming in, no matter how small. One week led to the next and finally I had two months under my belt. I must admit that had our meetings been spaced farther apart than once a week I could never have made it. Many times I just managed to hold on until the next meeting, which always left me with renewed hope and encouragement. During this time the phone calls between meetings were priceless. The G.A. theory of members calling one another worked like magic for me. Often while trying to help someone else I found myself benefiting as much as, sometimes perhaps more than, the other person.

My wife attended meetings with me and helped tremendously with her new understanding of the gambling problem which G.A. taught us. I don't want to imply that it was easy or simple. Although I had built up a strong resistance against the old urge, it did not entirely disappear. There were many trying days. The monotony of paying out money to my various creditors seemed at times intolerable. Frequently I felt dull and listless, but through it all the Thursday night meetings filled the void.

By now there existed an indescribable bond of friendship between the men who had started together on that Thursday night in August. As time went on, we realized more than ever that together we could reach our goal.

Other things started to happen: there were interviews on radio and television and we received recognition in newspapers and magazines. Most important, I found myself practicing the twelve steps of our recovery program. Making direct amends to the people I had harmed was a huge help, but the step that gave me the biggest inspiration was our twelfth, which deals with carrying the message of hope to other compulsive gamblers who still suffer. Answering all inquiries, calling members old and new, showing the understanding that perhaps only one compulsive gambler can have for another, all meant carrying out the twelfth step. The satisfaction I derived from such activity gave me more strength and determination in my fight to recover.

Then came August 24, 1961, which meant that one year had passed since I last gambled. The Boston G.A. chapter's celebration of its first anniversary was for me a dream come true. I now realize how little resemblance there is between my life before and my life now. I have that priceless commodity, "peace of mind." I have the love and respect of my wife and family, the respect of my friends and colleagues. These things I cherish too dearly to jeopardize. I know that for me to start thinking the wrong way again would cause my complete downfall.

This vast change in my personality took place after I was willing to admit to my innermost self that I was unlike other people. The delusion that I could some day control my gambling had to be smashed. These truths were embedded in my mind during all the weeks and months of my re-education in G.A.

It is now almost twenty-two years since I have gambled. When I walked into Room 101 I asked for a miracle. Let no one say that miracles can't happen. There were two in my life — first, I stopped gambling; second, I don't feel the need to gamble. I can't say that I don't sometimes have the desire. I am a compulsive gambler and always will be, but the important thing is that I have learned to control the compulsion. I am no longer helpless against the old, obsessive urge.

For these miracles I must thank God and the many others who made it possible: "Jay," who organized the Boston Chapter of G.A. and every member of G.A. past and present — my blood brothers; the members of Gam-Anon, the women of G.A., the wives of the compulsive gamblers.

They always had a word of encouragement for me. My wife, a member of Gam-Anon, also gave me much-needed help every step of the way.

I don't think I can ever write the final chapter to this story because for as long as I live I will continue to need G.A. I feel there will always be within me that little spark which, if rekindled, would blow me to kingdom come.

In conclusion I can only say that G.A. has brought me closer to myself, closer to my family and friends, and most important, closer to God.

Joe L.
Boston

It Wasn't My Fault

I thought about leaving my husband a thousand times when he was gambling, but I never had the confidence to think I could actually make it on my own. I also stayed because I feared that I had failed him in some way and I felt guilty. I was married at 18 and I looked up to my husband. I didn't mind his gambling at first — he took me to the track with him and I thought it was exciting. Besides, when we were first married, my husband was not betting the huge sums of money he would later.

I thought I could change him. I thought marriage would straighten him out and all he needed was to settle down in a good solid relationship. His father had died when he was quite young and I reasoned with someone to love him he wouldn't need to gamble any more. In the first year of our marriage everything seemed as if it were going to be all right. My husband told me he had borrowed money from a relative to consolidate and pay off his gambling debts. Nothing appeared to be wrong. He worked long hours but I didn't mind that because at least he wasn't gambling, or so I thought. He never made a bet from home and we had enough money to get by. I must have suspected deep down that he was still gambling — every once in a while I would ask him, and he'd say "no" very sincerely — but I just didn't want to admit it to myself.

Then one night when our first child was about a year old, he came home late from "work" looking tired and worn out. As he took off his jacket a loan book fell out. I picked it up and almost went hysterical when I saw how much money we owed. Maybe he wanted me to find out because after that he no longer hid his gambling from me. Things went from bad to worse. I was ashamed of my husband and our condition and I eventually cut myself off from everyone because of my shame. I had no friends and no one to turn to. I would sit alone in our apartment day after day terrified. My nerves were shattered too. If my child even moved the wrong way I would get angry and hit her. I couldn't stand the stress. And I was terrified that my husband would walk out on me, leaving me alone in a world in which I couldn't cope or make my way.

157

I became compulsive in my own way. To escape, I'd go shopping and run up huge bills I knew we could never pay. At times I used to clean constantly, running the vacuum cleaner for hours on end, sometimes through the night. By this time I had lost so much weight that I went to see a doctor, but even his help and tranquilizers did no good. Then I became pregnant again. We hardly had any sex life, but I thought another child might bring us together and help us focus on something else.

I wasn't in any shape to carry the baby. One evening my husband had to rush me to the hospital. There were complications and I almost died. During all this my husband was at the track. He dropped me off at the hospital and left. He didn't know if I were going to live or die and he didn't seem to care. I felt as if everything I had was lost. I became depressed and withdrawn. When I was back home I sank deeper into myself and I could barely function. I blamed myself for my husband's problem. I really thought it was my fault because I wasn't a good wife, a good person. I really believed that I drove him to gamble.

I never went out if I could help it. I just sat all day or watched television, but mostly I had no energy to do anything but sit like a vegetable fantasizing that my husband would die and I would be free, a "respectable" widow. I imagined that I had chest pains and found myself constantly complaining about them. I couldn't seem to catch my breath ever. I also thought I was going insane.

Then my husband stopped gambling. I didn't know why. He didn't tell me he was attending Gamblers Anonymous meetings. He thought if I found out he was really sick I'd leave him. I thought he had come to some horrible decision and I was frantic with fear. Finally I confronted him and he told me about Gamblers Anonymous. Then I received a phone call from a Gam-Anon member and I started going to a few meetings. But when I found out that his gambling wasn't my fault I became furious and bitter and I wanted to make my husband suffer as much as I had all those years. I was angry all the time and took it out on him continually until I began to hate myself for doing that.

Meanwhile, though, we were both trying hard to work the program, my husband in Gamblers Anonymous and me through Gam-Anon. Slowly, we began to work on our marriage and tried to rebuild our lives. I decided to go back to school — I wanted to get a college education. I was able to do that and have two more beautiful children. Today I have everything and I wish other people could experience the beautiful relationship I now have with my husband, but of course, without the pain we had to go through. We thank God He showed us the way.

Evelyn B.
Cherry Hill, N.J.

The Slip

The first night in Gamblers Anonymous we are asked to "Give the program ninety days. If you don't like what you see, ... you can always return to the misery. The games and action will still be there." I made ninety days of abstinence from gambling, and I vowed to return to Gamblers Anonymous for a lifetime, declaring that I had adopted a principle — I would not gamble — not for anything. This would be my foundation for a normal way of life and the means to overcome my compulsive sickness.

The night I celebrated ninety days without a bet I was given a bluebook dated and signed by all who attended the meeting. It was a reward and after the meeting I rewarded myself by stopping at the old hang-out for a nightcap. But I stayed too long. The doors locked and the remaining crowd assembled to start a crap game. I knew I wasn't supposed to tempt or test myself and inside my heart lay a principle and desire not to gamble. Many fellows knew of my problem and didn't notice me.

I watched, drinking and chatting with the small audience. After three hours the doors opened and I went into the night without making a bet but my blood bubbled from the old heat.

By my next Gamblers Anonymous meeting I lost the feeling that I came within a breath of gambling. I overlooked the fact that I knew the crap game started every night after a certain hour and that I overstayed intentionally. My therapy was light that evening. I joked about the incident, unconcerned. I received several comments. I was strongly warned that I might very well gamble the next time an incident such as this occurred, but I was not receptive to the advice at the time and it didn't help.

I was attending many Gamblers Anonymous meetings at this point. I became involved in the Gamblers Anonymous Program, visiting our intergroup, supporting smaller meetings and performing successful public relations work. When First Nighters appeared I would invite them to the next possible meeting to get them exposed to the program within days — not a week later. I used the telephone.

But during this period I was bombarded with problems; problems at home, at work and the ever-present gambling problem in my blood. I did not give strong therapy at meetings. I hedged. I remained in the past instead of revealing the current bug running through my veins. I tried to project a healthy recovery to the new members as evidence of success in the program. My very real and disturbing problems were kept within. I watched my deterioration with the feeling that my active participation in Gamblers Anonymous would overcome my problem. I felt that working one part of the program was an insurance policy. It did not work.

Then I became depressed, and my problems escalated. In the program I learned that I had for years avoided solving problems by gambling, but my defense against life's problems was gone — I had stopped gambling. Now I was faced with problems for which I hadn't the wherewithal to resolve or tolerate. I became hysterical. My therapy hinted at the disaster to come. Although I attended six consecutive meetings, I went back to gambling. I slipped.

Back at Gamblers Anonymous I was asked to face the reality that I had gambled and run from my problems for many years and hence, compounded most of the problems in my life. This awakening created an inward disgust. I was the cause and the effect of my miserable conditon.

I tempted myself and at the first opportunity gave up my principle just like a bankroll. I tempted myself because I was sick. After ninety days I had on account one principle in which I believed, but I gambled with my principle not to gamble. I discovered a new form of action.

Today in Gamblers Anonymous I am a better listener. I healed the wound of my slip, and I know that the first bet is made in the mind. Today I watch for the signals and the origins of disaster (the anger, the impatience) and attempt to alter my attitude immediately. Repair the moment, one day at a time and live free of the slip.

Stan L.
Teaneck, N.J.

From The Story of Frank P.

While I was recuperating from the suicide attempt, the words of Gamblers Anonymous came to me. I had laughed at these people before, now I knew it was the only hope for me. I went to my first meeting not knowing what to expect. It didn't do a thing for me, but I made myself go to another meeting the following night and something hit home. I went to five meetings a week for four months.

Today, thanks to Gamblers Anonymous, I have a better understanding of myself and my life. Gamblers Anonymous helped bring my family together again, with more love and understanding. When I joined Gamblers Anonymous I did it only to stop gambling. I didn't realize I would find so much more. Living just for today is a pleasant adventure for me. What is this power that Gamblers Anonymous has? Now I call it God.

From Ernie's Story

One thing I haven't mentioned was my constant search for help to rid myself of the compulsion to gamble. I took my problem to psychiatrists, psychologists, and clergymen, all to no avail. At last I reached a point where I no longer wanted to live, at the same time having a great fear of death. It was then that I sought and found G.A.

I attended my first G.A. meeting with the same feelings a drowning man must have when he sees a straw floating by. He knows the straw will not hold him up but he grabs it anyway. I grabbed at G.A. in that way, wondering how a group of strangers could do for me what imprisonment, hospital confinement due to beatings, loss of everything I held near and dear, and long sessions with psychotherapists and clergymen could not do. I went to that first G.A. meeting firmly convinced of three things. One, I was a very evil person because of what I had done and the many people I had hurt in the doing. Two, that I was alone with this problem and Three, that there was no help for me. I came in skeptical and walked out amazed.

There were about fifteen men at that meeting. As each one spoke, I heard my story repeated again and again. It was as if they had opened my diary and were reading from it. The most amazing part of all was that these men had changed their way of life, a thing I was convinced could not be done. They had managed to stay away from gambling for periods of anywhere from three weeks to three years. I learned from their talks that I was not an evil person but a sick one, that I was not alone with this sickness but one of millions similarly afflicted.

All I had to do to help myself was be willing to admit my life was unmanageable, and to unite with these others in their fight against the gambling compulsion. This I had done. I was the last speaker at that meeting. I told of all my hatred for mankind, my frustrations, my inability to cope with my problem, and my desire to become a member of the organization.

The need I once had for gambling I exchanged for a need for G.A. and G.A. meetings. As I continued to attend meetings, my life became better. Although the monies and the wasted years were lost forever, many things were restored: my own self-respect, the respect of my relatives, my superiors, my friends and my wife. I also regained my wife's love and the affection of my family. The ability to think clearly and to do an honest day's work returned, as did the desire to share my life with all those I cared for. The greatest of all benefits was — peace of mind.

Although I have been in G.A. two years, I still have financial problems, but they are far less acute than they were and in time, I am confident, will vanish completely. Everyday problems I'll always have, but with a mind no longer fogged with gambling they can and will be solved. Today, the need for G.A. as a crutch is no longer with me. In its place is a desire to help the sick, compulsive gamblers who still suffer. This wish can never be entirely fulfilled, but by my attempts to fulfill it I must be a lifetime member of G.A. I must give all I can for G.A., be willing to make twelfth steps calls whenever called upon regardless of distance, of time of day or night and to make meetings not just at my convenience, but many times at my inconvenience. I know that I will have to be on my guard against becoming so complacent as to forget those who need me. In return, I can expect to receive the help and blessing of those whom I need. I could not ask for more.

From The Story of Ray M.

On awakening the next morning I was still full of enthusiasm for G.A., but as the minutes passed my stinking thinking got the best of me (I later learned this was because I had not yet taken Step One). By 10:30 I was on my way to becoming the first "slipper" in G.A. I rationalized that I would go to the track for the last time that day, win a lot of money, pay off all my pressing debts, and then be a good G.A. member forever. I convinced myself that this was the thing to do, got in my car, and headed for the Pomona racetrack. I can vividly remember betting all twelve races that day and ending up winning $10.00, but because I didn't make the big kill as I had expected, I drove fifty miles to Gardena to try my luck with cards. I managed to go broke about five minutes before closing time. Driving home, I was a pretty sick individual, wondering what to say to my wife.

Twice more I had to go to Gardena before reaching the point of complete disgust with myself. On the last night of my gambling I didn't try to think up an excuse for my behavior. I was now at last ready to give up. I admitted complete defeat. In a period of less than sixty seconds, my entire life as a compulsive gambler flashed through my mind, and I saw with great clarity that I could not go on alone. Unequivocally I accepted the first three steps of the G.A. program. After making this decision, I felt like a re-born person.

From The Story of Bob M.

After ten months in the program I got the biggest urge. I had been beaten up by four thugs at the end of the line while driving a N.Y.C. bus. The bus company gave me a job sweeping out 50 dirty buses every night.

I told John, a member of A.A. how bad I felt, about the lousy job I had. I was going to get $200 pay the next day. I was going to the trotters, bet no more than $2 or $4 and make a safe $100 on a horse. I knew people who could give me a sure winner. Maybe if I had money in my pocket I could tell the bosses I wanted a better job. He explained to me about St. Francis of Assisi. How he gave up everything and became a beggar. John explained how I had gambled for 23 years and had stopped for ten months, that made me a success. "You don't have to be a big movie star or a president of a big corporation to be a success. All you've got to do is do your own thing and not gamble." I thought about this and the fact that even if I had a winner, I could never leave the track. I'd have to bet the next race and the next and the next day be back in action again.

From The Story of Jim H.

I took the long subway ride to Manhattan, sat in a bar nursing a beer until it was time to see the doctor. He didn't seem to be greatly concerned when I confessed I had gone to the track and lost all my money, but the things he said did nothing to relieve my depression. To begin with, he told me it would be some three years before he could take me on as a patient, and then, in his opinion, I would require from five to seven years of treatment, with five one-hour visits a week at seventy-five dollars a visit. I knew that my parents could never afford such an investment, though they had bailed me out of trouble time and time again. The situation seemed hopeless, especially when the doctor pointed out that he had had very little luck with gambling addicts.

Many other doctors had taken an equally dim view of my chances of recovering from compulsive gambling. One of them had said: "You would have a better chance of recovering from terminal cancer."

I had promised and tried to quit hundreds of times during a gambling career that started when I was thirteen and lasted until I reached the age of thirty-seven. I gambled through high school, three years of college and military service. Because of my insane way of life I was fired from forty different jobs, lost three businesses, was confined in three mental institutions, had assorted brushes with the law and several beatings. I became an alcoholic also, and after those years of misery and confusion came finally to see that one drink, like one bet, was for me pure insanity.

In late 1961 I read an article about Gamblers Anonymous in my local Ohio newspaper. I wrote to a Los Angeles post office box and received a pamphlet and a questionnaire containing twenty questions for people who thought they might have a gambling problem. I answered all twenty questions "yes." I corresponded with a Jim W., secretary of G.A. Later I was to learn that he was the founder of the G.A. Fellowship. I was invited to join with other people who were trying to recover from the illness which was called compulsive gambling.

The closest G.A. group to me at that time was in New York City. It was suggested that I start a group in my own town. I knew many gamblers like myself, but had tried unsuccessfully some seven years previously to interest several of them in giving up gambling. I abandoned this idea. I decided, instead, to use will power and the 12 suggested steps of recovery in the G.A. pamphlet that had been sent me. I lasted just seven months, then went back to gambling as insanely as ever. By this time I had so disgusted my parents, friends, relatives and employers with both my gambling and my drinking that I had nowhere to turn. I was given a plane ticket to Los Angeles by my father. He told me that he could no longer bail me out of my jams, and that whatever trouble I got into from then on I would have to suffer out on my own. My family was through once and forever. Of course I had heard this many times before, but somehow I felt this was *it*.

I was to change planes in Chicago and proceed to Los Angeles via Las Vegas. I learned that the flight out of Chicago, on this Labor Day of 1961, was full, but that I would have the first no-show standby seat. All the passengers showed up, leaving me to wait for a possible no-show on the next flight at midnight. As I walked away from the departure gate I heard a terrific explosion and saw people running in all directions. The plane I had hoped to board had crashed and all seventy-eight of the passengers and crew were dead.

I had often said that I wanted to be killed in a plane because it would be fast. For this trip I had purchased the maximum amount of insurance, 250,000 dollars worth. This would have repaid my father for everything he had expended over the years trying to cure me of gambling and helping me out of my self-created difficulties. Instead of being overjoyed at the fact that I had escaped death in the plane crash, I kept saying to myself, "Why couldn't it have been me?"

The next day I arrived in Los Angeles, and that evening attended my first G.A. meeting in the nearby Gardena. I heard some twenty-five compulsive gamblers speak about themselves and what gambling had done to them. Many had been habitues of the Gardena poker palaces, where local option laws made lowball and draw poker legal. Some of those who spoke had gambled only a few years, others for twenty to forty years. All admitted they were powerless over gambling, that their lives had become unmanageable. Their periods of abstinence from gambling ranged from a few months, to two three and four years. I was told that the new man, like myself, was the most important person in the room, that the survival of G.A. depended upon one primary activity: carrying the message to the men and women still suffering. I was the last person called on to speak. I remember saying, "Thank God at last I have found a home. There is hope."

The meetings helped me to grow stronger each day. The days rapidly went into weeks. I found myself watching the new people who came into the fellowship and hoping that they would find the same good things happening to them that G.A. had brought into my life. At first the hurt and fear would disappear from their eyes, and soon they were smiling and even laughing at the insane things they did as compulsive gamblers.

It took me thirty-seven years to find this peace of mind. I could not find it before because I did not, until coming to G.A., have an honest desire to do something about my gambling problem. After that honest desire, G.A. showed me the way to a new kind of life. It can do the same for all those who are sincerely searching for a way out of the nightmare of compulsive gambling.

From The Story of Howie C.

I realized immediately that the most important thing to do was to let people like myself know that G.A. existed in Las Vegas. So, we put a small ad in the newspaper. Later on we got an answering service, but in the meantime, we used my home phone for G.A. I did articles for the local newspaper, using alias names. They were happy to do the articles. As

G.A. in Las Vegas started to grow I started additional meetings. I realized how tough it was for me to go a whole week without gambling between meetings, so I started a 2nd meeting on a Thursday night to break up the week in the middle. I called every member, every day for the first six months or so. I guess that you could say that I was a sponsor to everyone in the program, but in reality, it was my calling them that saved me.

Monument to My Success

It was finally beginning to pay off. I had worked hard through college, medical school and internship and had finally established a thriving private medical practice in New Jersey. For most of those years I had been too busy to spend much time at recreation, but once success started to come the insidious disease awoke within me.

My gambling started before casino gambling was legalized in New Jersey. It was sparked, in fact, by a barrage of pamphlets and brochures from Las Vegas. I welcomed these invitations as a monument to my success. Soon I was going to Las Vegas frequently, sometimes with my wife and family, sometimes alone, but each time with a sense that I was accepting the rewards that were due me. My gambling started on a small scale, but then it increased to larger amounts. Occasionally I would win but that didn't really matter — it wasn't the money but the compulsion to gamble that kept me going back.

When I couldn't travel to Las Vegas I went to local racetracks. I'd tell my wife I was going to a meeting and I would gamble at the racetracks instead. Then the Atlantic City casinos opened up, making it all the easier to pursue what I enjoyed most — casino gambling.

No one who gambles compulsively comes out a winner. Soon I began to borrow money to cover my debts. Because of my profession and standing in the community, banks welcomed me, and loans and second mortgages were easy to get. Funds for repayment were supposed to come out of my big gambling wins, but of course they never did. This led me to the shylocks, who loved dealing with me because I was easy to find. They could put the finger on me. They lent and I paid, and paid and paid. It goes on forever because you are never able to pay back completely.

Because of my personal and professional circumstances, the thefts I later committed were of the white collar variety.

It was very simple. As a medical practitioner you deal with insurance companies. So from time to time I committed insurance fraud to obtain money. I never thought of the consequences; I thought that no one would bother checking. Well, someone did bother and I was indicted a couple of years ago. I was tried and found guilty of fraud.

The state judge who sentenced me for my crimes introduced me to Gamblers Anonymous. It was one condition of sentencing, along with restitution, community service and also incarceration for four weekends.

There were a number of appeals, which had the effect of delaying my entry into Gamblers Anonymous. I would not, could not admit that I am different than other human beings, that I cannot gamble normally. I think that that fact was especially hard for me to accept because of my considerable professional achievements. So the gambling continued.

The words of Gamblers Anonymous had made an impact on my wife, however, and after a while she took it upon herself to contact the Fellowship. Before I knew it two members, a man and his wife, came to my home. My first impulse was to throw them out. I looked at my wife, though, and figured I would go along with it to make her happy, and not to be discourteous.

Before I knew it I was at a Gamblers Anonymous meeting, that same night. The first thing I found out was that I wasn't different from those other fellows around the room. There may have been blue collar and white collar people there, but we all had the same problem. That night also helped to cure me of a reverse sort of snobbery: I thought that I had committed crimes of the grandest scale, and I wasn't about to associate with petty thieves. Through that meeting I found out I was a piker compared to some of the others — in terms of obtaining money, hurting people, and making life miserable for people around me.

I now realize the extent of the harm I have done. My wife became a dishrag and my children were emotionally distraught. I borrowed from my parents and my in-laws, who trusted me because I was a physician. They didn't think I could be in trouble since I was making so much money. That's an important point — there's no way that I ever made one eighth, one sixteenth, as much money gambling as I could have made as a medical practitioner.

My license to practice, which took me fifteen years to obtain, was revoked by the state of New Jersey, on the grounds of moral terpitude. So my life's work has gone down the drain. If I weren't a member of GA, I wouldn't have been able to deal with this on an adult basis. I accept the things I cannot change. It has been thirteen months since I gambled, and I certainly do not feel the need to gamble. But I know that if I don't attend a Gamblers Anonymous meeting at least once a week for the rest of my life that somewhere along the line a crisis could occur. The disease could rear its ugly head again and cause me to repeat the mistakes that have brought me all this pain.

A Lost Profession

I don't know when I became a compulsive gambler. I know that gambling dominated my life when I was young. It was very important to me. I went through grammar school and high school, and into the service. I always managed to get good marks. I had no history of any problems. I was what I would hope a mother would want as a child at that point in my life. I didn't steal. I didn't know how to steal. I couldn't conceive of it.

I went into the service, and then to college. I graduated with good marks. I played cards mostly at that time, and I went to the racetrack, not excessively. I went to law school and graduated and became an attorney. I started to develop a tremendous law practice, and I also started to develop a tremendous appetite for gambling; basically it was casino gambling. I built up in my law practice a real estate practice, if not the best, one of the finest real estate practices in the State of New Jersey. I had six secretaries for a one-man law office. I closed between five and six hundred houses a year out of the practice alone. I was making decent money. I was making big money. I could never make from gambling what I could make out of the practice of law. You hear dreams sometimes; people dream of cadillacs, new houses and yachts. This I could easily obtain from the practice of law, if that was what I wanted, but I felt the need, or had the compulsion, to gamble. I would get invitations from Las Vegas, go out on junkets and be treated royally. I would get magnificent four-bedroom suites, and in the suites was a game-room, with pool tables, a private swimming pool for just the two of us. It would all be on the house, obviously, and any restaurant that I went to in the city of Las Vegas I would be treated to. Anything I wanted was just about open to me.

I don't know if I was that dumb not to realize what they were doing and why they were giving us this, or if I just didn't care, but I was losing huge sums of money, much more than I could possibly earn and I started to borrow. When you start to borrow and you continue gambling, and you start to lose, you have two obligations instead of one: you owe the person from whom you borrowed as well as having a gambling debt to pay. I confused my mind, because I never thought I had a gambling problem. I was only gambling because I had debts to pay. I didn't have to go to shylocks and I didn't have to go to finance companies. I was important, in my own mind. I could go to banks and request money and receive it, and I would gamble with it.

As I continued to gamble, I found myself not only failing to pay the principal, but I couldn't even pay the interest on the obligations. So, I started to borrow from funds that didn't belong to me. And, I say "borrowed," because it was inconceivable to me that I could steal anything. I had never done it in my life. My parents brought me up in a decent house. How could I steal? It was only borrowing. I was temporarily borrowing money until I got lucky and until I was able to pay these debts.

Then the casinos opened in Atlantic City. Nobody drew me there. As a matter of fact, I made up my mind that I wasn't even going to go there. I could fight it. I didn't have a problem. I could resist it; I resisted it for about six months, then I started to go down with the delusion that I wanted to see what the casinos were all about, but I really knew why I wanted to go. When I went down there I knew a lot of people, because most of the people were from Las Vegas and knew just what to call me, Mr. G. It was the same story.

Again, I don't know if I was fooled, or my ego needed feeding, but I was sucked in by the entire picture. I thought I would be smart. I would not take a credit line at the casinos, so how much could I lose? But if I had a closing and the closing was cash, I would grab all the money and run down to the casino, and I would cash checks on accounts that were not mine. I happened to know people at certain casinos and they would invite me to have dinner on them, and they would invite me to stay over for the weekend. "Why don't you come down and enjoy it, and have a nice vacation on us." I was invited to fights, and I would receive magnificent invitations in the mail, one with balloons popping out of it inviting me there. Nobody dragged me there, I realize that.

My compulsion to gamble was so obsessive that I couldn't resist it. I didn't realize I had a problem. I don't know — and I don't believe there is a bottom to anybody until you are in the grave, but I reached a point where I just couldn't take it physically or mentally. I had lost so much money, and I had owed so much money and I had borrowed so much money; I really thought I had come to an end. I called up an attorney who was a very close friend of mine, and I told my wife for the first time what was happening. She knew I had gambled, but she didn't know the extent of it. She didn't know that we had a second, third, fourth, and fifth mortgage on the house. She didn't know that I had exhausted the bank accounts, because she believed in me and loved me and cared about me, and didn't want to believe anything else. My attorney said that my practice was the type that if I wanted to borrow millions of dollars from people, I could have gathered enough people together to do it. At that point, I started to realize that there was no way of paying this money back. There was nowhere I was going. My life was at an end; and, my attorney told me, "Look, you have to stop what you are doing. You have to stop your law practice. You have to just stop because you are either going to drive yourself out of your mind or kill yourself," and he was right.

At that point, my wife had gone to Florida, and I told her I would drive down. My attorney knew where I was, if he had to call me, and I closed my practice. It was a shock to everybody in the area. I drove down to Florida, but I prayed I wouldn't make it. I couldn't stay there. I stayed there one day, and I had to face people who wanted to know what had happened and what was going on, so I drove right back. I didn't know what had happened to me, and I didn't know what was happening around me. When I got back I found a note on my door, and it was from a member of Gamblers Anonymous who was a close friend of mine. And he said, why don't you call me and let's talk. My wife had come up and we sat down with him until about four o'clock in the morning. He never told me that I was a compulsive gambler. He was just unbelievable. He asked me to go to a meeting with him the next day.

I would have gone anywhere for any kind of help. So I went to a meeting. As I sat in the meeting it dawned on me that maybe I did have a problem. I listened to the stories, relating to some that I heard. Maybe finding out for the first time that I am not the only one in the world that has a problem — as a matter of fact, I had one thing that some didn't have. I had a family that was still together. My wife still loved me, despite everything that happened. My children still cared about me. I went to a meeting the next day and the following day and I think I made four meetings a week. As a matter of fact I still do. It has been almost three years now, and I haven't gambled on anything — not a lottery ticket, not a chance, not a pinball machine, nothing, not a penny.

Believe it or not, my life started to become manageable. I hadn't been in the house for several weeks. I was afraid to go to the house. I wasn't afraid of anyone hurting me, but I was afraid to face people. I went back into the house, and slowly I began to receive help and feel that there was hope. The last three years have been amazing. Before this, for the last five years, every time the phone rang either in the office or out of the office, I would jump. I would pace the floor at night. I can sleep now because I feel I am doing the right thing. I have been able to get a decent job. I am not making the money I did. I don't know if I ever will; but at least what I make I retain. I give it to my family, and, it is a decent salary. I am able to use the faculties I have in a correct manner. I get a chance to speak — I have become very active in the Fellowship. My job allows me to do so because I select my own appointments and time. We have been called in by many parochial and public high schools, because of the problems with seniors. I speak there, and I have spoken before parole boards. I realize that eventually I will face indictment, which is imminent, but I don't feel I am a criminal. I know I will have to pay for a criminal act that I committed, and because of GA I am able to face that; but, that is another part of my life that I will deal with.

I guess I would be remiss in telling you that my whole mind is changed. It has been difficult. The program teaches you to accept the things you cannot change, but don't think it doesn't sometimes hurt. Every time my children go to school, somebody will make a smart remark about their father, and every time my wife works, somebody will point at her. It is not fair to them. They didn't do anything. So, I try to do the best I can, and I just hope some day they can look at their father and say, "He tried. He may not have made it but at least he tried." I am trying through the Program.

My First Three Weeks in Gamblers Anonymous

I'm sitting on the davenport watching the face of my new friend as he speaks, for he has brought Gamblers Anonymous into my home for the first time. His words are about dark paths of disintegration and suffering in the grip of a terrible sickness, for he is a compulsive gambler. I am deeply stirred as my new friend describes in every detail the pattern of my own miserable and hopeless life. I struggle for self-control as the realization dawns that I am not alone, or even unique: others also suffer from this sickness which has caused so much torment and humiliation to my loved ones, to myself and to all others who have come within the range of my compulsive gambling. I had grown to believe that I was a freak and an outcast among my fellow human beings. I had lived without hope under the darkening shadows of approaching disaster.

Again the voice of the man beside me penetrates the confusion in my mind. He is speaking of the founders of the group he represents, and tells of their struggles with the same illness and how it led to the formation of the group, and what the group has done for him. Then he speaks the words I so desperately want to hear, that other men, with the help of Gamblers Anonymous, are living in freedom from gambling. Each has found a new life and is making restitution for his past abuses.

Now he takes his leave and I gratefully promise to be at the meeting on Friday. As I close the door behind him, I whisper a prayer of thanks to my God, for in my heart I feel the stir of something sacred which man cannot long live without. My friend has brought me hope.

Now it is Friday evening and my wife and I are at the entrance of the hotel where we are to meet. Our friend is there to greet us, and then we are at the open door of the meeting-place. We are welcomed with warm, friendly handshakes, and the meeting is underway.

The members, each in his turn, stand and speak of the evils that compulsive gambling has brought into their lives and of the recovery they are making through G.A. The humility and sincerity with which they speak pulls at my heart. A sense of peace pushes through me, and new hope inspires the interest with which I follow each speaker.

My mind reaches out to grasp the ideas that will help to form the pattern of my new life, free from gambling, which I hope to find here. I watch their faces and in some I see the marks of long-suffering; in others the way they stand, the sound of their voices, the look in their eyes, speak to me of the things unsaid. I am with men of my own kind, with understanding for each. I am grateful for their presence and their friendship, and I am no longer lonely. Often my thoughts turn to my friend and each time I am more grateful.

Reluctantly I see the meeting coming to a close. If only I may keep this new feeling that is moving inside me, I can build a new life. If only I can build a wall that will stand between me and this gambling sickness while my new pattern of life takes shape and grows strong, then I may stand among men in the outside world with equal dignity and usefulness. I scan the faces about me, searching for the answer, and my wall begins to take shape. It is not built of bricks, but of human beings, and as each takes his key place in my wall he is put there by his own achievement of living a normal, useful life free from compulsive gambling. I have lived so long in the grip of this awful sickness that I have ceased to believe in the wisdom of words and of advice given me through the years, for I have been unable to follow them. Now, the things that I see before me in these men are helping me to believe again, and I feel at last that I, too, with their help, can do what they are doing. This is the source of my new hope.

The meeting is over and we are driving home. There is peace and a deeper understanding between my wife and me. Again and again I think of my friend, for he stands in the very center of my wall, and I am grateful.

Day follows day, and as temptation flashes into my mind I retreat behind my wall and find strength.

It is Friday again and we are at the meeting. They greet us with the same warmth as before. I search the room with my eyes for my friend and then I see him conducting the meeting and I am glad. Again we sit and listen and I feel my new pattern growing stronger. I begin to realize how important each member is to me, and to each other. As men standing alone, we have been lacking in something vital — there has been an unfilled gap in each of us which has made us prey to compulsive gambling. It is in standing in a group that we can share our strong points, and make each of us whole. As the men talk, I hold myself open and feel the missing bits fall into place within, bringing greater peace and strength. I am grateful for all my new friends.

.If my friend could but read my thoughts tonight, he would know that if through Gamblers Anonymous I can heal the wounds in my soul, and right the wrongs to my loved ones and others, he will have done me a great and unforgetable service.

"An Open Letter to My Son"

I am about to unfold to you the imperfections, and weaknesses of me, YOUR DAD!

About fifteen years ago I was (and still am) a very happily married man — the father of two little boys. But the finger of FATE changed this man into a groveling figure of a half-man.

It was the summer of 1952 that this phase of my life began. I *always* had money in my pocket, from $30.00 to $50.00. At this time I was working for the *Chicago Sun-Times*. On this particular day we had a long "lay-in" (free time), and I was casually reading the morning paper. At the back of the paper is the "Turf Comments" section and I got to reading about the horses, so I circled two names. The comments on these were: "Could take all marbles" and another "Very sharp, watch out." I took $2.00 out of my wallet and asked another man (who I knew played the horses) to play these two horses for me. He asked "How do you want to play them?" I retorted, "I don't know? — whichever way I'll get the most money." So he played a $1.00 win and a $1.00 place parlay. The outcome was one horse won and one ran second. So I collected $28.60 and I thought, "Boy! This is a cinch!" So, needless to say, I was on my way to self-destruction.

I can't begin to express how much I hurt my wife, my children and, of course, myself. I became a worried, frustrated animal. I took on *all* the attributes of a compulsive gambler. I had to get four or five personal loans from loan companies. I lied, cheated, and stole. I reached the stage where I couldn't sleep, or eat, or even think straight. I stole money from an inheritance (about $7,000.00) I was betting $200.00 a day trying to get even. Nothing I did turned out right. I just went deeper and deeper into this bottomless pit.

When I started getting phone calls from "The Boys" I decided that maybe if I left home that would solve everything. It didn't work because my problems went with me, it solved nothing — just more headaches for my wife. So when I ran out of money and had no place to turn, I called my wife — and she sent me money to come home.

I made a clean breast of everything and promised I would never gamble again. BUT I failed to tell about one debt of $40.00. I figured I could pay that up without any trouble. I was only kidding myself. After six months I was back in "action" again (trying to pay back that lousy $40.00). So I lost another $5,000.00 before it had to come out. I would venture to say that in this 15-year period I have lost over $35,000.00. I will never get a dime of it back!

With the help of our minister I started going to "G.A." and that helped put me on the right track. I cannot stop going to G.A. because that helps me avoid those "urges." In my line of work we have gambling every night. There are "bookies" on all three shifts, so you see, I don't have to look for trouble — it is at my elbow every night. The only way for me to gain strength is to try to help others. I have to keep going to G.A. meetings, because I know that I'll be a compulsive gambler till the day I die.

Believe me, the cross that I bear is not easy, when I am engulfed on all sides by this evil.

With the help and understanding of my dear wife, and the courage and serenity from God, I will try so very hard to be the man my loved ones want me to be. With God and my family on my team (and, of course, G.A.) how can I lose?

Son, don't think too badly of me. I am a mere mortal man, who loves his wife and children very much. I am sorry for the past, but we can't bring it back. So bear with me. Give me your prayers and understanding. With this help I can face tomorrow.

Love,
Your Dad

Relapse

My first ten years of marriage were very good. My husband went to the track occasionally, but his gambling didn't seem to be a problem. Looking back, I can see that it built up slowly, then accelerated about fifteen years ago when he changed jobs. I noticed a big change in him almost right away. He was hardly home any more and when he was, things just went right over his head when I talked to him.

I didn't know what was happening at first. Then, as his gambling increased, it became apparent to me that his gambling was out of control. I found myself bailing him out a lot and making excuses to myself for doing it. He gave me money every week but I never saw a pay stub and I had no idea of what our financial condition was really like.

After about three or four years of his gambling I began to get very nervous and began to blame myself. I thought, this man was fine when we got married, why is he like this today? We were fighting a lot and it upset the whole household. My children were upset — every time we fought my son would go upstairs and throw up from nervousness. I kept thinking it was my fault but I could never figure out just what it was that I had done or what could have caused this.

Finally I demanded that my husband hand over his pay stub to me, which he did. He was working 70 to 80 hours a week and he made good money. He told me he needed an allowance of $90 a week and now I know that was his downfall. He kept borrowing money from other people, thinking he would pay them back with the next week's allowance but he just kept getting deeper and deeper into debt as he kept losing.

I also was working in a store all this time to supplement his income.

As my children grew older I found out my husband was borrowing money from them! He would borrow the money my sixteen-year-old made from baby sitting! People would also come to me and ask me for the money that my husband had borrowed from them years ago. My children were also antagonistic toward me. I never told them what was going on because I didn't want them to know about their father's gambling, and because they didn't know they hated me for nagging him and arguing with him all the time.

Eventually my husband began drinking. He went to the track evenings and as the gambling got worse, so did the drinking. He'd come home half bombed. In the beginning I'd go to the track once a week with him because it was a night out for me, but when the drinking started I couldn't handle it. I stopped going and I came to hate being with him. I would go out by myself and I found that I loved it. I just couldn't stand being with him any more. As a result, we completely separated. We just lived our own lives although we were living under the same roof. Even so, there were still scenes. He would beg me for money and he would swear that he would stop gambling and stop drinking. It was always the same and yet I never realized he was sick.

The straw that broke the camel's back came when I found out that he conned my daughter and her boyfriend out of $500 the boy needed to make a car payment. I just went crazy over that. I had found out about Gamblers Anonymous about a year before this but my husband always put it down and said he didn't need it. But by this time I knew he needed it and help for his drinking problem as well. It got so that I dreaded to hear his car in the driveway — I just didn't know what kind of shape he'd be in. I just wished he wouldn't come home sometimes. By this time his mind was gone and so was mine. We were both at the end of our ropes. We decided to give Gamblers Anonymous a try.

I was reluctant to come to Gam-Anon at first. I thought coming to the program was a big embarrassment. My husband believed he could never live his life without gambling. Neither of us were really convinced about the Gamblers Anonymous Program but we were desperate. I took to the Gam-Anon Program right away and I learned an awful lot about compulsive gambling. My husband even seemed to take to the Gamblers Anonymous Program, but during the first year we were in he was still drinking so it was still rough for me, although I was learning how to handle it now. After about six months he had to stop drinking because of his health and everything seemed to be working fine. Then about eighteen months after we joined the program I got an anonymous letter that told me my husband was gambling, that he had been for some time and that everyone knew it but me. I was devastated. I hit my real bottom then. I called some Gamblers Anonymous men and they told me to bring it up to him when he got home that night. If it hadn't been for them I think I would have gone out of my mind that day. I took the advice of Gamblers Anonymous members and confronted him honestly. He went into a rage and said he was leaving. I thought to myself: "Thank God, good riddance." But the next day when things had calmed down I suggested we have some Gamblers Anonymous people come over and discuss this. The next day three couples came over and that did it. After four or five hours of talking he really started a whole new life. That was six months ago. Now I have the relationship I had with my husband when we first knew each other. It's such a change after all those years of hurt and pain.

A lot of things have changed me. I found a great faith in God and it has given me patience and happiness. I know what my mind can accomplish today by just finding serenity, which I never had before. I still have a lot to work on but it's amazing how much you can do when you find this program.

Alice H.
San Diego, Calif.

174

Black Is White, Day Is Night

I am married to a compulsive gambler who at this point in time has arrested his illness. But, what I would like to talk about today is what it was like when he was actively gambling. When you marry a compulsive gambler, you usually don't know it. I didn't know. I knew he liked to gamble. I knew that gambling was a pastime to him, and I really didn't see any harm in that. I also realize now that his attitude towards money was very casual and I think I was attracted to that. We had some of our early dates at the racetrack, and I had fun. I thought it was an exciting way to spend a Saturday evening.

Compulsive gambling is a progressive illness, and some of the telltale signs start popping up — financial pressures, preoccupation with sporting events. They happen slowly and gradually and you don't always realize that they are happening in your life until you look back at them. But, that is what happened in my life.

At first, there was a loan that had to be paid, and I received a promise that he would never gamble again, that he realized he had gotten in over his head, and this was the lesson he needed. So, if I were to work with him, and help him pay back this loan, we would start clean, and I did help him, and I hoped that we were going to start clean. It seemed to me that every time we got close to paying off that next loan another loan appeared, and another and another, and there was a series of financial setbacks over a period of years that destroyed us financially. There were bills that went unpaid, children that didn't have shoes, furniture that ripped and could not be replaced. There were some months not knowing whether the rent would get paid or not. That was a gradual deterioration. It didn't start like that, but that is how it ended.

I stopped working after my first child was born, and wanted to devote myself to being a mother. I felt that I had looked forward to that since I was a young child. I grew up like most little girls in my era did, thinking that you live happily ever after, and you have a couple of kids and a home with a little white picket fence and that was really all I ever wanted.

What started to happen in my marriage was that I was losing my husband and I couldn't really understand why. Aside from the financial setbacks, there seemed to be a distance between us. There were fights for no reason, it seemed to me. I later realized that the arguments were so that he could leave the house. They were excuses for him. They didn't really have a basis. It was just so he could make a phone call, go to the track, or do whatever he was doing in his gambling. My husband used to gamble on anything that was available, anything.

I often wondered what it was that I could do to change the situation, and as the years went on, I began to question my abilities as a wife. I felt very inadequate. I felt that if I were loving enough or caring enough then my husband wouldn't need any outlet such as gambling, and I never realized how much he was gambling. I just knew that he was gambling. I knew that when I woke up at three o'clock in the morning and found him listening to the radio that what he was listening to was the sporting station, finding out the results of some sporting event he had bet on. I knew that when I would see him watching television and listening to the radio at the same time, that I was not very important to him at that time. I knew that he shushed the children away and threw them out of the room and told them to keep quiet or shut-up or threw something at them, which was not like him during other times — this was while he was listening to racing results.

I knew that we couldn't go out during certain hours, because he would have to be home to watch whatever he had to watch. I knew I would find newspapers all over the house, and I was not allowed to touch them, because he had to plan his next day's gambling. Everything got worse — financially, physically, emotionally. When I say physically, I suffered physical symptoms. I began to have pains in my chest. I began to see doctors about it. I was put on tranquilizers at one point. I started to isolate myself from the world. I withdrew. I thought that somehow or other I had to find a way to stop this person from gambling, to stop the destruction that was going on in my family and because I held myself responsible for it, I dare not talk to anybody else about it, and I never did. I stayed within the walls of my apartment. I occasionally looked out the window, but there came a point in my life when I stopped going out. I stayed home. I didn't answer the phone for fear that it was a bill collector. I didn't open the mail for fear that it was an unpaid bill, and I didn't answer the door. I knew what time my children would get home from school and that is when I started to function, as best I could, at that time.

So, when you ask for the effects, and you want to know dollars and cents, I can't give them to you, but I can tell you that there are women who are emotionally distraught, husbands who are emotionally distraught, because someone in their family is gambling. I can tell you that there are children who go neglected, financially neglected, which is bad enough, and it is almost a product of our times. My children went emotionally neglected as well. I couldn't be bothered. I couldn't play with them. I couldn't listen to them. I couldn't pay attention to their needs. I was too overwhelmed with the gambling problem in my family. So, they were affected in some unknown way that can't be measured in dollars and cents and can't be measured over a course of years. I don't know when the effects of that are going to come out in my children. One of my children is a drug addict. I don't know if that happened because I neglected her when she was a little girl, but it is very possible that happened because I neglected her because her father was gambling, because she didn't have the needs nurtured that a child needs. I don't know if there are going to be effects on my other children and the thousands of children that I know of in the program as it is today.

At one time, I was a Gam-A-Teen sponsor, and I met many, many children who lived with the compulsive gambling problem, and most of them had the same thing in common, and that was they did not know what was going on in their family. They just knew it was being destroyed. They knew that two people who should love each other and care about each other were fighting constantly. They knew that they couldn't dare ask for a pair of new sneakers for the track meet next week, because there was no money for it. Those are the effects of compulsive gambling. People go on welfare, wives go to work to pay the bills, not because they want to get out of the house, but because they have to pay the bills. Some women use alcohol. I used tranquilizers for a long period of time. It was the only way I could cope, and I wasn't doing a very good job even with that.

You don't know what is happening around you. I saw a television program once that hinted at Gamblers Anonymous, and I remember waking my husband up and telling him about it, and him telling me that he was different than they were, because he could stop any time he wanted to, and I wanted to believe that, and I did try to believe that for many, many years. A compulsive gambler is able to convince you that black is white and day is night. I would like to think of myself as a fairly intelligent person — not brilliant but certainly I could pass as intelligent. And yet, this man was able to convince me that a car that I knew was parked on one street was parked on another street — and something I knew I had told him he could convince me that I had never said it. If the bank sent a letter to the house saying that we were past due on something, he could convince me that the bank president was making a mistake. That is the nature of the compulsive gambling illness. And, there is usually somebody in his or her life that buys into that, and I was the person who bought into that.

There is a fantasy world built by the compulsive gambler, and the people in his family, and the people who are closest to him buy into the fantasy, "One more hit, and I am never going to gamble again; one more hit and you are going to get a car; one more hit and we are going to buy a house; just let me win this one time, and we are going to have everything." And, I believed that when he told me those things, that is what he meant. At that time, for that minute, that is what he meant. But, his compulsion to gamble overwhelmed him the next minute and I became less important and the children became less important.

I am one of the fortunate ones. I found Gam-Anon because my husband found GA. In most cases that I know of, in my experience in Gam-Anon, it is the spouse that reaches out for help first. Maybe that is who we need to reach first. The person who is living with the compulsive gambler is usually much more aware of the illness than the compulsive gambler himself. I was not one of those who reached out first. I was so caught up in my own depression and in my own anxiety that I didn't bother to reach out for help. I didn't think there was help. I felt alone; I

177

felt isolated, and I felt desperate, but I didn't know who to go to. As I said, I was one of the fortunate ones, my husband reached out for help first, and I went along with him. There I found out there were other people just like me. Prior to that, I really didn't know that anybody else lived with this problem, and I think that is the thing that we need to pay attention to, getting people to know that other people live with this problem, that there is help, that people can understand it and can help it.

I live my life now to the fullest, and I believe that I had the potential to be who I am today many years ago, but I was so devastated by this problem that I couldn't pay attention to my own potential.

Jim's Story

My name is Jim S. I have been a compulsive gambler for twenty years, though it is only since 1981 that I have been honest enough with myself and others to acknowledge and accept the reality of this.

I started gambling at age twelve, when I went to work at the racetrack outside of Seattle selling newspapers. Of course, I was not of legal age to bet, but that is no problem at the tracks because almost anyone would place a bet for me.

The next year I got a job on the backside (barn area) walking hots in the morning, and after the races in the afternoon. I decided that because of my size my future would be as a jockey, so I continued to work at the track. In 1960 I started riding at the small tracks in Washington during the summer. By 1962 I was old enough to ride at the major tracks. All this time I was convinced that I would become the most informed gambler that there ever was. After all, who should know more about the horses than the jockey?

I started off with much success as an apprentice jockey. I rode a lot of winners and gambled on almost every race. Whether I rode or not, I had to have a bet down. At the end of the year I had ridden over a hundred winners and had nothing in the bank and owed a good amount of money. I didn't let it bother me, though, because I knew that all I had to do was slow down on the gambling, and soon everything was going to be the way I had dreamed.

In 1964, I was ready for the "big win" that everyone hoped for. I was riding for the man that I had started out with and we were bringing our "big horse" back to the races after a year lay-off, which had been caused by a leg injury the year before. Thanks to the track clocker we were able to get some fast workouts with him in the a.m. without anyone else knowing. I had saved enough money to buy the house trailer that I had wanted and decided that by betting all this money on the "big horse" I would be able to get even a better house trailer than I had planned, and perhaps even a new car. As it turned out I bet all I had and was in front into the stretch and he broke both front legs. So there I was broken up, and broke. I had

178

to take time off healing a broken shoulder but I continued to go to the track every day, trying to get back the money that I had lost, once again borrowing and getting deeper in debt.

By the late sixties, I had started to have a weight problem and was having a lot of trouble trying to reduce, so like most jockeys with weight problems, I found the world of pills. By 1969, I was a hop head at the end of my riding career. When I quit riding I was flat broke.

I was offered a job selling the racing form at the track and was making $100.00 or more a day. When I quit that job 10 years later, I was again broke and in debt. I decided that the only way I was going to stop gambling was to leave the racetrack. I got a job right away as a waiter in San Francisco, was there about two years but still bet all my money. Went back to the racetrack and started working as a parimutuel clerk, believing once again that I would not gamble. For a year and a half I didn't bring home one pay check. I got tired of lying, stealing, bad checks, etc...and decided that the only way that I was going to quit gambling was to end my life. I had, in fact, tried to kill myself a few years earlier. I sat at home that night with a bottle of Gin and a gun, thinking that if I got drunk enough it would be easier to end it all. I sat there and cried until I couldn't cry anymore. Thinking that there must be some place to get help, knowing that there are programs for alcoholics, drug addicts, etc...I looked in the phone book and there it was under the G's (just like in bingo) Gamblers Anonymous. I made a call right away and the next night was taken to my first meeting in Pleasant Hill, California. I sat through the first meeting, read the "Combo Book", and listened to the others in the room, tell of their gambling experience.

I left that meeting and cried all the way home, crying not because I had just lost another paycheck at the track, but because for the first time in my life I realized what was going on. I was in the grip of an illness called "compulsive gambling" and for the time I was able to talk to someone that understood and had gone through some of the same experiences that I had been putting myself through all my life.

I think that when I walked out of my first G.A. meeting, I realized that what had been said was true: "I was in the grip of a progressive illness." This fact hit me so hard that I don't think I did anything for the next few days but read the whole Gamblers Anonymous Book and try to understand what was happening. I remember reading and hurting because everything I read had certainly been written about me.

I had gambled for 26 years and knew that I had enough and wanted to stop. I didn't know if what was said to me was true or not, but I remember thinking "what have I got to lose." I was told that if I did what the Combo Book said, I had a chance to recover from this illness. I was told to try to get to as many meetings as possible. I listened a lot, and talked a little and it did feel good right from the start to be able to talk about the things I had done. Most of the time I couldn't believe I was actually telling these people some of the awful things I had done. The bad dreams started to come after only a few days without making a bet. Going to work at the track each day was pure hell. Sometimes I would just start shaking and break out in a sweat. I was told that there would be a financial and psychological withdrawal from gambling. The psychological withdrawals were the worst, sometimes I was sure that it would be just as well if I had picked up the gun that I was going to use the night I made my first phone call to Gamblers Anonymous, and just put an end to all this. I cried a lot and that helped some, it seemed to ease the pain a little. A little guilt can create quite a lot of mental pain. The first few months I went through a lot of changes trying to deal with all this. By "all this" I mean I was going to lots of meetings trying to get all the strength I could from the G.A. rooms.

I heard a lot of talk from others, about how attending meetings was good for them because it gave them strength. What I didn't realize for a long time is that that is what I had been doing right from the start! The strength I get from others at the meetings is incredible. Now I know for sure that without the meetings and the unity in the fellowship, I would be gambling or dead!

Another thing that was a little hard to deal with was that in all the meetings I had gone to I hadn't met any other gays and I hadn't talked to anyone in the Program about my being gay, and having a lover of 12 years. I decided, after about two months into the program that I had to talk about my relationship and about the same sort of material problems that all couples go through, straight or gay. It was only because of my insecurity that I didn't bring it up from the start, but nonetheless it was still hard to talk to a room full of straight men. Bringing it out into the open has greatly helped my recovery from gambling. I have become so close to everyone in the program, without them all, I couldn't make it. My lover, Max, has attended a few meetings, and we now can talk about some of the things that I did when I was gambling, and also some of the things that I am going through now. I am trying to make amends to some of the people I harmed when gambling.

I was told to get involved in the program, which I have done. I go to all the G.A. functions that we put on, discussion meetings, and step meetings that I can. At least three G.A. meetings a week is a *must* for my recovery. Most of the time I go to more than three meetings. I also am secretary of the San Francisco meeting, Intergroup Rep., and Public Relations Chairman for Northern California. Getting involved is really a must, however one must be careful not to let this interfere with one's recovery. Being Public Relations Chairman can sometimes be very hectic. Since I started at this particular position it has put me through a lot of changes. Some of these pressures come from dealing with T.V. or radio stations, trying to get shows together concerning compulsive gambling. Since I have taken this position things have been going well as far as spreading a message of the Gamblers Anonymous Program.

Some of the pressures that have come from this work are within the Program. In the first few months we sent speakers to 20 different schools or colleges, two radio shows and three T.V. talk shows. When I started to get static from other members who had not yet been on one of these shows, it really got to me. I got to the point that I almost went back to gambling. Without other members in the Program to talk with I am not sure if the matter would be clear today. I have done none of this to build up my ego, but rather to help, or should I say, pass on a bit of kindness to a program that has helped save my life. Just a few weeks ago I called another member at midnight and he told me to come over and talk. I had been crying a lot thinking about all this. But after staying up till 3:00 a.m. I felt much better. Just another reminder of the type of fellowship in this program. As it turned out when I got to his home that evening there was another member there upset because of a spat with his wife. The member I went to talk to was going through changes because he had just decided to buy a house for himself and his family. It was quite a night. But none of us gambled the next day or since! The withdrawals at work are not as bad as they were in the beginning. At first I didn't tell anyone at the track that I was going to G.A. But once I did, it turned out to be the best thing that I could have done. I got so much support from the people at work. Being a Parimutuel clerk, selling and cashing tickets all day can make your mind wander. To keep the temptation away I don't ever look at the sporting pages or read the program. The hardest thing to give up was the racing form. I was a horse owner for most of my life on the racetrack, and I have also given this up. I sold my last horse last year. I found that I must give up a lot to keep the temptations away. I miss owning horses but that and the other things I have given up are a small price to pay in order for me not to go back to gambling. Not gambling and Gamblers Anonymous are the most important things in my life.

Jim S.,
San Francisco

Eulogy To A Friend

I have found starting this tribute to our dear friend extremely difficult. To put into words all my personal recollections of this beautiful human being would take a lifetime.

Love and respect from others must be earned; they do not come as a matter of course. In this respect he had no peers. Our friend has helped literally hundreds of GA people, whether making that "first call" to the new man still suffering or to the older man in the program needing his very special kind of strength.

During the therapy portion of a GA meeting, so many men associate their very first exposure to the program with their friend. To understand why he gave of himself so completely, I believe you first must understand him. He had a tremendous zest for life and thoroughly enjoyed every minute of it. He often stated that the years in GA were his and his wife's happiest — and he shared it with all of us. His desire was for each man in GA to be as happy and serene as he. I stated earlier he "shared" with others — after reflection, I see fit to make a correction. He didn't share —he "gave it all."

Not only would this beautiful person be the initial contact with the man entering Gamblers Anonymous, but he would invariably follow up with a personal visit or get others involved in helping the new man. He would, on numerous occasions, intercede on behalf of a new man, in dealing with a multitude of problems. He had talked to judges, bank officials, parole officers and others to explain the illness of compulsive gambling. The measure of his success can only be determined by the results. So many of us owe a tremendous debt to this great man. He has given us the strength and guidance necessary to return to a normal life. Our friend has personally caused the spiritual rebirth of hundreds.

In addition, he involved himself in every facet of the Fellowship. He was — as he put it — ready, willing and able to accept any responsibility — from trusted servant positions on the national, state and local levels — to cleaning ashtrays at the end of the meeting. He was the best example of total involvement.

This man was truly all things to all of us in GA. A person of untiring strength and conviction, he devoted his entire life to "helping another human being who is still suffering." To me, personally, he was a true and devoted friend in every sense of the word. I valued our friendship immeasurably, and I have no words to express my own personal sense of loss.

Our friend is gone but most certainly has gained immortality in the hearts and souls of those who loved him so very deeply... he was, truly, a "Man for all Seasons."

Epilogue

What causes a person to gamble compulsively? Is it some perverse complex of psycho-social factors, faulty genetic coding, or is each individual's case unique? We don't know and, except for a general interest in all matters relating to compulsive gambling, we cannot afford to care. Those who come to us need help immediately. There is no time for the intellectual luxury, fascinating though the investigation may be, to explore each compulsive gambler's history and to interpret the results. There is no place in our Fellowship's program for debate on the merits of differing theories of recovery, or on the conflicts between varying schools of psychological thought. Even after their initial crises have passed and their illness has been arrested, will our members know that it is only by helping others abstain from gambling and recover that they themselves will continue to grow. The benefits of introspection and speculation are paltry when compared to the rewards of helping others regain their lives.

How can Gamblers Anonymous help compulsive gamblers recover from their disorder when its causes are not fully understood? The Fellowship's program relies not only on the benefits of understanding, but on the power of faith. Belief in the effectiveness of Gamblers Anonymous is based on the solid evidence that thousands of compulsive gamblers have recovered by following the Fellowship's program. No other course of therapy has been successful without including regular attendance at Gamblers Anonymous meetings. Members are inspired to transcend their own inadequacies by faith in the Fellowship's ideals and are supported in their striving by the conviction that, should they falter, other members will be there to help. In short, Gamblers Anonymous is sustained by the faith of its members, and it is through this faith that the members themselves are transformed.

Unlike conventional psychotherapy, which focuses on the evolution and health of the individual under treatment, in Gamblers Anonymous it is the Fellowship and its groups that are the objects of analysis and debate. Members are imbued with a sense of the greater good of the group and therefore have the responsibility of collectively deciding which courses of action are best suited to aid compulsive gamblers to recover. Thus while the Fellowship is united in its purpose of helping compulsive gamblers to recover, it is also vibrant with a diversity of opinions on how best to continue this work. Each member is therefore also an advisor to his group, in that all lend energy and insight to the recovery of others. Rather than through the absorptive introspection encouraged by most traditional therapeutic approaches, it is through active contribution that each Gamblers Anonymous member pursues the realization of his or her own unique psychological and emotional potential.

As is the case with any other group of individuals who share a common problem or belief, compulsive gamblers offer each other a totality of support that cannot be found anywhere else. This support takes two basic forms: empathy and skepticism. Only those who themselves have endured the mania and degradation that the compulsive gambling disorder inflicts can truly feel the depths of this pain in others. And to know that another has suffered as bitterly and still has regained health is an unparalleled impetus to recover. With profound empathy, however, comes a healthy skepticism that is equally as profound. Many compulsive gamblers have perfected the "art" of deception to a point where their lies are detectable only by other compulsive gamblers, i.e. by others who have been similarly deceitful. Members force each other to remain honest, not just by invoking ethical imperatives but by the skill of their insight and wit.

Any organization that operates on faith is likely to be puzzling to those who do not share or are not familiar with its beliefs. It is the hope of Gamblers Anonymous that this book has shed enough light on the aims and procedures of the Fellowship for those outside of it to understand that it is the best, and only place for compulsive gamblers to turn for recovery.

Appendix I

JIM W. AND THE FOUNDING OF GAMBLERS ANONYMOUS

His Early Years of Gambling

Jim W., the man who founded Gamblers Anonymous, was born in Southern California in 1912. When he was six years old, Jim recalls, he heard the familiar fable about there being a pot of gold at the end of a rainbow. The boy waited and searched for months, and when he finally saw a rainbow he chased it for hours. Instead of a pot of gold, young Jim got soaked in the rain, caught pneumonia and almost died.

But the lesson didn't take; rather it was just the first step in his 40-year quest for "the big score."

When Jim was ten the death of his father plunged the boy into what was to become decades of self-destructive gambling behavior. Having learned the rudiments of card-playing from their father, Jim and his brothers Richard and Bill played furiously to relieve the pain of his absence. But rather than diminishing their grief, Jim recalls that both stakes and tempers mounted as time passed.

Forced by the loss of the family breadwinner to earn money at a very young age, Jim tried gambling to supplement his income. By the time he graduated high school Jim had become an adept poker player, prizing this proficiency as his single greatest skill. It was the era of the Great Depression and the job market was, of course, bleak, so Jim turned to poker for his livelihood. His early manhood years were what Dr. Robert Custer refers to as "the winning phase," and Jim repeatedly demonstrated his prowess for gambling with men who had to work, and therefore money to lose.

Although Jim eventually obtained steady employment, gambling still

185

dominated his life. He used wages to finance higher-staked poker games and for his new gambling passion — horse racing at Santa Anita. So consuming, did his new obsession become, that jobs were taken only to build up betting stakes, and left behind when the gambling went well. Unlike poker, however, Jim's betting systems for horses failed, miserably. The debts mounted more quickly than his horses ran.

At thirty years of age Jim W. entered military service, and was thereby introduced to a vast new arena of gambling action. During his years of service, Jim's compulsion worsened dramatically — to the point where he began to doubt his own sanity. He who had once been a skillful and methodical poker player had abandoned himself to reckless play. The agonies of losing were becoming intolerable, relieved only by the vain hopes of even heavier wagering.

After World War II, Jim returned "home" to Santa Anita, and resumed his life of losing at the racetrack. Jim soon blamed his losses not on himself or his illness, but on the frivolous atmosphere at the track — unsuited to a "professional" gambler like himself. Eventually he moved to Reno, Nevada, a place where Jim was convinced he could gamble on the horses more rationally, and with greater control. Betting was now "investing" in Jim's mythology, and he analyzed all appropriate data before placing his wagers. A brief period of prosperity resulted from this approach.

The discipline of analysis proved too great for Jim and was replaced by betting hunches based on the horses' name, color, etc. His interest in horse betting had begun to wane, outshone by the glitter of Reno's casinos. It was as though Jim's systems for blackjack and roulette had been secretly designed by the casino owners themselves, however, for Jim was soon shucked clean. The old patterns of taking menial jobs to finance betting kept him going for a few months, but it wasn't long before Jim "hitched" home to Los Angeles, broke and alone.

Jim got a well-paying job in home construction soon after he returned to California, but gambling still bankrupted him weekly. The glaring incongruity of high income, on the one hand, and deep debts, on the other, forced Jim to consider stopping gambling. He soon evinced a strong desire to quit, and he actually abstained for a while. A pocket full of cash outweighed his will, however, and soon he was back to Santa Anita, and debt.

Alcoholism and Alcoholics Anonymous

Demoralized by his losses and his failure to quit, Jim W. began to drink heavily. He drank to celebrate a win and to forget a loss. And to pass the time in between bets. Fortunately, Jim had the good sense to recognize that his drinking was a problem, and in 1946 he joined Alcoholics Anonymous. By following that fellowship's program, his drinking was brought under control. Membership in Alcoholics Anonymous brought an added bonus, for it was there that he met Sybil, the woman who became his wife in 1951.

The Algamus Society

Although his alcoholism had become manageable, Jim's gambling was completely out of control. Moving to Reno with his wife, Jim W. now plummeted two lives into destitution. Yet within the embattled marriage came the beginnings of an idea that would eventually save the lives of thousands of compulsive gamblers around the world.

Quite simply, Jim began to apply some of the principles of Alcoholics Anonymous to his gambling problem. Sybil saw that her husband was making some progress, and suggested that he contact others with gambling problems. Jim took the advice to heart and began talking to anyone who would listen about his gambling problem and his desire to stop. Rebuffs, ignorance and cavalier responses discouraged Jim, but not before he met Johnny W., a fellow AA member and a compulsive gambler.

At the time they met Jim hadn't gambled for five months, Johnny had long wanted to stop gambling, so the two decided to stick together to support each others' resolve. Together with two others, the four alcoholics/compulsive gamblers met to discuss their mutual problems and needs. The name, "The Algamus Society," was coined, and the spirit of camaraderie prevailed. Despite the auspicious start, however, the Algamus Society fell apart after one more meeting. As Jim W. recalls, a major reason for the failure was that the second meeting's conversation strayed away from therapeutic discussions of gambling to shop talk and other matters of lighter import.

Discouragement and Hope

However worthy the attempt to quit, failure always seemed to plunge Jim into even worse periods of gambling than before. As Jim remembers, he "hit bottom" after the collapse of the Algamus Society. Earnest hopes to quit, once dashed, were perverted into equally fervid dreams of winning big. Driving to the Boulder Club in Las Vegas, Jim spun fantasies of wealth and generosity, grandeur and esteem. Of course, he lost badly. But from that loss came a triumph of sorts — Jim W. had $25 left after his drubbing at the crap game and he did not blow it. The self-discipline required to walk out of the casino with that pittance still in hand took every ounce of concentration he had, but he did it. Jim had come to realize that gambling hurt, and that he no longer wanted to be a slave to its pain.

Jim returned home after that night in Las Vegas determined to control his gambling, but at a loss for a way to do so. All of the three other members of the Algamus Society had resigned, each denying any problem with alcohol, gambling or both. Such discouragement could have once again plunged Jim into the compulsive gambling void but instead Jim took heart. There was hope, Jim felt, because a group had met to help compulsive gamblers, even if only for two weeks. Perhaps this meant that a more permanent program could some day be established.

A Second Attempt

Jim's faith in the possibility of recovery from gambling was sorely tested in the months after the Algamus Society collapsed. In his solitude Jim's thoughts strayed frequently to gambling. Fortunately, his wife Sybil was able to help him out. She worked for the Alcoholics Anonymous Central Office, where she occasionally received calls from those with problems other than drinking. Whenever a gambler called, she referred that person to her husband. In November, 1955, Jim arranged to meet with Art M., also a compulsive gambler, to discuss their mutual problem. Also invited to the meeting at Jim's apartment were some friends who were trying to control their gambling, including the former members of the Algamus Society. Art M., who had agreed to attend only on the promise of a $20 loan, never was seen again. Nonetheless, the meetings at Jim's apartment continued sporadically for several months. Eventually attendance dwindled away to the point where Jim was alone once again. Reflecting on the failure of this second attempt to establish an ongoing group meeting, he concluded that the apartment setting was too informal; there was no commitment from the group to support the meeting place. Also, as Jim now acknowledges, the $20 loan/bribe was a poor way to launch a program for recovery. The gloom that surrounded him also darkened what should have been a joyous occasion — the one-year anniversary of Jim's abstinence from gambling.

In early 1956 Stan R., a local newspaper reporter and an addict of horse betting, contacted Jim, referred by the AA central office. Jim could offer no group meeting, but suggested that the two of them meet and talk regularly. Stan R. took Jim's advice, and eventually stopped gambling.

A second referral by AA proved even more helpful to the future development of Gamblers Anonymous. Fred Shields, a prominent radio announcer, asked Jim, along with his wife Sybil and Stan R., to appear on his talk show to discuss their efforts to control the gambling problem. All eagerly agreed.

Fred Shields introduced the three as representatives of "Gamblers Anonymous." Thus the name was coined and the Fellowship, as such, was conceived. The show seemed to be a great success as each told his or her story, but Fred's suggestion that interested listeners call in appeared to have fallen on deaf ears. Hours passed and no one called. By the end of the night just one man had telephoned, asking Jim for advice on how to win at the track.

All, including Fred Shields, were dismayed, but Stan R. was crushed. His hopes had soared even higher than Jim's or Sybil's upon learning of the opportunity to be on the Fred Shields' show; now he was plunged into the abyss. Stan R. went back to gambling and fell away from the Fellowship. Gamblers Anonymous, such as it existed, had only one member.

In late 1956, Jim received a call from Sam F., an insurance salesman, who was also referred by the AA central office. They arranged to meet at Jim's apartment that same night. In Sam, Jim found two character traits that he valued highly: a willingness to admit that a problem existed, and a sense of humor. The two became instant friends, and because of their mutual support, neither gambled. This was the true beginning of Gamblers Anonymous.

The Paul Coates Interviews

Some six months after their meeting, Sam and Jim responded to a call by a woman who sought help for her husband's gambling problem. Upon visiting the couple at home, the two Gamblers Anonymous members quickly learned that the husband just wasn't interested in quitting. Grateful for their attempt to help, the woman offered to put them in touch with Paul Coates, an influential newspaper columnist for the *Los Angeles Mirror*.

Much to Jim's surprise, Coates called the following day. An article soon appeared in the *Mirror*, describing the fledgling Gamblers Anonymous program. Despite this excellent exposure, Jim and Sybil once again met with disappointment — no one responded. The reporter persisted, however, and he and his producer invited Sam and Jim to appear on their weekly television show. Once again their hopes burned brightly.

Jim's excitement at the prospect of appearing on a popular television show was cooled unexpectedly. Sam told him that he would not go on, fearing that he might be recognized and thus jeopardize his insurance business. Jim W. did not tell Coates of this, afraid that the arrangements would fall through. Instead, Jim brought along a "ringer" from Alcoholics Anonymous, Floyd M., and introduced him to Coates as a new member of Gamblers Anonymous. While Jim was not pleased with this deception, he reasoned that a fellowship, such as Gamblers Anonymous purported to be, must have more than one member. Paul Coates spotted the subterfuge, and directed most of his questions to Jim W. Despite the confusion, and also the fact that Jim and Floyd both appeared with paper bags over their heads, the show went well. Coates ended the broadcast with an offer to handle any inquiries the audience might have.

The First Gamblers Anonymous Meeting

In the days that followed, Jim received about fifteen inquiries about the time and location of the next Gamblers Anonymous meeting. Jim responded to each with an address and a date: Friday, September 13th, 1957.

Jim, Sam, Floyd and Sybil, along with some friends, assembled to greet the newcomers. They had prepared literature on the Twelve Steps of Recovery and had planned out the format for the meeting. Five gamblers came.

Jim W. chaired the meeting, gave therapy and described the Fellowship's Recovery Program. Some of the newcomers were silent, others barraged Jim with questions. The formal meeting lasted for only an hour and a half, but the informal discussion that followed lasted into the small hours of the morning. More importantly, a second meeting was planned, and held.

The history of the founding of Gamblers Anonymous is the story of one man's dream, realized through the help of many others. Today that dream not only lives but flourishes far beyond its humble beginnings. Through it, tens of thousands of compulsive gamblers have been able to recover their own dreams for normal, healthy lives.

Appendix II

STUDY BY DR. ROBERT L. CUSTER
Questions and Responses

GAMBLERS ANONYMOUS SURVEY QUESTIONS

I. DEMOGRAPHIC DATA

1. AGE:
   Range   24 - 72
   Mean   47

2. SEX:
   Male   96%
   Female   4%

3. RELIGIOUS BACKGROUND:
   Catholic   42%
   Protestant   30%
   Jewish   25%
   Other   3%

4. MARITAL STATUS:
   Married   84%
   Separated   4%
   Divorced   6%
   Widowed   1%
   Single   5%

5. EDUCATION:
   Some High School   24%
   High School Grad   30%
   Some College   25%
   College Graduate   20%

6. NATIONALITY:
   Irish   )
   Italian   )   The leading three
   German   )

7. EMPLOYMENT:
   Yes   94%
   No   6%

8. MILITARY SERVICE:
   Yes   67%
   No   32%

9. STATE OR COUNTRY RESIDENCE:
   (15 States and Canada)

10. LENGTH OF GAMBLERS ANONYMOUS ATTENDANCE:
    Range - 1 to 238 months
    Mean - 87 months (7 years 3 months)

11. REGULAR ATTENDANCE:
    Yes   98%
    No   2%

12. AGE WHEN FIRST ATTENDED GAMBLERS ANONYMOUS:
    Range - 22 - 61
    Mean - 39.7 years

13. HOW LONG CLEAN:

Range - 1 - 238 months
Mean - 73 months (6 years 1 months)

14. HOW MANY SLIPS:

One	32%
Two	10%
More than two	16%
None	42%

15. CHAPTERS WITHIN ONE-HOUR DRIVE:

One	6%
Two	10%
More than two	68%
None	42%

54. SPOUSE ATTEND GAM-ANON REGULARLY:

Yes	56%
No	36%
Don't Know	8%

59. SEE MENTAL HEALTH PROFESSIONAL BEFORE GAMBLERS ANONYMOUS:

Yes	40%
No	60%

74. GO TO GAMBLERS ANONYMOUS ONCE A WEEK:

Yes	97%
No	3%

75. WAIT 6 MONTHS AFTER HEARING OF GAMBLERS ANONYMOUS:

Yes	40%
No	60%

76. FEEL POSITIVELY TOWARD GAM-ANON:

Yes	84%
No	8%
Don't Know	8%

77. FEEL POSITIVELY TOWARD GAM-A-TEEN:

Yes	72%
No	8%
Don't Know	20%

II. TWENTY GAMBLERS ANONYMOUS QUESTIONS	YES
18. LOSE TIME AT WORK	85.0%
19. HOME LIFE UNHAPPY	99.5%
20. AFFECTING REPUTATION	93.0%
21. REMORSE	99.5%
22. TO PAY DEBTS	93.0%
23. DECREASE AMBITION	94.0%
24. AFTER LOSING - RETURN	97.0%
25. AFTER WINNING - RETURN	98.0%
26. LAST DOLLAR GONE	97.0%
27. BORROW	99.5%
28. SOLD PROPERTY	79.0%
29. MONEY - GAMBLING - EXPENSES	93.0%
30. CARELESS OF FAMILY	94.0%
31. GAMBLE LONGER	98.0%
32. TO ESCAPE WORRY	92.0%
33. THOUGHTS OF ILLEGAL ACTS	86.0%
34. DIFFICULTY SLEEPING	72.0%
35. ARGUMENTS	92.0%
36. CELEBRATE	84.0%
65. SUICIDAL THOUGHTS	36.0%

III. TRAITS:

38. COMPETITIVE:
Yes 90%
No 6%
Don't Know 4%

39. ATHLETIC:
Yes 62%
No 36%
Don't Know 2%

47. HIGH ENERGY LEVEL:
Yes 76%
No 25%
Don't Know 6%

48. SQUANDER ASIDE FROM GAMBLING:
Yes 72%
No 25%
Don't Know 3%

78. HABITS	YES
Smoking	52%
Drinking	34%
Over-eat/Weight	56%
Over spending	58%
Insomnia	14%

IV. CHILDHOOD HISTORY & FAMILY HISTORY:

57. RAISED AWAY FROM PARENTS 2 YEARS:
Yes 8%
No 82%

58. LOST PARENT BEFORE AGE 15:
Yes 13%
No 87%

62. PHYSICALLY BEATEN AS A CHILD
Yes 13%
No 87%

63/ ANTI-SOCIAL CHARACTERISTICS AS
64. CHILD/ADOLESCENT:
Yes 5%
No 95%

67. CLOSE RELATIVES SUICIDE:
Yes 4%
No 96%

68. EITHER PARENT ALCOHOLIC:
Yes 18%
No 82%

COMPULSIVE GAMBLERS:
Yes 14%
No 86%

SERIOUS PSYCHIATRIC ILLNESS:
Yes 4%
No 96%

V. GAMBLING BEHAVIOR HISTORY

16. AGE WHEN FIRST GAMBLED:
Range - 4 - 40
Mean - 14

17. AGE FIRST LOST OR WON 420:
Range - 7 - 40
Mean - 17

37. EGO BUILDING ACTIVITY:
Yes 94%
No 6%

41. WIN AMOUNT = TO ANNUAL SALARY:
    Yes   44%
    No   56%

42. WIN $5,000:
    Yes   50%
    No   50%

52. ALSO AN ALCOHOLIC:
    Yes   8%
    No   92%

53. ADDICTED TO DRUGS ALSO:
    Yes   2%
    No   98%

55. STILL HAVE URGE TO GAMBLE:
    Yes   60%
    No   40%

60. HATE TO ADMIT YOU WERE A
    COMPULSIVE GAMBLER:
    Yes   72%
    No   28%

61. FEEL A BIG SHOT:
    Yes   92%
    No   4%
    Don't Know   4%

70. GAMBLING AVAILABLE WITHIN
    ONE HOUR:
    Yes   98%
    No   2%

71. IS GAMBLING NOW AVAILABLE
    ONE HOUR:
    Yes   100%
    No   0%

72. PREFERRED FORM OF GAMBLING:
    Horse Racing   21%
    Harness Racing   16%
    Sports Betting   21%
    Card Games   24%
    Dice   15%
    Dog Racing   3%
    Slots   1%
    Bingo   0%
    Other   2%

73. WOULD HAVE PREFERRED CASINO:
    Yes   60%
    No   28%
    Don't Know 12%

VI. PROBLEMS RELATED TO GAMBLING:

40. LOSE JOB OR BUSINESS:
Yes 60%
No 40%

43. EVER HAVE BAILOUT:
Yes 90%
No 10%

44. EVER BEEN ARRESTED:
Yes 21%
No 79%

45. EVER BEEN IMPRISONED:
Yes 9%
No 91%

46. CAUSED SERIOUS FAMILY PROBLEMS:
Yes 98%
No 2%

49. FAILED TO MEET BASIC NEEDS:
Yes 70%
No 30%

50. BORROW FROM ILLEGAL SOURCES:
Yes 50%
No 50%

51. DEFAULT ON DEBTS:
Yes 66%
No 34%

56. BRAG ABOUT WINNING WHILE LOSING:
Yes 75%
No 25%

66. ATTEMPT SUICIDE:
Yes 18%
No 82%

69. EVER DECLARE BANKRUPTCY:
Yes 21%
No 79%

VII. PROGRESS SINCE JOINING GAMBLERS ANONYMOUS:

79. HEALTHY SUBSTITUTES:
Yes 82%
No 10%
Don't Know 8%

	YES
80. PERSONAL APPEARANCE	92%
81. MANAGING FINANCES	98%
82. PROVIDE BASIC NEEDS	99%
83. PAYING BILLS	96%
84. NEW FRIENDS	94%
85. MORE FAMILY TIME	96%
86. AVOID IRRITATING BEHAVIOR	90%
87. PLAN CAREFULLY	84%
88. KEEPING JOB	93%
89. MORE TOLERANCE	93%
90. NO GAMBLING	96%
91. THINKING CLEARLY	99%
92. PROBLEM SOLVING	96%
93. SELF-RESPECT	97%
94. DEALING WITH ANXIETY	92%
95. DEALING WITH DEPRESSION	87%
96. DEALING WITH ANGER	87%
97. HELPING OTHERS	98%
98. MORE HONESTY	97%
99. GIVING LOVE	97%
100. RESPONSIBILITY	99%
101. RESTITUTION	98%
102. OTHER	

103. OVERALL IMPROVEMENT

Poor 0%
Fair 26%
Good 74%

Appendix III

STUDY BY DR. JULIAN I. TABER
Questionnaire and Responses

COMPULSIVE GAMBLING QUESTIONNAIRE AND RESPONSES OF VARIOUS GROUPS IN PERCENTAGES

1. Compulsive or excessive gambling is most probably a symptom of some deeper emotional or personality problem.

	Agreed	Disagreed	No Opinion
Members of GA	82%	11%	7%
Treatment Experts	66%	10%	24%
Psychologists	77%	19%	4%
Psychiatrists	91%	9%	0%

2. Compulsive gambling can and should be treated as the primary problem when there is no evidence that other areas of life are being affected except by gambling.

	Agreed	Disagreed	No Opinion
Members of GA	82%	16%	2%
Treatment Experts	76%	10%	14%
Psychologists	88%	8%	4%
Psychiatrists	75%	19%	6%

3. I think it is appropriate to view compulsive gambling as a disease or disorder.

	Agreed	Disagreed	No Opinion
Members of GA	96%	0%	4%
Treatment Experts	90%	3%	7%
Psychologists	62%	31%	7%
Psychiatrists	75%	6%	19%

4. Compulsive or habitual gambling is a habit resulting from long experience and should not be viewed as a disease or disorder.

	Agreed	Disagreed	No Opinion
Members of GA	7%	84%	9%
Treatment Experts	7%	83%	10%
Psychologists	31%	65%	4%
Psychiatrists	13%	75%	12%

5. Once set into motion compulsive gambling continues because of an overwhelming urge to gamble, an urge which makes good judgments difficult or impossible.

	Agreed	Disagreed	No Opinion
Members of GA	96%	2%	2%
Treatment Experts	100%	0%	0%
Psychologists	77%	8%	15%
Psychiatrists	91%	3%	6%

6. Compulsive gambling is probably an addiction similar in nature to other addictions such as those created by drugs or alcohol.

	Agreed	Disagreed	No Opinion
Members of GA	91%	4%	5%
Treatment Experts	83%	7%	10%
Psychologists	88%	4%	8%
Psychiatrists	63%	19%	18%

7. A psychological "high" or altered mood associated with risk-taking is probably what motivates most compulsive gamblers.

	Agreed	Disagreed	No Opinion
Members of GA	73%	11%	16%
Treatment Experts	83%	3%	14%
Psychologists	50%	8%	42%
Psychiatrists	59%	16%	25%

8. Compulsive gambling is probably a result of some character or personality defect that existed prior to the onset of gambling.

	Agreed	Disagreed	No Opinion
Members of GA	73%	18%	9%
Treatment Experts	62%	28%	10%
Psychologists	42%	27%	31%
Psychiatrists	84%	3%	13%

9. Compulsive gamblers usually have many other severe problems in living caused by basic character disorder rather than by an illness or addiction.

	Agreed	Disagreed	No Opinion
Members of GA	34%	43%	23%
Treatment Experts	24%	48%	28%
Psychologists	35%	38%	27%
Psychiatrists	31%	25%	44%

10. During periods of intense gambling the compulsive gambler usually shows a marked change from his ordinary mood or personality.

	Agreed	Disagreed	No Opinion
Members of GA	93%	7%	0%
Treatment Experts	97%	3%	0%
Psychologists	46%	15%	39%
Psychiatrists	47%	13%	40%

11. Self punishment is what motivates most compulsive gamblers.

	Agreed	Disagreed	No Opinion
Members of GA	32%	46%	22%
Treatment Experts	10%	62%	28%
Psychologists	8%	54%	38%
Psychiatrists	9%	41%	50%

12. I don't really believe that there is such a thing as compulsive gambling.

	Agreed	Disagreed	No Opinion
Members of GA	0%	98%	2%
Treatment Experts	0%	97%	3%
Psychologists	0%	100%	0%
Psychiatrists	3%	88%	9%

13. The number of compulsive gamblers probably depends upon the availability of gambling games in our society.

	Agreed	Disagreed	No Opinion
Members of GA	50%	41%	9%
Treatment Experts	59%	24%	17%
Psychologists	23%	42%	35%
Psychiatrists	25%	66%	9%

14. Most compulsive gamblers are probably emotionally immature.

	Agreed	Disagreed	No Opinion
Members of GA	82%	16%	2%
Treatment Experts	76%	7%	17%
Psychologists	65%	19%	16%
Psychiatrists	66%	19%	15%

15. A compulsive gambler is not very likely to have had any enduring attachments to family, job, or community.

	Agreed	Disagreed	No Opinion
Members of GA	41%	57%	2%
Treatment Experts	21%	66%	13%
Psychologists	15%	62%	23%
Psychiatrists	6%	69%	25%

16. A compulsive gambler is no more likely to have other addictions than anyone else.

	Agreed	Disagreed	No Opinion
Members of GA	30%	64%	6%
Treatment Experts	14%	72%	14%
Psychologists	38%	38%	24%
Psychiatrists	22%	28%	50%

17. Money is the primary motive for most compulsive gamblers.

	Agreed	Disagreed	No Opinion
Members of GA	20%	73%	7%
Treatment Experts	3%	90%	7%
Psychologists	8%	65%	27%
Psychiatrists	0%	72%	28%

Questions in the next section call for opinions on treatment.

18. With compulsive gamblers there is very little hope for significant improvement regardless of what therapies are tried.

	Agreed	Disagreed	No Opinion
Members of GA	11%	84%	5%
Treatment Experts	0%	83%	17%
Psychologists	0%	81%	19%
Psychiatrists	3%	81%	16%

19. In working with compulsive gamblers, group therapy is to be preferred over individual psychotherapy whenever a choice is available.

	Agreed	Disagreed	No Opinion
Members of GA	91%	4%	5%
Treatment Experts	55%	31%	14%
Psychologists	50%	27%	23%
Psychiatrists	47%	9%	44%

20. Any treatment given to compulsive gamblers should place a high priority on the development of discipline and self-control.

	Agreed	Disagreed	No Opinion
Members of GA	75%	18%	7%
Treatment Experts	72%	10%	18%
Psychologists	73%	27%	0%
Psychiatrists	44%	22%	34%

21. Any treatment given to compulsive gamblers should place a high priority on developing insight into the causes of gambling.

	Agreed	Disagreed	No Opinion
Members of GA	23%	64%	13%
Treatment Experts	38%	55%	7%
Psychologists	42%	42%	16%
Psychiatrists	41%	31%	28%

22. Any treatment given to compulsive gamblers should place a high priority on finding ways to stop gambling and to resist the urge to gamble.

	Agreed	Disagreed	No Opinion
Members of GA	84%	4%	12%
Treatment Experts	97%	0%	3%
Psychologists	88%	8%	4%
Psychiatrists	78%	13%	9%

23. Compulsive gamblers probably have unusually high frequencies of stress related illness such as high blood pressure, ulcers, etc.

	Agreed	Disagreed	No Opinion
Members of GA	66%	25%	9%
Treatment Experts	66%	10%	24%
Psychologists	15%	23%	62%
Psychiatrists	34%	3%	63%

24. Brief hospitalization (3-6 weeks) with professional help is desirable for those compulsive gamblers who really want to stop gambling.

	Agreed	Disagreed	No Opinion
Members of GA	43%	34%	23%
Treatment Experts	55%	17%	28%
Psychologists	38%	38%	24%
Psychiatrists	44%	19%	37%

25. Some form of professional help is necessary if compulsive gamblers are to arrest gambling permanently.

	Agreed	Disagreed	No Opinion
Members of GA	36%	52%	12%
Treatment Experts	52%	34%	14%
Psychologists	88%	4%	8%
Psychiatrists	72%	9%	19%

26. Professionals such as psychiatrists, psychologists and social workers have very little to offer the compulsive gambler with respect to the gambling problem.

	Agreed	Disagreed	No Opinion
Members of GA	54%	34%	12%
Treatment Experts	21%	62%	17%
Psychologists	15%	65%	20%
Psychiatrists	13%	59%	28%

27. Organizations such as Gamblers Anonymous (similar to Alcoholics Anonymous) are all the help compulsive gamblers need.

	Agreed	Disagreed	No Opinion
Members of GA	30%	50%	20%
Treatment Experts	3%	86%	11%
Psychologists	8%	73%	19%
Psychiatrists	16%	53%	31%

28. An alliance of professionals and self-help groups working together is an ideal arrangement for helping the compulsive gambler.

	Agreed	Disagreed	No Opinion
Members of GA	73%	18%	9%
Treatment Experts	100%	0%	0%
Psychologists	92%	0%	8%
Psychiatrists	91%	3%	6%

29. Only those who have themselves suffered from compulsive **gambling** are really able to understand the compulsive **gambler**.

	Agreed	Disagreed	No Opinion
Members of GA	73%	27%	0%
Treatment Experts	3%	93%	4%
Psychologists	4%	85%	11%
Psychiatrists	6%	72%	22%

30. If one can afford it, professional psychotherapy is **superior to** Gamblers Anonymous or similar self-help groups and should **be used** instead of such groups.

	Agreed	Disagreed	No Opinion
Members of GA	4%	86%	10%
Treatment Experts	3%	93%	4%
Psychologists	15%	58%	27%
Psychiatrists	16%	50%	34%

31. Professional people who work with gamblers should be thoroughly familiar with the workings of such groups as Gamblers Anonymous.

	Agreed	Disagreed	No Opinion
Members of GA	100%	0%	0%
Treatment Experts	100%	0%	0%
Psychologists	85%	4%	11%
Psychiatrists	91%	0%	9%

32. Teaching a few simple self-control techniques should help compulsive gamblers stop gambling.

	Agreed	Disagreed	No Opinion
Members of GA	9%	82%	9%
Treatment Experts	7%	90%	3%
Psychologists	8%	69%	23%
Psychiatrists	0%	91%	9%

33. It is a good idea to remove all financial pressures from the **gambler by** using consolidation loans and/or bankruptcy so that he/she **can** devote full attention to the control of gambling.

	Agreed	Disagreed	No Opinion
Members of GA	11%	82%	7%
Treatment Experts	10%	76%	14%
Psychologists	12%	62%	26%
Psychiatrists	16%	47%	37%

34. Behavior modification techniques which reward good behavior and punish bad behavior would be appropriate in treating the compulsive gambler.

	Agreed	Disagreed	No Opinion
Members of GA	9%	59%	32%
Treatment Experts	38%	38%	24%
Psychologists	69%	8%	23%
Psychiatrists	41%	19%	40%

35. Any mental health professional with an advanced degree would need very little specialized training in order to work effectively with the compulsive gambler.

	Agreed	Disagreed	No Opinion
Members of GA	11%	70%	19%
Treatment Experts	7%	83%	10%
Psychologists	8%	77%	15%
Psychiatrists	3%	81%	16%

Questions in the next section call for opinions on the proper goals for treatment.

36. I believe a good behavior such as hard work should be encouraged as a substitute for gambling.

	Agreed	Disagreed	No Opinion
Members of GA	50%	36%	14%
Treatment Experts	62%	17%	21%
Psychologists	31%	46%	23%
Psychiatrists	28%	34%	38%

37. The development of a more relaxed lifestyle and of personal serenity is very important for compulsive gamblers.

	Agreed	Disagreed	No Opinion
Members of GA	96%	2%	2%
Treatment Experts	62%	17%	21%
Psychologists	50%	19%	31%
Psychiatrists	34%	16%	50%

38. Therapy for the compulsive gambler should have total abstinence from all forms of gambling as a primary goal.

	Agreed	Disagreed	No Opinion
Members of GA	91%	7%	2%
Treatment Experts	93%	3%	3%
Psychologists	62%	23%	15%
Psychiatrists	78%	13%	9%

39. Some types of minor social gambling might be acceptable for the compulsive gambler who has stopped gambling.

	Agreed	Disagreed	No Opinion
Members of GA	7%	82%	11%
Treatment Experts	3%	90%	7%
Psychologists	15%	58%	27%
Psychiatrists	6%	69%	25%

40. An important goal of therapy with any compulsive gambler should be a complete understanding of the laws of chance and probability.

	Agreed	Disagreed	No Opinion
Members of GA	25%	66%	9%
Treatment Experts	7%	79%	14%
Psychologists	4%	54%	42%
Psychiatrists	6%	72%	22%

41. A mental health professional working with a compulsive gambler should encourage a lifetime commitment to a group such as Gamblers Anonymous.

	Agreed	Disagreed	No Opinion
Members of GA	82%	9%	9%
Treatment Experts	66%	24%	10%
Psychologists	50%	19%	31%
Psychiatrists	62%	9%	29%

Questions in the next section call for opinions on our social policies for gambling.

42. "Innocent by reason of insanity" might be an appropriate defense for a compulsive gambler accused of stealing to get money to gamble.

	Agreed	Disagreed	No Opinion
Members of GA	54%	34%	12%
Treatment Experts	31%	59%	10%
Psychologists	4%	88%	8%
Psychiatrists	3%	88%	9%

43. Professional people working with compulsive gamblers should not use "compulsive gambling" as an excuse for misbehavior of the client.

	Agreed	Disagreed	No Opinion
Members of GA	41%	48%	11%
Treatment Experts	72%	21%	7%
Psychologists	85%	12%	3%
Psychiatrists	94%	3%	3%

44. In the case of an admitted gambling-related crime, anyone trying to help the gambler should encourage full restitution for the victim.

	Agreed	Disagreed	No Opinion
Members of GA	93%	0%	7%
Treatment Experts	93%	3%	3%
Psychologists	81%	0%	19%
Psychiatrists	84%	0%	16%

45. If legalized, gambling games should be run only by private corporations.

	Agreed	Disagreed	No Opinion
Members of GA	14%	39%	47%
Treatment Experts	7%	59%	34%
Psychologists	4%	42%	54%
Psychiatrists	0%	34%	66%

46. If legalized, gambling games should be run by charities, schools, churches, the state and/or private corporations.

	Agreed	Disagreed	No Opinion
Members of GA	25%	16%	59%
Treatment Experts	41%	21%	38%
Psychologists	12%	27%	61%
Psychiatrists	28%	13%	59%

47. Gambling revenues should never be used for private profit.

	Agreed	Disagreed	No Opinion
Members of GA	43%	9%	48%
Treatment Experts	31%	34%	35%
Psychologists	31%	31%	38%
Psychiatrists	19%	19%	62%

48. Legal gambling is harmless for the vast majority of the population.

	Agreed	Disagreed	No Opinion
Members of GA	36%	41%	23%
Treatment Experts	59%	31%	10%
Psychologists	65%	23%	12%
Psychiatrists	62%	16%	22%

49. Legal gambling should be carefully regulated to decrease the chances that people will become addicted.

	Agreed	Disagreed	No Opinion
Members of GA	66%	7%	27%
Treatment Experts	59%	14%	27%
Psychologists	42%	31%	27%
Psychiatrists	19%	53%	28%

50. Society should not be concerned about what happens to the compulsive gambler.

	Agreed	Disagreed	No Opinion
Members of GA	2%	93%	5%
Treatment Experts	10%	90%	0%
Psychologists	4%	88%	8%
Psychiatrists	6%	88%	6%

51. I am not in favor of any form of legalized gambling.

	Agreed	Disagreed	No Opinion
Members of GA	36%	20%	44%
Treatment Experts	21%	66%	13%
Psychologists	19%	54%	27%
Psychiatrists	0%	97%	3%

52. It would be a good idea to license gamblers so that only those who can be responsible and prudent can gamble.

	Agreed	Disagreed	No Opinion
Members of GA	11%	48%	41%
Treatment Experts	10%	76%	14%
Psychologists	0%	69%	31%
Psychiatrists	3%	69%	28%

53. Young people in their teens should never be permitted to gamble for money.

	Agreed	Disagreed	No Opinion
Members of GA	46%	25%	29%
Treatment Experts	38%	45%	17%
Psychologists	23%	54%	23%
Psychiatrists	16%	59%	25%

54. Organized professions such as psychiatry, social work and psychology probably should come forward with public positions with respect to legalized gambling.

	Agreed	Disagreed	No Opinion
Members of GA	66%	9%	25%
Treatment Experts	55%	41%	4%
Psychologists	42%	19%	39%
Psychiatrists	38%	41%	21%

55. I think it is a good idea for the state to raise money through gambling so that we will pay less in taxes.

	Agreed	Disagreed	No Opinion
Members of GA	25%	46%	29%
Treatment Experts	17%	66%	17%
Psychologists	27%	38%	35%
Psychiatrists	41%	22%	37%

56. The treatment of compulsive gambling by professionals should be covered by health insurance plans.

	Agreed	Disagreed	No Opinion
Members of GA	77%	0%	23%
Treatment Experts	90%	3%	7%
Psychologists	85%	12%	3%
Psychiatrists	84%	9%	7%

57. The government should take no position on gambling, any and all forms of gambling should be legalized.

	Agreed	Disagreed	No Opinion
Members of GA	9%	54%	37%
Treatment Experts	7%	76%	17%
Psychologists	0%	77%	23%
Psychiatrists	16%	50%	34%

58. Compulsive gambling is not likely to become a major problem as more states legalize gambling because it is the type of person, not the existence of gambling, which creates the problem.

	Agreed	Disagreed	No Opinion
Members of GA	23%	64%	13%
Treatment Experts	10%	90%	0%
Psychologists	50%	31%	19%
Psychiatrists	53%	31%	16%

59. All gambling games, and places in which gambling takes place, should warn the gambler in some clear fashion that gambling can be hazardous to mental health.

	Agreed	Disagreed	No Opinion
Members of GA	75%	7%	18%
Treatment Experts	69%	21%	10%
Psychologists	46%	38%	16%
Psychiatrists	31%	47%	22%

Appendix IV

STUDY BY DR. DURAND F. JACOBS
Survey Results

FACTORS ALLEGED AS PREDISPOSING TO COMPULSIVE GAMBLING

Description of the Sample

The first group, numbering 58, volunteered to complete the survey during their attendance at the International Conclave of Gamblers Anonymous held at Palm Springs, California in 1981. A second group, composed of 25 individuals, completed the survey while attending a national convention of Gamblers Anonymous held at Anaheim, California in 1982. The vital statistics and general background of the respondents revealed no statistically significant differences between the two groups. Consequently, they were consolidated into a single sample of 83 persons for the analyses that follows.

The reader is cautioned to bear in mind that the findings reported here are of a highly preliminary nature. They cannot be assumed to describe compulsive gamblers in general, nor even to represent an authoritative profile of GA members throughout the country. This material is offered as a means of enhancing the meager store of documented accounts about compulsive gamblers, and in the hope that this report will stimulate further systematic investigations of this type.

Vital Statistics

- There were 71 males and 12 females in the group surveyed for this study.
- Their mean age was 48 years (range 28-72).
- Their mean educational level was one year beyond high school graduate (i.e., one year of college).
- Only 7% of the group were unemployed. Of the remainder, 74% were employed full-time, 7% part-time and 11% retired.
- Eighty percent were married and living with spouse at the time of the study was completed; 18% were divorced or separated and only 2% were single.
- Fifty-two percent of the sample had been in the military service.
- Religious affiliations were listed as 18% Catholic; 34% Protestant; 41% Jewish and 7% Other. The proportion of Jewish members in this sample is much greater than what one might expect from the 1980 U.S. Census figures which report that Jews constitute less than 3% of the general population in company with 23% Catholics and 32% Protestants.
- The racial and ethnic backgrounds of the sample varied widely across many European countries. Striking was the extremely small proportion of blacks (2%) in contrast to their 11-12% representation in the general population. Asian and Pacific Islanders and those identifying themselves as Arab Americans both constituted 2% of the sample. This is consistant with the 1-2% representation these two groups have in the general population. Hispanics comprised 3% of this sample, compared to their 6% representation in the general population
- The mean age at onset of gambling was 18 years with a range of six to 43 years. They had been compulsive gamblers for an average of 21 years.

General Background

Family history items revealed the following:
- 25% reported a family history of compulsive gambling.
- 27% reported a family history of alcoholism (the presence of both alcoholism and compulsive gambling in a given family was relatively infrequent).
- 12% suffered loss of a parent before they were fifteen years of age.
- 13% admitted to having attempted suicide. (This is an extremely high rate when compared to general population statistics).
- 16% of the group had been in prison for 30 days or more.
- 5% had legal action pending against them at the time of the survey.
- An average of one traffic ticket during the previous three years was reported with a range of 0-8.

Quality of Life

Respondents were asked to rate their present circumstances as being better, about the same, or poorer than others their age. Overall, this group of G.A. members perceived the quality of their lives as distinctly superior to that of others their age. Specifically:

- 51% reported their general health as better, while 11% rated it as poorer. Twenty-five percent were currently under a doctor's care.
- 59% were happier, while 7% stated they were less happy than most people their age.
- 19% admitted they spent a considerable amount of time worrying about the future, while 41% did this rarely if at all.
- 54% replied they were sleeping better, while 14% reported they were sleeping poorer than others their age.
- 61% responded that they were doing better on their jobs than most people. Only one person claimed an employment situation worse than most.
- In response to the question, "How are you getting along with people in general?" 72% reported "better than most other people" with only one respondent believing he was getting along worse.
- 60% rated themselves as getting along better than most with the person closest to them, while 12% said they were getting along worse.
- 77% reported that their appetite was better than most. Only one person complained of an appetite worse than others.
- 65% said they were presently overweight. When asked when they had attained their highest adult weight, 43% replied this had occured *after* they had stopped gambling; 39% replied *during* their gambling years, and 14% said that occurred *before* they began gambling.
- When asked to describe their attitudes about money 69% portrayed themselves as open handed, e.g., "generous," "spendthrift," "easy come, easy go," "don't care," while the remainder characterized themselves as preoccupied and tight-fisted, e.g., "thinking about it all the time," "frugal," "stingy," "stash it."

Use of Drugs

A series of items in the survey sought information regarding use of tobacco products, alcohol and street or prescription drugs.
A. Use of tobacco products:
- 48% reported they did not use cigarettes at all; 9% smoked less than one pack per day; 34% smoked between 1-2 packs per day; and 9% smoked more than 2 packs per day.
- Cigar and pipe use was denied by 35%; 55% admitted to occasional use; and 10% to heavy use.
- Only one person stated he used snuff or chewing tobacco.

- 78% stated that their greatest use of tobacco products was *during* their gambling years. Ten percent said their greatest use occurred before they started gambling, while 12% said it occured after they stopped gambling.

B. Use of alcohol:
- 90% admitted to "light" use of alcohol throughout the years before, during, and after their gambling careers.
- 20% indicated "moderate" to "heavy" use of alcohol in the years *before* their gambling commenced. Moderate to heavy use of alcohol peaked to include 42% of the sample *during* the gambling years, and dropped to 34% *after* gambling stopped. This trend was particularly striking in the "heavy" use category which included 2% *before*; 15% *during* and 4% *after* gambling had stopped.

C. Use of other drugs:
Only a small minority of the total sample reported any use of mood or mind-altering drugs other than alcohol. Such drug use was typically "light" in the years both *before* and *after* their gambling careers. Less than 3% reported "moderate" to "heavy" use at these times. *During* the gambling years, however, moderate to heavy use of drugs other than alcohol doubled over the pre-gambling years. After gambling stopped, moderate to heavy use dropped precipitously to levels only half as high as the pre-gambling years. Overall, this group of gamblers tended to use mood-enhancing drugs (e.g., "uppers" and stimulants) with almost twice the frequency that they used mood-depressing drugs (e.g., "downers" and tranquilizers). This preference was particularly striking during their gambling years.

Childhood and Adolescent History

Responses to items relating to childhood and adolescent history generally tended to support the theory.
- Slightly more (30%) compulsive gamblers recalled their youth as being "less happy" rather than "more happy" than others their age. The remainder recalled no difference.
- Fifty-five percent indicated that their need for acceptance and approval was greater than those of their peers, while only 15% said their needs were less.
- Forty-six percent reported that their feelings of insecurity and inferiority were more intense than most other teenagers, while 29% said their needs were less intense.
- When asked "what was your most typical reaction to rejection by important adults in your life," only 7% reported aggressive retaliation against them, and another 5% recalled displacing their anger onto someone or something else. Thirty-eight percent said they had

responded to rejection by important adults by doing "things that would please them." However, the greatest number (50%) either denied rejection by "pretending I didn't care" or reacted by "losing myself in a fantasy world where my behavior gained their love and approval."

The dominant tendency of this group to respond to the stresses and frustrations of childhood and adolescence through a combination of denial and wish-fulfilling fantasy conceivably set the stage in later life for them to compulsively seek to return to experiences met while gambling where they were accepted as "big shots," "highly-skilled," "big spenders," and generally "treated like I was somebody!"

Perhaps the most direct and dramatic support for the theory emerged from responses of this group to four items which were specifically designed to capture evidence of a dissociative state (i.e., living another life) while gambling. Responses to the items were distributed on either a four or a five point Likert-type scale that ranged from "never" to "frequently" or from "never" to "all the time."

Item: "When you gambled, did you ever feel like you had taken on another identity?" Eighty-five percent admitted that this was so to some degree; of these 18% reported such an experience "rarely" or "occasionally"; 28% "sometimes"; and 39% "all the time."

Item: "After a gambling episode, did you ever feel like you'd been in a trance?" Eighty-seven percent responded they had to some degree: 11% rarely; 38% occasionally; 38% frequently.

Item: "While gambling did you ever feel like you were 'outside yourself' — watching yourself gamble?" Sixty-nine percent reported yes to some degree: 18% rarely; 28% occasionally; 23% frequently.

Item: "Have you ever experienced a 'memory blackout' for a period when you had been gambling?" Fifty-three percent reported yes to some degree: 15% rarely; 24% occasionally; 14% frequently.

Clinical reports in the literature have noted that similar dissociative reactions are common among alcoholics and drug addicts, but this is the first time that such experiences have been systematically verified in a sample of compulsive gamblers. One might speculate that toxins in the substances ingested by alcoholics and drug addicts contributed to the dissociative features observed in their behaviors while under the influence. However, such an argument falters as an explanation for the extremely high incidence of clear-cut dissociative reactions reported by this sample of compulsive gamblers. Only 11% of this group used drugs at all during their gambling years, and no more than 4% reported moderate to heavy use during this period of their lives. Forty-two percent of this sample did state they had used alcohol to a moderate to heavy extent during the years when they were gambling.

The survey did not inquire whether drugs or alcohol were used while actually gambling. Results of this study would suggest that use of alcohol and/or drugs alone cannot explain the extremely high frequency of dissociative reactions experienced by this group while gambling. Further research is needed to provide more definitive answers about the relative roles of physiological and psychological mechanisms in the dissociative reactions experienced by those indulging in various addictive patterns of behavior.

Reflections on the Gambling Years

The survey sought to ascertain what were the typical emotional states of this group in the years before, during, and after gambling stopped. Before gambling they recalled few persistent extremes of mood, while only 4% reporting they were painfully "tense" and 10% "feeling dead inside." During the gambling years feeling "tense" increased more than five-fold to include 22% of the sample, while those "feeling dead inside" (18%) almost doubled over their pre-gambling state. In the years after gambling stopped, reports of persistent emotional extremes virtually disappeared.

In recalling how they felt the first time they gambled, 12% said they were very fearful and tense, while 46% found the experience extremely exciting. After gambling for a year or two, only 6% reported feeling fearful, while 59% found it extremely exciting. When they decided to quit gambling, only 14% still found it extremely exciting, while 50% said it made them feel very fearful and tense.

In a related set of items 54% of the group reported that from the time they first started to gamble until just before they quit the thrill they received from gambling continued to increase. Forty percent of these said their pleasure increased to a point and then decreased. An additional 31% reported that for them the thrill steadily decreased. Over the same period of time 57% reported they felt progressively worse when they were not gambling, and 21% said they felt progressively better.

In looking back on their gambling careers this group checked a variety of objectives they were trying to obtain. In order of importance they listed the following three objectives above all others:
1. To escape from emotional tension (i.e., unhappiness with themselves) and a humdrum existence.
2. To find stimulation.
3. To find relaxation.

"The thrill of the action" was overwhelmingly reported as the single most important influence that kept them gambling, followed in order by "wanting to make a lot of money fast," "just couldn't stop," "wanting to escape a humdrum existence," and "wanting to give my family and friends the good things in life."

Recovery

The three top reasons given for admitting to oneself that their gambling was out of control were:
1. "when my marriage was threatened by my gambling"
2. "when I was gambling heavily and steadily"
3. "when I stole to support my gambling"

The influences that kept them "clean" were ranked in the following order of importance:
1. The G.A. program
2. Fear of falling back into my old ways
3. A family member of close friend
4. My own will power
5. Personal faith in God

When asked "what gives you the biggest thrill these days," their most frequent responses were:
1. Family and friends
2. G.A.
3. Work
4. Mental peace and self respect
5. Recreational activities

They said of all the problems facing them as recovering gamblers, the toughest were:
1. to establish better relationships with spouse or parent
2. to establish better relationship with family and friends
3. to fight the temptation to gamble again
4. to find activities to fill free time
5. to get out of financial difficulties
6. to stay in the G.A. program
7. to make new friends

The survey closed with three questions probing their attitudes towards professional treatment:

Item:	Yes	No	Undecided
Do you believe that some recovering compulsive gamblers could profit from a month of inhospital treatment?	56%	15%	29%
Would you have considered such treatment for yourself, if it had been available?	46%	32%	22%
Would you make use of such treatment now, if it were to become available?	24%	50%	26%

Appendix V

GAMBLERS ANONYMOUS OFFICES

Local Group Meetings

There are Gamblers Anonymous chapters in most states, as well as in Puerto Rico, Canada, England, Ireland, Northern Ireland, Scotland, Wales, the Netherlands, Belgium, West Germany, Argentina, Brazil and Uganda. Most are in or near major urban centers and can be located by consulting local telephone directories.

International Service Office

At the heart of the Fellowship is the International Service Office (ISO). A not-for-profit office supported by contributions from Gamblers Anonymous groups, the ISO handles correspondence and other administrative matters. The office also issues a monthly bulletin, "Life Line," which keeps members informed of news about the Fellowship.

The International Service Office performs an important public relations function, providing information on compulsive gambling and the Gamblers Anonymous Fellowship. The office also prepares starter kits for beginning groups. In addition, the ISO prints and distributes films, books and pamphlets.

BIBLIOGRAPHY

BOOKS:

American Psychiatric Association. *Diagnostic and Statistical Manual.* Third Edition. Washington, D.C.: American Psychiatric Association, 1979. (the diagnostic category — "Pathological Gambling" is listed as No. 312.31 under: disorders of impulse control, not classified elsewhere)

Bergler, E. *The Psychology of Gambling.* New York: Hill and Wang, 1957.

Eadington, William R. "Excitement: The Gambler's Drug" by William Boyd, pp. 371-75. "Compulsive Gambling and the Conscious Mood Perspective" by Tomas Martinez, pp. 347-70 (distinctively *social* psychological, puts the c.g. in perspective) (order the Eadington book from Charles C. Thomas Pub. 301-327 E. Lawrence Avenue, Springfield, IL 62717 $45.00)

Eadington, William R. The Gambling Papers: Proceedings of the Fifth National Conference on Gambling and Risk Taking. Lake Tahoe, Nevada, University of Nevada, Reno, 1982.
  Volume   I: Pathological Gambling: Theory and Practice.
  Volume II: Pathological Gambling II: Theory and Practice.
  Volume III: Pathological Gambling: The Johns Hopkins
              Compulsive Gambling Treatment Center Studies

Gamblers Anonymous. *Gamblers Anonymous: Big Book.* Los Angeles, CA: Gamblers Anonymous Publishing Co., 1974. (a book which includes the goals etc. of GA as well as testimony to the success of the organization. Order from National Service Office, Gamblers Anonymous, P.O. Box 17173, Los Angeles, CA 90017)

Halliday, Jon and Peter Fuller, (eds). *The Psychology of Gambling.* New York: Harper and Row, 1974. (psychoanalytically oriented reader on the topic. Has articles by Fuller, France, Freud, Bergler, Greenson, Lindner, Jones, Ferenczi, and Fachinelli. Has a selected bibliography at the end which may prove useful to researchers. Order from Harper and Row Publishers, Inc., 10 E. 53rd Street, New York, NY 10022 $4.25)

Herman, Robert D., (ed). *Gambling.* New York: Harper and Row, 1967. (has articles on gambling as well as the following on compulsive gambling: The Psychology of Gambling by Edmund Bergler, pp. 113-30: The Gambler and His Love by Iago Galdston, pp. 131-35: Inspirational Group Therapy: A study of Gamblers Anonymous by Alvin Scodel, pp. 152-68. Order from Harper and Row — same address as above)

Herman, Robert D. *Gamblers and Gambling.* Lexington, Mass: Lexington Books, 1976. (has a chapter on compulsive gambling which takes a "labeling theory" approach to the topic) order from: Lexington Books, D.C. Heath and Company, 125 Spring Street, Lexington, MA 02173 ($12.00).

Journal of Social Issues (a periodical). Volume 35 (no. 3), 1979. (these articles are written by participants and consultants to the gambling commission. The most important piece of the commission's work with relevance to the study of compulsive gambling is included in the article by T. E. Dielman "Gambling: A Social Problem?" which reports on the gambling commission survey data on attitudes of American populace toward gambling, notes that probable cg's had more family problems, higher migration and heavier alcohol use.)

Lesieur, Henry R. *The Chase: Career of the Compulsive Gambler.* Garden City, NY: Doubleday Anchor, 1977. (intensive interviews with fifty compulsive gamblers and 25 others in the social works of c.g.s. Included are discussions of how people become c.g.s; how gambling interferes with family life; the relation between c.g. and work; how c.g.s and bookmakers interact; how they get loans and manipulate money; how gamblers cooperate to con and deceive others; and the relation between c.g. and illegal behavior. Order from: Doubleday & Co., 501 Franklin Avenue, Garden City, NY 11530 $2.95)

Livingston, Jay. *Compulsive Gamblers: Observations on Action and Abstinence.* New York: Harper and Row Pub., 1974. (social psychological treatment of the personality and career pattern of c.g.s. The second half of the book includes an in-depth discussion of Gamblers Anonymous. Order from: Harper and Row Pub., Inc. — name and address as above $3.45)

Moore, Robin. Compulsion: *The True Story of an Addictive Gambler.* Doubleday, 1981.

Roston, Ronald A. Some Personality Characteristics of Compulsive Gamblers, unpublished Ph.D. dissertation. University of California, Los Angeles, CA 1961. (personality study of GA vs. non-GA members using MMPI and a modified Rotter Level of Aspiration Board. Gamblers found to be more hostile, aggressive, active, rebellious, magical thinking and socially alienated. Gamblers compared with psychiatric patients and a normal control group. Order from University Microfilms, Ann Arbor, Michigan)

ARTICLES and MONOGRAPHS

Anderson, G.M. Compulsive gambling: talking to the experts. *America* (Feb. 3, 1979).

Ardiola, Rocco C. "When Kids Go To The Race Track." *New York Times* (January 28, 1979).

Aubrey, William E. "Altering the Gambler's Maladaptive Life Goals." *International Journal of the Addictions,* Vol. 10 (no. 1), 1975: pp. 29-33.

Birmingham, Stephen. "The Big Losers: What Chance Has a Woman Against Her Man's Gambling Fever?" *Cosmopolitan Magazine* (September 1969): pp. 76-81.

Bolen, Darrell, Alex B. Caldwell and William H. Boyd. "Personality Traits of Pathological Gamblers." Presented at the Second Annual Conference on Gambling, 1975.

Boyd, William H. and Darrell W. Bolen. "The Compulsive Gambler and Spouse in Group Psychotherapy." *International Journal of Group Psychotherapy,* Vol. 20 (no. 1), 1970, pp. 77-90.

Cady, Steve. "The Gambler Who Must." *New York Times Magazine* (January 27, 1974), pp. 12-13, 51-58. Discusses c.g.s., Brecksville VA Hospital and Robert Custer.

Chapman, Sanford R. "An Argument Against the 'Unconscious Need to Lose' Concept in the Compulsive Gambler." Presented at the Second Annual Conference on Gambling, 1975.

Cotler, Sherwin B. "The Use of Different Behavioral Techniques in Treating a Case of Compulsive Gambling." *Behavior Therapy,* Vol. 2 (October, 1971): pp. 579-84. (behavior modification & aversive conditioning)